GW01339091

'Love as Brethren'

'Love as Brethren'

A Quincentennial History of the Coopers' Company

by

PAMELA MARYFIELD

WEST PARK PRESS
for
THE WORSHIPFUL COMPANY OF COOPERS
M M

Text © Pamela Maryfield, 2000

Published by
WEST PARK PRESS LTD
PO BOX 17728, LONDON N5 1WQ

for
THE WORSHIPFUL COMPANY OF COOPERS
COOPERS' HALL, 13 DEVONSHIRE SQUARE
LONDON EC2M 4TH

First published 2000

ISBN 0-9537845-0-9

British Library Cataloguing in Publication Data
A catalogue record for this book
is available from the British Library

No part of this publication may be reproduced,
stored in a retrieval system, or be transmitted in any form
or in any means, electronic, mechanical, photocopying,
recording or otherwise without the prior permission
of the relevant holders of copyright.

Printed by St Edmundsbury Press, Bury St Edmunds
Manufactured in Great Britain

Contents

List of Illustrations		*vii*
Acknowledgements		*ix*
Illustration Acknowledgements		*x*
Prologue	July 1538	*1*
Chapter one	Origins: Fraternity to Company 1250–1550	*7*
Chapter two	The First Hall and the First Charity 1550–1570	*27*
Chapter three	Consolidation 1570–1630	*47*
Chapter four	Rebels, Radicals and Civil War 1630–1660	*67*
Chapter five	Restoration, Plague and Fire 1660–1680	*81*
Chapter six	Fighting for the Charter 1680–1700	*97*
Chapter seven	A New Direction 1700–1750	*113*
Chapter eight	Marking Time 1750–1800	*127*
Chapter nine	Part one: Schools, Schoolmasters and Reformers 1800–1870	*143*
	Part two: Surviving Change 1800–1870	*163*
Chapter ten	Men of Property 1870–1900	*185*
Chapter eleven	Holding Fast 1900–1952	*201*
Chapter twelve	Rejuvenation 1952–1980	*221*
Chapter thirteen	Into the Future 1980–2000	*241*
Captions to Colour Plates		*250*
Appendices	Appendix one: Casks and their Capacities	*252*
	Appendix two: Apprentices: social and geographical origins	*253*
	Appendix three: Revised Income of the Ratcliffe Pension Charity	*254*
Glossary		*255*
References		*259*
Indexes	Index of People	*267*
	Index of Subjects	*272*

List of Illustrations

Black and White Illustrations

Endpapers   Detail of the 1658 Faithorne Map of London

Page	
3	Croze
9	Cooper's off-set axe
12	Quarterage list, 1487–88
16	Mark of Anthony Dirikson
18	Mark of Anthony Bleek
22	Mark of John Bray
23	Mark of Thomas Bray
28	1561 map-view of London ('Agas' map)
31	Mark of John Heath
36	Accounts for 1571–72
41	Mark of Henry Gamble
43	Accounts for 1575–76
44	Mark of Edmund Byrde
51	Hammer and driver
55	1658 map-view of Ratcliffe (Faithorne map)
61	Accounts for 1579–80
62	Mark of Thomas Gybson
78	Mark of Robert Cheslyn
84	Mark of Richard Winch
91	Mark of John Stutzberry
92	Coopers' Hall, 1831–32
94	Mark of Henry Strode, senior
104	Mark of John Fleet
110	Mark of Arthur Bray, junior
116	Mark of William Alexander
122–3	Lord Mayor's Show, 1740
124	Mark of Benjamin Carter
131	Fire at Ratcliffe, 1794
145	Heading knife and round shave
157	The Ratcliffe Charity, 1857
178	Cartoon of Sir David Salomons

180	The old school at Ratcliffe
197	Coopers' School, Tredegar Square
198	Coopers' School, Tredegar Square, a detail
212	Topping plane and inside shave
218	Adze
223	13 Devonshire Square
229	Exhibition at Coopers' Hall, 1976
237	Museum of coopering

Colour Illustrations

The colour illustrations are inserted between pages 150 and 151. Full captions for each illustration can be found on pages 250–1.

Plate
1	Dame Alice Knyvett
2	The Egham Charity
3	Woodham Mortimer Hall
4	Memorial to William Alexander
5	Memorial to William Alexander: the inscription
6	Plan of the Egham Charity's Lands at Staines
7	Drawing the Lottery at Coopers' Hall in 1803
8	Sir David Salomons
9	Henry Capel
10	Chapel in the Ratcliffe Charity
11	Dining Room in the Company's third Hall
12	Sir Henry Murray Fox
13	Dining Room at 13 Devonshire Square
14	Coopers' Court, Maplin Street, Bow
15	Jonathan Manby, the last brewery apprentice of the twentieth century
16	Cooper Lew Jones at work

Acknowledgements

THIS BOOK IS NOT a 'house' history, concentrating exclusively on the central subject and portraying only its worthiest achievements. It attempts to trace the development of a middling City livery company which was not particularly wealthy or influential against the background of civic and national history.

Many members of the Company were generous in answering my questions about the recent past and helped in matters of accuracy in the final chapter. In particular, I am grateful to past Master Peter Allington and the Company's Clerk, John Newton, for help with many of the practicalities in preparing this book.

Most of the research was done in the civilised and congenial atmosphere of the Manuscript and Print departments at Guildhall Library, whose staff were always helpful. I was fortunate to have practical guidance in the art and craft of coopering from Peter Coates, formerly of Theakston's brewery and Lew Jones of the St Austell brewery.

I am grateful to Dr Davina Lloyd and liveryman Martin Jolly for access to archives held by the Coopers' Company and Coborn School at Upminster; to Mrs C. E. Doe for sharing with me her research into Woodham Mortimer Hall; to staff of the Local History Library and Archives in the Bancroft Library, Tower Hamlets; to the staff of the Surrey History Service at Woking; to Wilson's School for permission to use extracts from Alexander Jephson's family history; to the artist's family for permission to use William Luker's painting of the Company's third Hall (plate 11); and to Geremy Butler who took many of the photographs.

My archaic manuscript was processed with amazing speed and accuracy by Kath Roe; Tony Paynting worked his word-magic to remove the roughest corners of the text and contributed encyclopaedic knowledge and Sue Mercer's encouragement was constant. The remaining mistakes, ambiguities and infelicities are mine.

Illustration Acknowledgements

Black and White Illustrations

Worshipful Company of Coopers: pages 3, 9, 12, 36, 43, 51, 61, 145, 157, 212, 218 (photographs by Geremy Butler), pages 223, 229, 237 and all examples of cooper's marks throughout the text.

Museum of London: page 28.

London Borough of Tower Hamlets, Local History and Archives Library: endpapers and page 55 (photographs by A. J. Bartram).

Guildhall Library, Corporation of London: pages 92, 122–3, 131, 178.

Coopers' Company and Coborn School: pages 180, 197, 198 (drawings by G. D. Clay)

Colour Illustrations

Worshipful Company of Coopers: Plates 1, 9, 12, 13 (photographs by Geremy Butler).

Reproduced by permission of Surrey Historical Service: Plates 2 and 6 (photographs by Roy Drysdale).

C. E. Doe: Plates 3, 4, 5 (photographs by Geremy Butler).

Guildhall Library, Corporation of London: Plates 7, 8, 10, 11.

Bailey • Garner, Architects for Coopers' Court: Plate 14.

Theakston's Brewery, Masham: Plate 15.

St Austell Brewery Co. Ltd.: Plate 16.

Prologue
July 1538

On a summer's evening in July 1538, preparations were being made to mark the anniversary of John Baker's death in 1490. He was a citizen and cooper of London. He had been Warden of his craft guild five times and he had left his property at the sign of the Swan by the Guildhall gate in Basinghall Street to the Fraternity of Coopers. One of the conditions was that the Coopers should observe his *obit* each year. He believed, in common with many devout men and women, that prayers for his soul would shorten its time in purgatory.

John Baker's parish church was St Michael's in the Ward of Bassishaw. Unusually, parish and ward coincided and even by London standards, the parish was tiny. It consisted of one street, Basinghall, and several side alleys. On the western side were several merchants' houses and Blackwell Hall, the City's wool exchange. The rest of the buildings were tenements like John Baker's, which served as home, workshop, lodging for apprentices and other servants. Some tenements included a cottage or two tucked away from the street in the yard of the main building. These were the homes of the poorer residents whom John Baker remembered in his will.

St Michael's church had recently been rebuilt. Its larger windows meant it was filled with the evening sunlight. It was a warm summer and the harvest promised to be one of the best, a comfort to everyone, for not even Londoners escaped the high prices, hunger and poor trade which resulted from a poor harvest. The church had been swept clean on the orders of Coopers' Clerk, John Moore. The dirty old rushes were replaced with clean ones, scattered with herbs which smelled sweetly as they were crushed under foot. There were no seats in the nave, but a few benches were placed by the walls between several altars which were in daily use. Before one of these, dedicated to the Virgin, was an empty coffin draped with the blue velvet pall cloth of the Coopers. Two chantry priests began the evening service of Vespers with the antiphon *Placebo*. When they had finished, they had a supper of bread, ale and cheese and spent the night in a small bed-chamber above the church porch.

Soon after dawn on 19 July, the parish clerk and sexton arrived to complete the preparations for John Baker's requiem mass. Two beeswax candles each weighing one pound were lighted on the Virgin's altar. Children who would earn a penny each for leading the congregational singing, were assembled and given a lighted taper each. The bells began to toll as the chantry priests appeared to say Lauds. Soon a procession of 18 Coopers arrived, led by their Master, John Charley and the two Wardens, Harry Maxfelde and John Clarke. They looked like scholars, dressed in their livery of dark blue gowns and hoods of red and black. They were followed into the nave by about 30 parishioners. The group formed a half circle about the altar and stood or occasionally knelt from the opening *Dirige* of Matins for the dead to the *Agnus Dei* which concluded the requiem mass. It was a long and complex service conducted in Latin, with nine readings from the Book of Job, and the penitential psalms sung as antiphons. The priest and people took alternate verses. This was where the children took the lead and earned their pennies.

The service was more than a commemoration. The presence of John Baker's coffin was a reminder to the living of their communion with the saints, the faithful who had preceded them through death's gates into purgatory and eventually into paradise. The prayers of the faithful on earth were an important part of that process; they could be sustained wherever there was a community dedicated to the care of souls and to the well-being of the living. The Coopers' Fraternity had this two-fold purpose. It had been founded in the Lady Chapel of St Paul's sometime after 1250. It was dedicated to the Virgin and its members met at her altar to hear mass on her many feast days and then to attend to secular business. The Fraternity gave its members security and fellowship. It ensured a dignified burial, the coffin covered by the pall cloth and followed by most of the Livery. For a suitable bequest, it would continue its prayers for the departed in years to come. More practically, the Fraternity would look after its weakest and most vulnerable members: the aged and the sick who could not work; the widows burdened with children; and the orphans.

At the end of the service, the children were given their pennies and the parishioners a groat (four pence) each, together with a note to redeem a sack of coals. These were John Baker's reward for their prayers. The Coopers left their Clerk and Beadle to complete payments to the priests, parish clerk, sexton and bellringers. The latter were given ale. The Coopers made their way towards Cheapside and an Inn called the Dagger, where a substantial meal had been cooked for them to break their fast.

Their route along Basinghall Street, across Ketton Street to Old Jewry and Cheapside took them past the Swan. It occupied a large site and contained

A croze. This distinctive tool is used to cut the groove inside the cask into which the head of the cask fits. The capacity of the cask can be adjusted by altering the distance of the groove from the rim. Here, the croze is shown on top of the oak pall chest made in 1591.

Baker's house, two cottages and an extensive cooper's yard. As a widow, Agnes Baker had continued to run the business for about ten years. On her death the property passed, according to the will, to two trustees for ten years, at the end of which, or earlier, it was to pass to the Coopers' Fraternity once it was incorporated. The Coopers had complied and sought incorporation by royal charter, which was granted in April 1501. The transfer did not go smoothly, for there are many items in the Company's first surviving account book in 1523 relating to legal fees connected with John Baker's bequest.

Some of the older Coopers dimly recalled John Baker and knew that his father, William, had several times been Warden. William Baker was prosperous enough in trade to be able to purchase his entry to the Fraternity in 1443. His 'redemption' cost two marks, sufficient to pay the rent of a house and workshop for half a year. Within four years he was listed among the leading men of the Livery and was elected Junior Warden in 1453. He was responsible to the Fraternity for collecting subscriptions each quarter (quarterage) and to the Lord Mayor for fines levied on defective work. He served as Warden three times more. In 1469, John Baker first paid quarterage and was elected Junior Warden three years later. He served as Warden on four more occasions, the last two in 1484 and 1485 as Upper Warden, the most senior official in the Fraternity. Until the grant of the Charter, there was no office of Master.

Since the Swan had become the Company's property, it had been used as the Livery Hall. It was not grand nor was it large enough for the annual gathering referred to as 'Common Hall', when the election of Master and Wardens took place. The oldest liveryman walking along that July morning, looking forward to his breakfast, was Roger Tyrrys. He had been presented as an apprentice to Hugh Crompe, the Senior Warden, who became the first to hold office as Master in 1502. He had, in his turn, become Master in 1531 and he was aware of the Hall's limitations. His immediate predecessor, Thomas à Wood, had supervised extensive renovations which involved replacing a whole wall. The cost had exceeded the Company's ability to pay. Tyrrys and John Charley, the present Master, had each lent £3; John Cloker had given £1 and had been generous in undercharging for the timber he had supplied. The bills had somehow been paid and there had been enough money to spare for some new white glass and painted hangings to make the main hall feel warmer and more comfortable.

The reminiscences of the elderly were interrupted by the sudden noise and clamour of Cheapside, London's main market where in addition to the open counters of the shops lining the street, there was a clutter of stalls, baskets and wooden casks occupying most of the space, obstructing carts and riders, trying to pick a way through the crowd. It tended to be densest near the Eleanor Cross at the western end and the Standard, a water conduit, opposite Honey Lane at the eastern end. There was little doubt that the coopers' art was an essential one. Most of the wares displayed by stall-holders were packed in wooden casks; salmon and herrings, soap, pewter ware, arrows, butter as well as beer, ale and wine. The latter came in the finest 'tight' barrels, kilderkins and firkins, which were the pride of the craft.

The talk over breakfast at the Dagger may well have touched on the question of a new, large Hall. How could the Company raise the money for such a costly enterprise? It was small in number: about 25 full members 'of the cloathing', admitted to the Livery. But there was the possibility that a few of the wealthier brethren would be able to help. Not all depended on coopering for their livelihood. A few, such as Thomas à Wood, John Cloker, John Charley and John Heath were wholesale traders, merchants taking risks but also taking advantage of the buoyant trade with Antwerp and along the Channel and North Sea coasts. Wood and Charley had wealthy friends, one of whom was Nicholas Gibson, a Grocer who had just been elected Sheriff. He was rumoured to pay one of the highest tax assessments in the City.

Perhaps the optimism and day-dreaming became less inhibited as the Company settled to serious feasting. Their bill of fare included three necks of mutton stewed with six rabbits, a whole boiled gammon, three roasted geese and piles of bread arranged among the meat dishes the length of an oak table. The Coopers sat on benches on either side and made a hearty start to their feast with a toast to the memory and generosity of John Baker. The ale was good quality, cool and fresh from a well-made firkin. The drinking on that particular morning was modest, a mere 16 gallons to serve 18 hearty men, their cook and servants. By ten o'clock they had to be sober enough to go their separate ways to their workshops, counting houses and homes to make certain that their journeymen and apprentices were at their various tasks.

CHAPTER ONE

Origins: Fraternity to Company 1250–1550

> *The Coopers' Fraternity came into being in the thirteenth century, a time when uniquely English institutions, Common law, Parliament and the legal system of royal courts were established. In the next century, Edward III (1327–77) began the Hundred Years' War; the Black Death killed one third of the population and wool became the staple export and source of wealth. His grandson, Henry IV (1399–1413) was the first English King to use English instead of French. He had usurped the throne from Richard II. Henry V beat the French at Agincourt but the English lost the war and France, except Calais. Feeble rule by Henry VI (1422–61) and rival magnates caused sporadic civil war until Henry Tudor won the throne at Bosworth, in 1485, and restored royal authority. Henry VIII (1509–47) showed its might in breaking with Rome, dissolving the monasteries and creating a national church.*

THE ROYAL CHARTER which Henry VII granted to the Coopers of London in 1501 was a landmark. It created a company where formerly there was a fraternity and trade guild. It granted the legal status of a corporation, able to own property in perpetuity. It enabled the Coopers to come into the inheritance, bequeathed them by the will of John Baker, of two tenements in Basinghall Street, near the rear gateway to Guildhall. At last, they could look forward to owning a Hall of their own, even though it might be no more than a prosperous tradesman's home with a workshop and yard.

By 1501, the Coopers had an organisation which was over a century old. In 1396, 'the goodmen of the Mystery of Coopers of London' petitioned the Mayor and Aldermen to grant an ordinance which would strengthen their control over the craft in London and the suburbs. A century earlier, in 1298, Coopers had appeared before the Lord Mayor's Court to plead as though on behalf of their trade but no further references appear until 1396. Then they sought to prevent coopers from using oil or soap tuns for making casks to hold beer and other liquors and, further they asked for powers to search cooperages for any casks which contravened this rule. Any which were defective would be brought to Guildhall and destroyed. The Coopers' request was granted. The episode illustrates that the organisation was recognised by the City authorities and was a capable body, well able to contribute to the orderly government of the City.

The coopers' craft was an essential one. Wooden casks, which were so accurately made that they were watertight and of exact and standard volume, were the universal storage system throughout mediaeval Europe. The skilful cutting, shaving and bending of staves (over steam and dry heat) to fit snugly against each other to produce a container of the correct volume, was an art perfected in Germany, though known and practised by the Romans. There is plentiful evidence of the continued strength of this craft tradition from the numerous German, Dutch and Flemish coopers who came to work in London during the sixteenth century.

The tightness of a cask depended on good craftsmanship and sound materials. Any goods which needed to be stored through the winter or a long sea voyage had to be kept in sealed conditions. Ships were dependent on coopers doing their job properly to keep their crews fed and supplied with sweet drinking water during voyages which became longer and more hazardous as the Atlantic and the coast of Africa were being explored. If the staves were made from wood which was not properly seasoned and remained green and sappy, water or food stored in such casks would go bad.

The point was not lost on Francis Drake. The spectacular 'singeing of the king of Spain's beard' by sending fire-ships in among the great armada as it prepared to invade England and lay in Cadiz harbour, certainly impeded the preparations. But possibly ultimately more damaging, but less spectacular was the time Drake spent in the days after the Cadiz raid, cruising the coastline and capturing small boats carrying staves and hoops for the armada's coopers. In making his report to the Secretary of State, Sir Francis Walsingham, Drake wrote, 'The hoops and pipe staves were above 16 or 17 hundred ton in weight, which cannot be less than 25 or 30 thousand ton, if it had been made in case, ready for liquor, all of which I commanded to be consumed into smoke and ashes by fire, which will be to the King no small waste of his provisions beside the want of his barks'. Certainly bad water and rotten food played a part, along with the elements and Lord Howard's broadsides, in the armada's destruction in 1588.

So specialised was the cooper's craft that all ships maintained a cooper on board for substantial voyages to repair casks and check that all was well. The earliest settlers in North America ensured that each small settlement had at least one cooper. Most supplies sent out to them from England to the Plymouth Plantation, for example, were packed, as far as possible, in barrels. These were used for the settlers' winter stores, repaired, as necessary, by the resident cooper. The specialist character of the craft is also apparent in its unique tools. Beautifully made of beechwood, some with handles of ash,

ORIGINS: FRATERNITY TO COMPANY

A cooper's off-set axe; handle and blade are on different planes to protect the hand when cutting and trimming (or 'listing') staves. A pair of axes is depicted on the chevron of the Company's arms.

they were usually passed down the generations from father to son or master to apprentice.

The craft organisation which eventually came to control the coopering industry in London and the suburbs, that is, within two miles of Cornhill, initially had a religious and social purpose which was paramount. As in other towns such as Bristol, Coventry, Norwich and York, the craft organisation developed from a fraternity or guild. These were part of the fabric of late mediaeval society, the essential elements which bound it together, whether in town or village. They had a religious focus in that each was dedicated to a saint whose intercessionary powers were invoked on behalf of members. The Coopers' saint was the Virgin Mary and their motto was *Gaude Virgo Maria* probably derived from one of the many hymns to the Virgin whose cult reached an apogee of fervour in the fourteenth and fifteenth centuries. The grant of arms, made in 1509, bore this motto and it featured on festive banners and most likely on the pall cloth which covered the coffin at corporate funerals.

The Coopers' Fraternity was identified in 1440 as the one founded in the 'Newerk' at St Paul's. There it maintained an altar light most probably in the Lady chapel which was where the Coopers met for mass on the many holy days dedicated to the Virgin in the pre-Reformation calendar. The 'Newerk' was the eastern part of the cathedral re-built between 1256 and 1283 and therefore provided the earliest date at which the Fraternity could have been founded. Such evidence as exists suggests that the Fraternity came into being at the end of the thirteenth century. The maintenance of the altar light was often helped by penitential punishments such as William Swift's in 1456. For his 'great obstynacye and dys obedyence against his Wardens' he had to pay two pounds of beeswax for the Fraternity's light before 'our lady of the Newerk at Powles'.

Devotion to the Virgin was popular because she was regarded as one of the most effectual intercessors for men before God on the day of Judgement. Her prayers and assistance were sought when members of the Fraternity prayed together at her altar on her major festivals. So strong was the tradition that the practice continued after the Reformation had officially swept away many of these observances and condemned the beliefs, which sustained them, as idolatrous. In 1570, when the Protestant church settlement had been in existence for over a decade, two senior members, Master William Bate and Master John Williamson, were fined for being absent on Candlemas day (the feast of the Purification) 'being warned to go to Powles'.

On major feast days there was a holiday, or at least a half day for apprentices and journeymen at the cooperages and all were expected to attend church. Afterwards, there was usually a prolonging of the heightened sense of fellowship with a 'brotherly drynking' at a tavern and perhaps a meal as well. This mix of religious and social activities created bonds of loyalty and a sense of community in a world which could be very insecure, often threatening and sometimes savage. The members valued their Fraternity because they knew it was stronger than they were as individuals. It secured them against the loneliness of death. They were assured of the prayers of their brethren to help their passage through the pain of purgatory. As John Baker's provision for prayers and remembrance demonstrated, there could be assurance of continued, regular intercession providing that there was a bequest sufficient to sustain remembrance of the deceased.

An orderly, seemly funeral, well-attended by one's brethren, with the use of the Fraternity's pall cloth was another comfort and assurance. It was a benefit, which, for a fee of 2s 6d, was extended to wives and widows. In addition, the fellowship offered security to the living, in particular, relief in times of illness, when one was too old to work or if one's children were left as orphans.

It was natural for people to form fraternities where they already had a common purpose and shared the same craft. Apprenticeships often linked families, and practitioners of the same craft often lived near each other. In London, coopers were scattered throughout the City and suburbs but, even so, there were numerous groups: soap-barrel makers and brewers by the river in Southwark; others in and near Fenchurch Street (where a Coopers' Row survives); on Tower Hill; Dowhill; without the walls in St Aldgates and at Whitefriars. Other unifying factors were the specialist skills, vocabulary, tools of coopering and common grievances against sharp practice. At some time, probably in the late thirteenth century, the Fraternity of the Virgin Mary, founded in St Paul's, became the Fraternity of Coopers.

Until they acted collectively, individuals or small groups of coopers had made representations in the Lord Mayor's Court to defend their craft. It was, however, far more effective to be represented by the Wardens of a Guild. They could give the dignity and authority to their representations which would be hard for individuals to match. By the beginning of the fifteenth century, the Fraternity of Coopers had a constitution and a programme.

Many of the rules, or ordinances, which they wanted to be applied generally in the City, had support from the City authorities. It was, for example, in the public interest that the cask, the universal container, should be made in recognised sizes and that these should be made accurately so that the number of bushels or gallons would be known immediately from the container. It was

THE WORSHIPFUL COMPANY OF COOPERS

A page from the Company's earliest surviving manuscript, a book recording quarterage payments. Each dot indicates the quarter's subscription has been paid. The entries for 1487–88 begin half-way down the left-hand column. The first two are the Wardens, William Randolffe and Watt (Walter) Coke; the third is John Baker. At the end are two widows, Sister Long and Sister Achler followed by the entry fees of 3s. 4d. made by new members.

12

equally important that the customer should not have goods which were damaged or bad because the casks had been badly made. Wine, beer, oil and sweet water should not smell or taste of fish or soap, so there must be strict rules governing how casks were repaired and staves re-used. From the cooper's point of view, there needed to be control over the number of people coming into the trade and their training so that the labour market in the craft was not swamped and wages driven down. The careful control of apprenticeship would ensure the quality of workmanship and maintain prices and wages. This is not the classic capitalist consideration. Although in time the Company came to be dominated by its wealthiest members, it represented the best interests of the self-employed, small-scale masters and employees. All these matters were addressed in the Fraternity's ordinances at an early stage. The power to enforce the rules was critical and hence the importance of seeking, in the petition brought to the Lord Mayor in 1396, City authorisation, or more likely re-inforcement, of the Fraternity's power to conduct searches of all coopers' shops, breweries and soap-boilers' premises. The City ordinance of 1420, requiring every cooper to have a distinctive, personal mark, to be branded on all the casks he made, improved the effectiveness of the search operation. Defective vessels could be more easily traced and the maker punished by a fine. The faulty cask would either be returned for re-making or adjusting, depending on how badly it had been made; or, if it were beyond amendment, committed for burning. The system of coopers' marks was, at first, jointly governed by the Lord Mayor's Court and the Fraternity. Both authorities kept a record.

Similarly, in the conduct of the search, the Lord Mayor's officer, or serjeant, accompanied the Wardens of the Coopers, and thus indicated a shared responsibility. He was paid a fee by the Coopers and made the arrangements for dealing with defective casks. When all the evidence pointed to systematic cheating and the casks were incapable of being put right, the Lord Mayor would order a bonfire, usually at the Standard in Cheapside. This water conduit was a meeting place where proclamations were made and occasionally where executions were carried out. A bonfire there, in the midst of London's main market would attract attention, as it was meant to do. In 1464, a search had produced 60 defective barrels, kilderkins and firkins, mostly used for herrings. These were burned in Cheapside in the Mayor's presence. It was a most effective piece of publicity. The flames and flying sparks and the smell of burned, bad fish would have sent a pungent message to all downwind retailers, customers and coopers.

As well as regulating the craft, the Fraternity developed rules for regulating its own members. Entry to membership as a freeman carried a standard charge of 3s 4d if qualification was the result of serving apprenticeship or by right of patrimony (being born to a cooper who was already a member). A few entered by redemption, paying a much higher charge of 20 shillings, and these members were often not practising coopers but men who wanted to gain the freedom of the craft and thereby, the freedom of the City. This allowed them to follow a trade in London. When apprentices were formally indentured to a master, a fee of 20 pence was paid to the Fraternity. Membership subscriptions were levied quarterly at ten pence a member. Together, these entry fines and quarterage made up most of the Fraternity's income in the early years.

Rules of conduct for members were an important means of maintaining internal discipline. The annually elected officials were the two Wardens. Their authority had to be respected since they were the Fraternity's representatives. 'Trespass' against the Wardens, 'reviling' them, defying them, abusing them, were all transgressions which were severely punished, not only with a fine, but with public penance. In 1443, Richard Wienne had abused the Wardens, calling them extortioners, probably because he had been fined for faulty work. He had to pay 6s 8d and was ordered 'to go on his knees on the ground and humbly beg remission of his Wardens and all his Brethren'. Robert Hewet was similarly charged and fined for 'trespass against his Wardens' in 1456 and ordered to 'meekly kneel upon one knee and ask remission'. His penalty was to pay for three pounds of wax and a taper costing eight pence which would have been used to furnish the altar in St Paul's Lady chapel. Small gestures of disobedience such as failing to attend a Fraternity mass at St Paul's or 'not coming to *Dirige*' to commemorate a deceased member, carried fines. Sometimes matters got out of hand and on one occasion five members attempted to settle an argument by fighting at a meeting. They were duly fined and threatened with presentation at the Lord Mayor's Court if they did not behave with restraint and decorum. The practice of settling disputes between members over trade matters and debts, by means of arbitration, was well established in the mid-fifteenth century. A small panel of respected members would be proposed by the Wardens and put forward for approval by the two sides to the dispute. The fighting episode was referred to a panel of four in 1443, and another example of arbitration in 1456 was noted by the scrivener in the quarterage book.

The fifteenth century record is tantalising in giving brief glimpses of the Fraternity's routines. These are provided by notes made occasionally by the scrivener who kept the record of members' names and their payment of quarterage. Between annual lists he noted gifts, arbitrations, fines and events as though maintaining an aide memoire, or acting at the suggestion of a

Warden that a note should be made. The first recorded mark is that of Thomas Blake in 1495. The official record was kept at Guildhall but it is likely that there was also a record with the Coopers. Similarly, there may have been a record of apprentices, if only to keep a check on the number with each cooper and the date of presentation. Apprentices were first listed in the quarterage book in 1491.

The Fraternity's possessions were as minimal as its record books. They were kept in a chest which had two keys, one for each Warden. When the Wardens were sworn in, the keys and chest would also be committed to their safe-keeping at the Upper Warden's house for the year and the contents, including money, would be checked in the members' presence. The contents noted in 1456, were a 'bord cloth' (for the table) embroidered in gold and silver, one box with a key — petty cash, perhaps — and £16 13s 4d. There was also a decorative girdle or belt embellished with silver which John Scherman had bequeathed in 1441. It may have been used as a symbol of office for the Upper Warden.

Membership was also small, creeping up from 40 in mid-century to 80 at the end. There were a few women who, having been widowed, but not re-married, were able to continue their husband's business. Their presence in the annual membership lists was noted in the heading as 'sisters' of the fraternity of Coopers. Coopers from other parts of the country (foreigners) and from abroad (strangers) were able to practice legally by licence from the Fraternity and were few in number. The Coopers' own records made no distinction between livery and householders but a return made to the City Corporation in 1501 listed 17 members as liverymen. These were the members with the privilege of wearing the Coopers' gown and hood, hence they were subsequently referred to as 'being of the clothing'. They had the right of voting at the annual election of officers, and the hope of aspiring, in their turn to become a Warden.

The grant of the royal charter which is dated April 29 1501 was important in giving the Fraternity a more secure position in City affairs, in confirming the new Company's control over the trade with a legal force far greater, far more potent than any ordinance of the City Corporation.

The grant was made to eight Coopers, who included the current year's Wardens, Richard Cock and Robert Thurgood, to form a Fraternity 'to the praise, glory and honour of God and His Most Famous Mother, Mary the Virgin'. It was to consist of a Master and two Wardens from the freemen coopers of the City of London and its suburbs and the brethren and sisters who were already freemen of the Craft and any others who might wish to join. It was to be a perpetual corporation able to acquire, hold and dispose of property for the support of poor men and women of the Fraternity. It could plead and be sued in any court as a corporation and it could use a common seal to authenticate its corporate actions. Election Day remained on the Sunday next before Pentecost when the Master and Wardens for the next year were to be chosen.

The new Company was granted the power to make all lawful, honest and reasonable rules to regulate the trade, provided always they did not conflict with the laws and customs of the realm. The Master and Wardens were authorised to govern the members according to the rules and ordinances and to punish offenders. Their powers in this respect extended to all freemen of the City and all foreigners in the City who practised the craft, even though they might not be members of the Company. Coopers in the City were not compelled to join the Company but they had to be freemen of City to practise their craft. Normally citizenship would be granted by joining one of the livery companies. There were wax chandlers who were members of the Coopers' Fraternity in the 1480s. They may have entered the Fraternity by patrimony or redemption. Apart from the very important grant of corporate status, the only new element introduced by the Charter was the office of Master. The rest of the grant is a confirmation and clarification of powers already exercised by the Fraternity for over a century and probably for two.

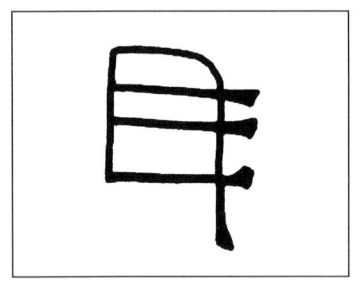

Mark of Anthony Dirikson, c. 1580. For many years he headed the list of 'Dutch' householders

The Charter made more explicit the dominance of the small livery and, within the livery, the concentration of power in the hands of a few families, often connected by marriage or by apprenticeship. Admission by patrimony sometimes ensured continuity in two, more rarely three, generations. The Thurgoods, father and son, were dominant from the 1480s. The younger man, Robert, was admitted as a freeman in 1473. He was crippled, with 'crooked hands', so he was unlikely to have served a trade apprenticeship or worked as a cooper. His admission by patrimony, or his father's copy, allowed him to enter into part of his inheritance very much as a yeoman's son would inherit his father's copyhold land. Robert was senior Warden in 1496 and 1500, led the campaign for the Charter and then was three times Master between 1503 and 1512. Once he had served his first term as Master he would have held a particularly respected position in the Company as one of the 'Ancients'.

Other recurring names in the lists of early Masters are Hugh Crompe who first held that honour, in 1502, and had previously been Warden four times between 1480 and 1499; Thomas Elnore, Warden three times from 1494 and Master in 1504 and 1513; and John Harvey, four times Warden between 1488 and 1498 and Master in 1510 and 1515. All these men were in a position of great authority in the Fraternity and must have played an important part in petitioning for the Charter.

Two leading families of the next generation, Tyrrys and Cloker were connected to Robert Thurgood by having members apprenticed to him. These were Roger Tyrrys, Master at least four times and William Cloker, brother of the elder John Cloker. John was Warden in 1508 and 1513 and Master four times from 1517 to 1534. His son John was Under Warden in 1528 when his father was Master but seems not to have fulfilled early promise or else he became more absorbed in business affairs than in those of the Company.

The elder Cloker was a successful man of business, probably trading wholesale as well as running a cooperage. He had bought property in Crooked Lane near London Bridge, probably two or three tenements, one of which was bought by the Company in 1560 and may have been the subject of a disputed ownership. Mr Cloker's 'matter' and deeds relating to it were the subject of a legal case referred to several times in the Company's records but never explained. He settled some of the Company's debts personally when he was Master in 1528 and during his next mastership he was energetic in trying to obtain statutory restrictions on the large numbers of overseas coopers in London. He was diligent in seeking support for any petition or favour by keeping the Lord Chancellor supplied with an occasional hogshead of good wine. His special place in the Company's regard was marked by his well-furnished funeral feast when 27 liverymen sat down at a table laid with brawn, a stew of rabbits, four roast capons and two geese stuffed with apples. The food was accompanied by bread and ale, four quarts of Gascon wine and five of Malmsey. It was a heartfelt commemoration.

The two decades after the grant of the Charter are hardly covered by any surviving record. There are no minutes and only one year's accounts, those for 1523–24. Even the names of the officers are missing for 1524–26. The accounts for 1523 record a large number of legal expenses as if the Company were involved in litigation and some entries suggest that the will of John Baker was in dispute and an attempt, probably by a relative, was being made to prevent the inheritance passing at last to the Company. During these years, the Company shared with other livery companies a great concern about how to enforce the control of guilds over the influx of foreign and stranger coopers. The Coopers obtained a copy of a list of their names and met representatives of the Joiners at Three Cranes Wharf to consider how to set about strengthening the law against foreigners. There are many expenses listed which indicate renewed lobbying in 1528, when the Company accounts begin: horse hire to meet 'my Lord Cardinal [Wolsey]'; boat hire for the Clerk, John Moore, to go to Westminster; and other legal fees and presents. Great fears about a flood of immigrant craftsmen had been fuelled by an Act of 1523 relaxing the absolute ban on alien, but licensed craftsmen, employing alien journeymen.

The Company was eventually successful in obtaining an Act in 1531 which gave them statutory powers to search, view and gauge all ale, beer and soap vessels made for sale in London and the suburbs. Approved vessels were to bear the St Anthony Cross, in the form of a branded letter T, to assure wholesalers, retailers and customers that the measurements were true and the workmanship sound. Most important of all, the Act set the prices for each size of vessel and repeated the restriction on brewers, to keep only two coopers to repair vessels. At the time it was a triumph for the Company, but as inflation took off in the next decade, the fixed prices became a liability.

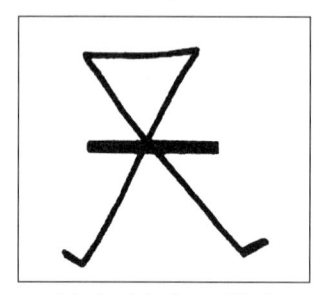

Mark of Anthony Bleek

The first officer to take charge of branding casks was John Basley, who became Sealer, paying an annual rent to the Company of £6 and hoping to make a profit for himself from the income of one farthing charged to seal each vessel. The seal became increasingly profitable even as its rent rose. It reflected the expansion of London's trade both inland and overseas and the great influx of immigrants to London from all over the British Isles. By 1556, the rent for the seal had risen to £10 a year.

The search for defective vessels and other illegal practices was nothing new but it became an important back-up for the Sealer. Usually two major searches were conducted each year, in April and October. The Master, Wardens, Beadle and Lord Mayor's Serjeant usually composed the essential search party and spent at least two days at work during each search. They might well search in Islington, Ratcliffe and Westminster as well as taking a boat from Tower Hill to Southwark, which was very well supplied with cooperages. Southwark was also favoured by unlicensed foreigners and strangers, so their vessels might be seized and rowed over to John Charley's Wharf near the Tower Watergate, thence to be carted to the Lord Mayor. A search was regularly conducted at St Bartholomew's-tide among the booths and great crowds at the fair at Smithfield. There were usually a dozen or more unlicensed coopers at work turning out poor quality household goods such as water buckets, wash-tubs, churns for making butter or cheese. The other major fair was in Southwark: Lady Fair, in honour of the Virgin, and it too, was a source of illegal coopering and poor quality goods. Sometimes a search was arranged at short notice to follow up a rumour or information, as in 1528, that Flemings were working on wharves near the Tower, without licence. After a hard day of walking or being rowed from one cooperage to another, the search party would relax over dinner at one or other of their homes, and celebrate any success with a few cups of good wine.

The search was carefully focused on areas, cooperages and individuals whose work and activities had aroused the suspicions of the Company's Beadle, who was often out and about warning and summoning members to meetings. The Company continued, after the passing of the 1531 Act, to pay an annual retainer fee to the Lord Mayor's Serjeant. He accompanied the main searches but earned, in addition, fees for seeking out and reporting instances of unlicensed foreigners or strangers and poor workmanship. He might just go 'out and about' for 12 pence; or warn members against breaking the rules for the same amount; or he might charge 20 pence for 'going about to find out defaults among them that mark vessels too little'.

The Company's anxiety about foreigners and strangers practising the trade in London without licence was well-founded for an organisation whose purpose was to maintain good standards of workmanship. Some restriction of supply was implicit in the system of control exercised by the Coopers and other organised trades. Their concern was to maintain a good income which unfettered competition might threaten. In addition, the state's role was a controlling, interventionist one: Parliament had fixed prices in the 1531 Act. In this carefully controlled, balanced market, however imperfectly it worked in practice, there could be no free-for-all. Hence the influx of coopers into London had to be controlled. The strangers, usually known collectively as Dutchmen, included not only Dutch and Flemings from the Spanish Netherlands but also Germans and French. Many sought and were granted naturalisation, after which they were known as denizens. Even as early as 1500, there were already about 3,000 alien craftsmen in London with some neighbourhoods almost entirely inhabited by French or Flemings. A census taken in 1573 indicated this number had risen to over 4,000 alien immigrants. The government's views were ambivalent since many of the newcomers brought new skills and techniques and they provided an extra source of taxation. This in turn meant that the many attempts made by the Coopers, occasionally in conjunction with other affected trades, to lobby the Privy Council or Parliament, when it was in session, failed to secure the protective legislation they sought against the strangers.

The most effective and constructive means of controlling the trade was the apprentice system. It has been claimed as 'the most positive contribution of the craft guilds to late mediaeval and early Tudor society'. It provided a period of at least seven years practical, vocational training and education. The boys were usually 13 or 14 years old when they took indentures and became members of the household of their master. It was the commercial equivalent to the contemporary practice of placing the son of a knight or nobleman as a page in another noble's household. The indentures and the ceremony of the master presenting the apprentice in open Court, before the Company, marked a solemn agreement. The master promised to provide education in the trade, to have a care for the lad's moral and spiritual welfare and to feed, clothe and lodge him. The boy would promise loyalty, obedience and diligence in serving his master and learning the trade.

Until the second half of the sixteenth century, the records give no place of origin for apprentices, but it is likely that, given the rapid growth of London, most came from beyond its confines. What is certain is that they were not paupers, nor were they casually seeking an apprenticeship. They usually had some education and basic numeracy and were sent by carrier or brought by a friend or relative to a London connection. Most Londoners in the sixteenth century were of the first generation and had retained their country or small town links.

Some coopers' wills indicate that first and second generation Londoners continued to hold property in their home town or village. Clusters of apprentices originating in the same small area suggest that links of kinship, friendship and obligation were strong enough for London coopers to arrange apprenticeships for lads from 'home'.

In October 1586, Lawrence Horsman of Kettlewell, a hamlet in Upper Wharfedale in Yorkshire, was apprentice to John James and subsequently 'set over' to Helen, James' widow. Between 1588 and 1590 he was joined in London by another Kettlewell boy, John Topper and two more from a neighbouring hamlet, Arncliffe. Together with two boys from Ribblesdale and one from the nearest market town, Skipton-in-Craven, they all probably travelled south in the care of the Skipton carrier.

Apprentices might change masters by being formally 'set over' if they felt ill-used or badly trained, or if their master became ill or died. In 1555, Thomas Bleek, the younger, asked to be moved from his master, Richard Bartlett, complaining of 'misbehaviour and ill-usage'. His request was granted. But it is good to know that whatever the ill-feeling, it had dispersed sufficiently for Richard to be a beneficiary of Bleek senior's will.

Between presentation as a new apprentice and the grant of freedom, seven or more years later, there was a great wastage in numbers. Country boys were very susceptible to the diseases of the City, in particular sweating sickness, influenza and the bubonic plague. The latter was widespread from 1535 to 1539, although the 'sweat', a virus disease to which people in the prime of life, between 20 and 30 years old, were most susceptible, was absent from London from 1528 to 1551. Some boys absconded, perhaps to live by their wits in London, or because they felt they had learned enough to earn a living back home. Because the length of apprenticeships varied (some were apprenticed earlier than the normal 13 or 14 years of age) it is difficult to match numbers gaining the freedom with the numbers of indentures seven years earlier. But rough comparisons suggest that the freemen were seldom as many as two-thirds and usually one quarter of the original number of apprentices.

An indicator that apprentices were considered as part of their master's family, is their inclusion as beneficiaries in Coopers' wills and the remission of one or two of their years of service. Forty shillings was a usual amount of a legacy and perhaps a suit of clothes. John Baker left his apprentice 53s 4d and his violet, furred gown.

Most apprentices, on completing their term of service, were granted the freedom of the Company (and of the City) and often remained as journeymen working in the same household where they had been apprenticed. It was a big step to become an independent householder, with one's own workshop, mark and apprentices. The sons of the wealthier Coopers tended to move quite quickly to this status. At a ceremony in open Court, they were granted their mark, a personal logo, often derived from their initials, which had to appear on the bevel edge on the chime of their casks. For this they paid 3s 4d, and from 1547 they were encouraged to give a silver spoon to the Company or its cash equivalent, which was calculated at 6s 8d. These were goodwill payments and were introduced to alleviate the effect of inflation. The spoons also provided a useful source of capital which could be quickly exchanged for cash to meet extra taxation from Crown or City.

Entry to the Livery was the privilege of relatively few householders. From 1529 when there were 23 liverymen, there was only slow growth in numbers to reach 35 in 1566. This was a little under half the number of householders. The choice of new liverymen was made by the existing Livery from among the most substantial and longest-serving householders. Elections occurred when a few vacancies had accumulated. For example six entered in 1529 and eleven in 1547. An oath of loyalty was taken before the Court, the new liveryman received his hood and gown, the symbol of his new status and was then entitled to take part in all Court meetings, feasts and drinkings.

No distinction was made between liverymen and assistants. However, there was always a small core of up to a dozen who attended Court meetings regularly, had served as Warden or Master at least once and were occasionally referred to as assistants. There was no automatic succession from Warden to Master, although it was customary to proceed from Under to Upper Warden within one or two years. The Company relied heavily on the experience of those who had served as Warden or Master, but without being exclusive. It was a mirror of early Tudor society which gave great respect to status and birth but accepted talent and kept open the ladder from the ranks of humble birth to the highest levels of society. Self-made men of enterprise and good fortune were liberally scattered across the highest echelons of society.

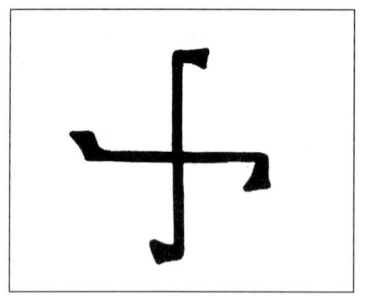

Mark of John Bray. Marks were recorded in a special book by the Clerk. When the owner died, his mark could be chosen by another new householder. This mark became Arthur Bray's, Master in 1624.

The Charter of 1501 had fixed Election Day on the Sunday preceding Pentecost. It was most likely confirming long-established practice. All the Livery were summoned by the Beadle and fined subsequently if they were late, absent without good cause or improperly dressed. The wearing of gowns was required. Until the late 1540s, the election was held in the hall of one of the other livery companies, since John Baker's old house was neither large enough nor sufficiently dignified for such an important ceremony. In 1530, the Pewterers' Hall was hired and its keeper paid extra to ensure clean rushes had been spread on the floor.

The day usually began with mass, either in the chapel of Guildhall or in the parish church of St Michael Bassishaw. Singing clerks and children were hired to ensure the service was pleasant and dignified, and the church was provided with new tapers and clean rushes. From 1547, the Company's own newly-built Hall was used for the election, which was by acclaim from two nominations for each office. The Hall was always decorated with 'flowers and bowers' and 'strewing' herbs, usually rosemary and juniper, were mixed among the rushes on the floor. The table would have been spread with the best of the stock of napery, the damask, and have as its centrepiece a large silver gilt bowl used for rose water. The food was simple; spice bread and ale but these basics were augmented by a gallon each of strong beer, Gascon wine and muscadine.

Adding a touch of brightness, were the silk banners stretched between white staves and bearing the Company's motto and arms, the arms of the City and specially commissioned banners for recent royal events: Henry VIII's coronation, Anne Boleyn's coronation and the reception of Anne of Cleves at Greenwich. Propped against the walls, they would have made a scene of riotous colour. The contemporary taste was for strong and contrasting colours, so purples and yellows, scarlets and pinks would be further picked out in gold and silver thread. The Election Day meal in 1537 had the added excitement of a serving-man with a grievance, presenting himself in his armour with bow and sheaf of arrows. The Beadle took control, sent for the Serjeant and together they took the man off to the Compter, the Lord Mayor's gaol.

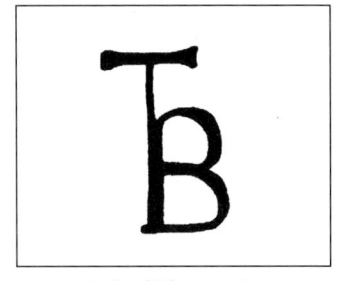

Mark of Thomas Bray

Whether a ceremony of confirming the election of the Master and Wardens took place immediately after they had been acclaimed, or more likely, later at their first court, when they were sworn into office, it is fairly certain that the ceremony took the form of crowning them with garlands. Among the few items in one of the earliest surviving inventories, are three garlands and two red streamers. These are mentioned again in the inventory for 1570 with the comment 'to choose Master and Wardens with red ribbon' .This probably referred to circlets of laurel leaves, fashioned from pewter or silver, decorated with red ribbon.

The first court to be presided over by the new Master, usually held in mid-June, was a special occasion and marked as such in the Company records with more than usually elaborate initial letters, titles and flourishes of the scrivener's art. The whole Livery was summoned and those householders with business to transact. There was usually one of the largest lists of apprentices to present. This was the Court for setting over discontented apprentices and when debts were settled or sent to arbitration by senior members. Missing this court meant a certain fine of four pence, equivalent to a labourer's wage for a day. Arrangements were made for the annual audit and inventory, normally held in July and four liverymen were appointed to scrutinise the accounts of the retiring Wardens and agree the balances which they handed over to their successors.

Often the Upper Warden was owed money which he had spent on the Company from his own funds and he would be reimbursed from the Under Warden who was more likely to show a profit. From time to time generous and wealthy colleagues would lend any deficit so that the Wardens were not personally out of pocket. Income from fines, quarterage and admissions were vital to the Company's cash-flow and their efficient collection depended very much on the assiduity of the Beadle as the chief collector of such dues. He also seems eventually to have kept the iron chest with double locks in which the treasures and cash were stored. Disaster struck in 1545 when it seems either both keys were lost or the locks jammed irrevocably. A smith was sent for to take a side panel out of the chest.

Court business had a rhythm and regularity which gave a sense of security to members. It gave authority to a small number of leading liverymen to control and discipline their fellow coopers within the City and suburbs. It dealt with the imposition of routine fines for lateness, absence, being improperly dressed either without gown, or worse, in an apron. It adjudicated on members' breach of rules such as swearing, reviling the officers, giving away trade or Company secrets, stealing another's customers and just occasionally, brawling in street or tavern. It acted as a court of justice, hearing evidence, hearing the defence as well as offering arbitrators in the more difficult cases. It heard from the Sealer whose task was to bring to court offenders who had made vessels too small, not tight enough, used green wood or sappy binding hoops, and worst of all tried to re-use old strongly-smelling staves from soap or fish barrels for kilderkins, firkins or barrels for ale, beer or wine. Fines were awarded according to a tariff for offences and the miscreant ordered to pay by the next court. Hardship was respected and many householders in difficulty because of illness or poor trade were given time to pay, or even a lower fine. There existed, not just occasionally, but over the decades, a true brotherly concern for all members and sternness was usually tempered by charity.

Fines were charged for keeping an apprentice without bringing him to court to be admitted, having more than the allowable number of apprentices, failing to mark casks and evading or obstructing the Sealer. Predictably some coopers' names recur for 'unworkmanlike' casks, 'naughty' kilderkins, and 'sappy' tubs and pails. Serious, multiple or repeated offences, where the mistake could not be amended, led to a public burning—of the cask, not the cooper—and sometimes the cooper might be put briefly in the Compter.

Many fines originated in a trade matter but then led on to a dispute between the accused and the Court. Often quite senior liverymen were involved, tempers were lost and the eventual outcome was a fine for disobedience. John Wylles, Master in 1535, was in serious trouble in 1531 when he was Upper Warden. His fine was a hefty £4 10s. 'for his disobedience and trespass'. Robert Swayne, Master in 1552, was fined ten shillings for disobedience in 1536 and John Whitehead, one of a coopering dynasty, and Master in 1551 and 1564, was sent to the Compter for his disobedience in 1539. Swayne and Whitehead were probably sowing a few wild oats.

Loose tongues and quick tempers were the cause of many incidents and fines. From its earliest days, the Company took a strict view on abusing fellow members with words or fists. Nicholas Long misused Master Parkin in 1558, calling him knave and was lucky to escape with a fine of 20 pence, one quarter the normal fine. John Miller struck John Bray's servant. The lad almost lost an eye, 'to the great reproach and ignominy of the fellowship', since the incident took place in front of several strangers. George Dodson, who often could not hold his tongue, rebuked the Warden in front of journeymen and was fined 3s 4d. A few months later he was in trouble for 'disclosing secrets', and was fined ten shillings. Richard Cooke had to pay the same amount for pretending he had the authority of the Master and Wardens. The result was he deceived John Edwards, who lost his temper, reviled Cooke publicly and called the Master and Wardens 'vagabonds'. Cooke was no stranger to disputes and had probably been cheating on his business partner in 1562, when the Court intervened and appointed arbitrators to allocate debts arising from purchases of wood from a Suffolk farmer.

Friction could arise when members lent money to the Company to pay the various taxes (to purchase wheat or equip soldiers, for example) imposed by the Crown or the City. Such extraordinary expenditure usually left the Company in debt with the immediate charge being borne by the Upper Warden at the end of the Company's financial year at midsummer. A special arbitration took place in 1564 because Thomas Busby, when Upper Warden in 1561, had been unable to balance his account. Accusations were made against Busby, led by Richard Charley, then the Sealer, and James Nicholas who was himself no stranger to controversy. Twelve arbitrators were chosen and met on the afternoon of 29 June 1564. They came to the conclusion that

Busby must personally bear the loss. The term 'assistants' was used to describe the arbitrators.

Arbitration by one's brethren could avoid the delays and expense of the law courts. For some coopers, who were more than usually disputatious, this must have been a relief. One such was Thomas Bleek who had been apprenticed to John Charley, was made free in 1540 and became Under Warden in 1559. He was fined for his loose tongue in 1545; then two years later he was in dispute with Stephen Heath (Master in 1559, 1563, 1573 and 1579) and each was fined for falling out and 'rebuking each other in unbrotherly fashion in the street'. There followed a run-in with his former Master, John Charley, where each was fined; Bleek paying three times Charley's fine; a fine for slander against Stephen Heath when the latter was Master for the first time and Bleek his Warden, and a long-running dispute with Ralph Boughey (or à Bough) another senior member, Master in 1555 and 1560. To avoid the Courts of Law, the pair agreed on arbitration and Bleek was found guilty of slander against Boughey.

The decision cost him a dinner for Boughey, the Master and Wardens and some of the 'Ancients'. For all his misdemeanours, Bleek appears not to have been vindictive: he quarrelled and lost another arbitration with his journeyman, William Wright, but William was left a worsted jacket in Bleek's will. This was entirely in accord with the Company's desire to see disputants, in the end, shaking hands on being commanded by the Court 'to be as lovers and friends'. The Company was anxious to remain a Fraternity.

CHAPTER TWO

The First Hall and the First Charity 1550–1570

> *Edward VI's guardians promoted Protestantism. The Prayer Book in English replaced the Latin Mass, images of saints were destroyed as idolatrous, chantries confiscated, prayers for the dead ceased. Mary (1553–58) reversed some of these changes but made no attempt to restore monastic lands. Support for her evaporated because she allied with Spain and burned too many Protestants. Elizabeth, her half-sister, was welcomed as a national saviour, the earliest manifestation of the 'nation'. She was beset by enemies abroad; France and Spain, who regarded her as a heretic, and challenged at home by northern rebels, the Earls of Northumberland and Westmorland and the Duke of Norfolk. Mary, Queen of Scots, the legitimate heir, fled to England and became a focus for Catholic plots against Elizabeth.*

JOHN BAKER'S BEQUEST of two tenements at the sign of the Swan in Basinghall Street came, at length, into the Company's possession not later than 1522. Various improvements and major repairs were made in 1528–29. These were probably to extend the property, for there are bills for making walls, erecting lath and plaster above brickwork, glazing windows and fixing a gable frame. There were further works in 1531–32, 1533, when a chimney was repaired, and 1534 when timbers, boards, tiles and laths were supplied. More repairs of a fundamental kind were carried out in 1536. It appeared that good money was being squandered on an old building which was too small for the Company's major events.

The initiative to build a proper Hall was made in 1543, when John Heath, the Upper Warden, provided the inspiration and much of the money needed for this ambitious project. Heath was a grocer, that is, a wholesaler, by trade, though his father was a member of the Coopers' Company. At the head of the accounts for 1543–44, John Heath is described as 'the first provoker and founder of the Craft's new Common Hall and for the new building of it out of the ground... he freely gave all the principal timber... moreover he gave and well and truly paid from the 29 August until Christmas Eve... the payment of the workmen that built the same hall and the other premises thereto belonging... and besides sundry other gifts... praying to god to send many more such good benefactors to the said craft'. John Baker's house was pulled down and the new building was sited in its yard and thus set back from Basinghall Street.

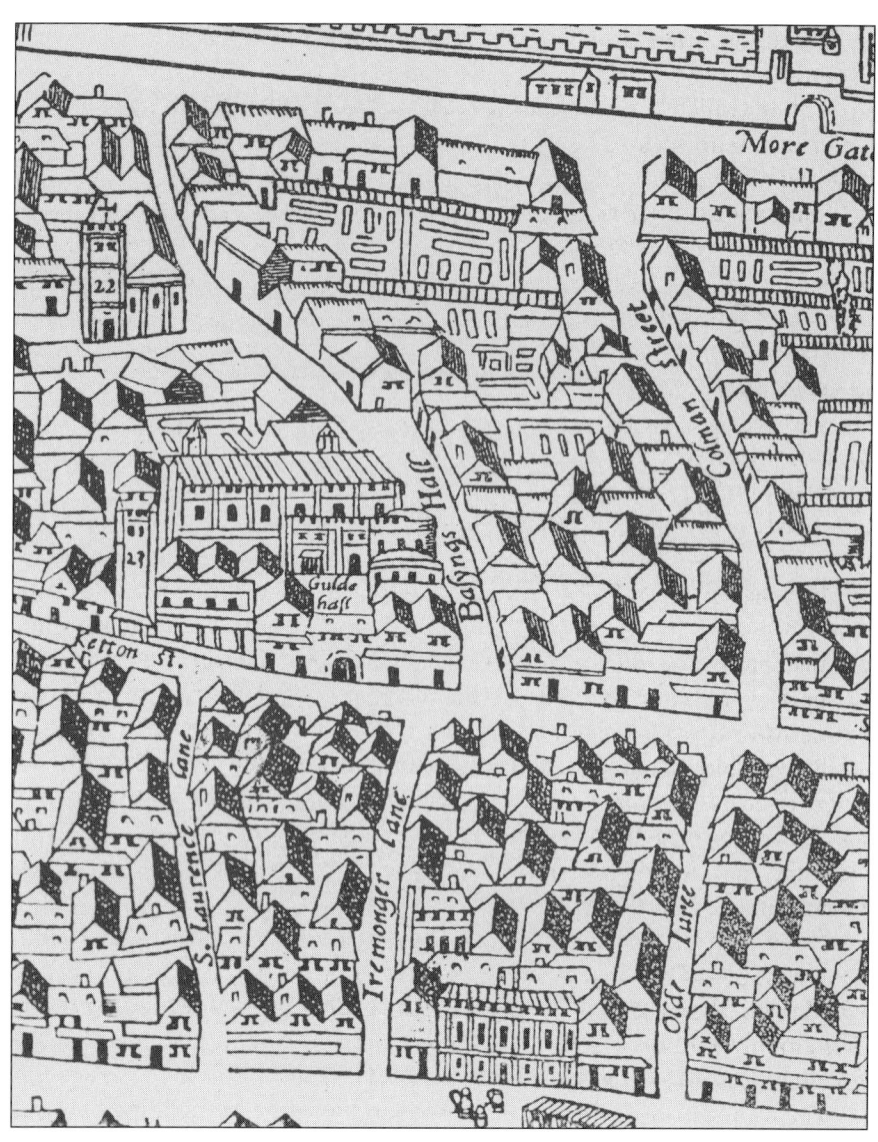

Map-view of 1561, the so-called 'Agas' map of London. The recently-built Coopers' Hall and its neighbouring tenements, bequeathed by John Baker, occupy the corner of Basinghall Street behind Guildhall and in front of St Michael's church (no. 22). Beyond is London Wall with its ditch (broken lines) and northwards are the tenter-frames and open fields: Finsbury due north and Moor Fields, north east. Ketton Street follows the line of present-day Gresham Street and Cheapside forms the southern boundary. A market stall and three large wooden water vessels can just be seen. The vessels were used to take water to houses. They are examples of the Coopers' craft.

THE FIRST HALL AND THE FIRST CHARITY

The timbers were brought from Godstone in Surrey, first to Croydon and then transported partly by river to Basinghall Street. The cost of transport was £12 13s 4d, which included tolls and tips to the 'wyffe that toke the tolls for the bridge'. With six loads costing 16 shillings, there were at least 90 loads. The building was a timber-framed structure, like most buildings in London, with no foundations other than timber 'groundsills'. There were probably some brick courses and certainly brickwork chimneys, but the major part of the walls, internal and external, were of lath and plaster. Such building materials provided good shelter for the rats which carried the bubonic plague.

The building was modest and soon proved too small. Extensions were made as early as 1546–47 when more ground was cleared and foundation 'groundsills' laid. At the same time, there were second thoughts about the parlour, which had a gable added with a new window. All the work was done on site from the cutting of the timbers into 'quarters' by the sawyers, the construction of the main frame by the carpenters, to the finishing processes of the joiners, fashioning banisters, panelling and wainscot. In between came bricklayers, plasterers, tilers, the ironmonger and the smith, the plumber, who laid piping across the yard to carry away water from the kitchen and the upholsterer to add a little comfort to window seats and settles. 'Hary' the Dutchman arrived to sort through the old glass from John Baker's house and re-use what he could. Glass was still a precious commodity, though more easily available since a new manufacturer had been established at Crutched Friars after its dissolution as a monastery. The old glass was set in new lead and 70 feet of new glass was put into the lower windows. The main rooms were the hall, which may have been partly wainscotted and had painted fabric hangings on the upper walls, and two parlours, the larger of which, was used for Court meetings. The hall was the height of the building with roof windows. On the first floor was the counting house. The hall had wooden benches, the parlours had settles and one large table painted green. The employment of a skinner and an upholsterer suggests that some of the furniture was padded and covered with leather.

The roof was tiled but it is possible that the span over the hall was large enough to merit a lead covering. The payment to the plumber indicates he was paid for more than pipe-laying in the kitchen. He was probably also employed fixing lead on the roof. The outer walls were protected by the over-hung roof to keep them as dry as possible. The infill between the timbers consisted of horizontal laths slotted into a framework, then covered and filled with clay and straw daub to make a solid panel. When this dried out, the cracks were covered with a lime-base plaster, coloured red and ochre.

That it was a fragile structure is clear from the many and frequent repairs, sometimes replacing a panel, sometimes a whole section of wall. Finishing touches were the paving of the yard and street outside, building a wall with a gate at the street boundary, and as a final flourish, in 1544, building a porch over the gate with one bench seat on either side. It made a pleasant spot to sit under cover and watch the world go about its business. Unfortunately, one bench was soon broken by an unruly horse, hired possibly to carry the Clerk or a Warden on a visit outside the City on the Company's business.

John Heath generously paid off £13 of the Company's debts and all members were invited to subscribe towards the completion costs. Some gave money, some goods but the details are lost. The scrivener got no further in recording the details than a flourishing heading in the account book.

To have acquired a Common Hall of their own was a matter of great pride and rejoicing. Several other companies had recently taken advantage of former monastic property coming on to the market: the Leathersellers, for example, had obtained the dormitory of the nunnery of St Helen in Bishopsgate in 1542. The Coopers felt good to be keeping pace with some of the larger livery companies. It called for a celebration.

Once again, the chief provider was John Heath. He offered a venison which was carried from his house to the Hall for roasting. A special cook and labourers for two days were hired, as were pewter vessels and silver decorations for the table. The Company had taken some years to build up its stock of wooden trenchers and white, ash wood cups. The Company's treasures, gowns, garlands, the girdle, the Master and Wardens' hoods, silk banners and few pieces of silver were also brought to the Hall for the feast from the houses of John Charley and John Heath, where they had been securely held.

There was no economy about the menu and the wealthier members contributed £2 10s towards the costs. With three pence buying bread and beer for a Court meeting, and 5s 8d buying 12 shoulders of mutton, it went a long way. In addition to the dozen shoulders, and the venison, there were two legs of mutton, three dozen bread loaves, a barrel of ale, several gallons of wine, cucumbers, radishes, various, unspecified root vegetables, pepper, rosemary, parsley and, most expensive of all, marzipan cakes. To add to the comfort of the occasion, there were clean rushes and herbs on the floor, garlands on the tables and walls, and minstrels in the hall's gallery. At the gate there were porters to keep out intruders and within the hall, stewards to serve. When the accounts were drawn up by the Wardens at the year's end, there was general satisfaction that, in spite of all the expenses of the Hall, the

THE FIRST HALL AND THE FIRST CHARITY

great feast, the provision of wheat for the City granary and the equipping of six soldiers for the King, there was £9 surplus on the year.

The duty of providing wheat was a form of taxation laid upon the livery companies by the Lord Mayor. It was aimed at avoiding public disorder and relieving distress among the poorer citizens should the harvest fail and the price of bread rise beyond the ability of the poor to pay inflated prices. Increasingly, the City Corporation and the central Government regarded poverty as a new problem, new, at least, in its scale, and a threat to public order. As London grew in population and extent, drawing in fortune-seekers, the dislocated and the destitute, there was much hand-wringing among the ruling classes about the ills that would ensue from the increase in the numbers of masterless men. One of the several weapons to fight this de-stabilising influence was to maintain a City grain supply which could be released on to the market to lower prices when there was a dearth. When Edward VI gave the royal palace of Bridewell to the Corporation in 1553, it was used in part as a hospital, a house of correction for vagabonds and unruly apprentices and a City granary. The usual precept for the Coopers was £20 towards filling the granary. The Livery appointed four trusted members, to apportion the cost on the basis of individuals' ability to pay. The range of payments was from 2 shillings to 40 shillings and regarded as a loan to the Company which, in turn and at length, reimbursed members. Usually they had to wait a year, sometimes longer for repayments. Gunpowder was another commodity for which a precept was issued occasionally, (e.g. in 1574) so that the City could maintain its readiness for military action.

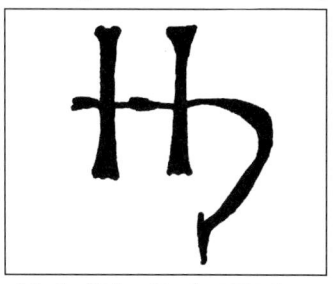

Mark of John Heath, 1509, later assigned to Henry Hinchlit, 1601 and then to Hamlet Hawks, 1637.

Another form of taxation in kind, was the obligation placed by the Crown on the City of London to impress and equip soldiers. This duty was passed down to the livery companies, each being required to provide a number deemed fair for its size and wealth. In 1543, when Henry VIII went to war with France, in alliance with the Emperor Charles V, the Company was required to arm and clothe six men. Again, there was the same levy in 1547 when Scotland was invaded. Some items of 'harness' (armour), girdles and weapons—bows, sheafs of arrows, swords, daggers—were kept at the Hall, maintained from time to time by an armourer and by one of the Company. There is a note about an elderly freeman, old Asplin, who 'scoured the harness' in 1538. To some extent, compulsory archery festivals at midsummer were a means of ensuring that the City companies kept their military equipment in good shape.

During Henry VIII's French wars, the Company had to equip three groups of six armed men, two bowmen and four billmen, on each occasion. It involved a great deal of activity; not only had the armour to be scoured to remove rust, it had to be oiled, leather attachments checked and possibly replaced, but also swords needed sharpening, arrows feathered and clothing purchased. In 1542, the men were required in plain white coats, doublets of white fustian and canvas, and white upper slippers. Red cloth was also purchased to make crosses for the jackets and chain was sewn on the archers' sleeves. At 5s 4d a yard, the material was relatively expensive. Two swords and two daggers cost 5s 2d. Usually, the Company had no reserves from which to meet the full costs, so loans were raised from members. In 1544, the full cost was £6 9s 9d; in 1558, when 12 men were required, it was £9 13s 8d. The Company raised a loan of £13 13s 4d in 1563 to send eight men to Newhaven, (not the English port, but Le Havre). These men were provided with pay and rations to sustain them during their march possibly to Portsmouth.

When the Earls of Northumberland and Westmorland raised rebellion against Elizabeth in 1569, London was taxed with supplying 4,000 men, of whom half were to carry the light musket, the caliver. These rather unreliable guns cost 6s 8d and had to be provided with powder and shot, in special pouches. Again, the Company's levy was to find and equip six men, this time with blue uniforms. There seems to have been little difficulty in raising small loans from members to pay these costs. Concern for security and a developing sense of patriotism were enough to bring in contributions from among all categories of Coopers, journeymen and 'Dutchmen', householders and liverymen. Often the loans were duly and fully repaid, but the Company's finances were sometimes precarious so there was no guarantee of this.

These demands from the Lord Mayor illustrate the role the livery companies were called upon to play in ensuring the security of the King's government. The first Tudor kings were keenly aware of the fragility of their power and their dynasty. The machinery of government at their command was slender, as were their resources. When Henry VIII became king in 1509, there were only five ships in the Royal Navy. It was therefore vital that the Crown worked in partnership with London, which increasingly dominated the economic and political life of the country and grew rapidly from a population of 50,000 in 1500 to 200,000 in 1600. The Crown needed London's

THE FIRST HALL AND THE FIRST CHARITY

loyalty and obedience and to be able to tap its wealth. The great state occasions of coronation, victory celebrations, royal funerals and marriages demonstrated the partnership of City and Crown.

Henry VII's funeral, in April 1509, was an occasion of magnificent ceremony lasting three days. The King himself had left detailed instructions for his obsequies. He left money for 10,000 masses to be said for his soul's repose and, with an accountant's exactness, specified the payments and the details of his funeral procession. He required 300 hooded penitents in white, bearing torches, to accompany his hearse. Of these, all provided by livery companies, the Coopers provided, and clothed, 30, a surprisingly large number for their relative size and status in the hierarchy of companies (ranked 37 out of 50 in 1501). The great companies had, in addition, to provide 104 black-clothed riders to accompany the Lord Mayor's procession which met the royal cortège at St George's Bar on London Bridge. While the King's body lay in state, after its journey across London to Westminster Abbey, there were two more processions in the City ending with a barge procession taking the Lord Mayor, Sheriffs and Aldermen with the black riders upstream to Westminster for the funeral service.

The route of all royal processions through the City was lined with special stands belonging to the livery companies. Each had its allotted space, each provided its own 'standing' which had broadcloth as a covering, railings to protect the liverymen from the crush of other Londoners, and a brave display of their banners. A royal funeral or coronation would always merit a new banner, made of silk, or sarcenet-taffeta, embroidered and painted with the Company's arms, motto and other devices appropriate to the occasion. The route from London Bridge began at St Magnus the Martyr, continued along Gracechurch Street, where the Coopers had their standing in 1509, and then into Leadenhall Street, reserved for foreign merchants and craftsmen. In Cornhill and the eastern part of Cheapside were more standings belonging to the lesser livery companies, ending with the Twelve great companies in West Cheap nearest to St Paul's.

A similar route was followed for coronations, when it was customary for the new sovereign to lodge at the Tower on the eve of the service at Westminster Abbey. In 1533, Henry VIII spared no effort or expense to celebrate Anne Boleyn's coronation. The Eleanor Cross in West Cheap was regilded and there was a spectacular barge procession from Greenwich, in which some of the Company took part, to bring the Queen to the Tower. Henry's efforts were in vain. Although the companies went obediently to their standings, the new Queen was greeted by silent crowds. In the privacy of their Common Halls and homes, Londoners called her a harlot and continued to honour and respect Queen Catherine whom the King had set aside and humiliated.

The Company took part in a barge procession, in January 1540, to welcome Henry's fourth bride, the Princess of Cleves. This time it was Henry's turn to feel unenthusiastic and embarrassed. The politic match failed, and its instigator, Thomas Cromwell, fell from power. What little the liverymen understood of these matters did not interfere with them doing their duty. They seem, metaphorically as well as literally, to have pushed the boat out. Whereas a mere 15 shillings had been expended for Anne Boleyn, for Anne of Cleves they had 14 new escutcheons made to decorate the barge, had two blue velvet cloths repaired and hired musicians for entertainment as they were rowed down to Greenwich. It was dark when they returned, it being January, and they needed a link man with his torch to guide them back through muddy lanes to the Hall. It was cold, too, so the drink allowance for the bargemaster, shipwright and the Coopers themselves, was generous.

There were other celebrations, which punctuated the calendar, of a more domestic and regular kind. Until the Reformation and the drastic reduction of Saints' days, which meant holidays, the Company joined the celebrations of the two midsummer feasts of St John the Baptist (June 24) and St Peter (June 29) with traditional processions, bonfires, cakes and ale. For the procession, large quantities of cotton cloth were purchased every year and cut in four possibly to be used as targets in 'clout shooting' (long distance archery). Eight cresset bearers were hired to provide light. Traditionally, Baptist-day was a time for making up quarrels with neighbours, for being charitable and merry and for good-natured archery competitions between the apprentices and young journeymen of the different companies. At the Hall, there was a great deal of activity in preparation for these midsummer junketings. The Company's small stock of archery gear needed attention, arrows re-feathered, lost gloves replaced. On each of the two nights, there was a feast for the Livery. In 1547, which may well have been the last celebration in London, the Company added red crossed keys for St Peter to their white cloths and, in addition to their badges, the cresset bearers were also provided with straw hats.

All this was swept away by the Protestant reforms put in place during Edward VI's brief reign. The cult of Saints came under attack during 1547 and, by September, royal officers ensured that in St Paul's and many City churches, all images except those of the Virgin and St John on the rood screen had been removed. Processions, bells, feasts of saints, candles at

Candlemas, ashes on Ash Wednesday, wooden crosses on Palm Sunday, maintaining candles for the dead on altars in chantry chapels and elsewhere, were all swept away. With them went the midsummer bonfires.

A serious financial consequence for the Company was the Chantries Act which completed the despoiling of endowments to say masses for the dead and support chantry priests. It dissolved the chantries, as the monasteries had already been dissolved by Henry VIII. John Baker's bequest was threatened since part was to ensure the annual *obit* commemorating his death and praying for his soul. There was consternation throughout the City as hundreds of similar, and better endowed, bequests to livery companies were threatened with forfeiture and extinction. Fortunately, the royal bureaucracy was unable to locate and collect the dues from these endowments. A deal, therefore, was worked out between the City and the royal officials that the City companies would 're-purchase' their theoretically forfeited endowments. In 1549, the Coopers scraped together £19, their share of almost £19,000 raised by the livery companies to secure their inheritances. Leading liverymen contributed, as always, to a loan for the Company. The Master gave £1, John Heath £2, the Wardens and several others, 13s 4d. It was three years before they were repaid. There were no more masses said or sung on 19 July for the soul of John Baker. But the Company kept faith with the living and each year gave alms and coal to the poor of the parish.

It was probably at this time that the old motto *Gaude Maria Virgo* was abandoned and *Love as Brethren* adopted. Whatever were the doctrinal views of members, the Company had to bow to the law of the land. To contemporaries, the years 1548–49 appeared as a watershed. The familiar ceremonies and liturgy which had comforted the faithful for centuries were swept away for ever. Queen Mary tried to restore them when she succeeded her brother in 1553, but only partially and patchily. For Londoners, the ending of the 'sensyng of Powlles'—the swinging of a great censer from the roof of St Paul's and the release of doves to represent the coming of the Holy Ghost at Whitsun—symbolised the passing of the old religion. It was the 'tyme of scysme when the Realm devyded from the Catholic Churche'.

It was also a time of great significance for the Company. In 1549, it became the tenant of a garden at Ratcliffe, then a small settlement of mariners and shipwrights, and one of the hamlets of the ancient manor of Stepney. The garden was part of the estate of Nicholas Gibson, in 1526, Prime Warden of the Grocers' Company, and Sheriff in 1539. He had left it in trust to his widow, Avice, who shortly married Sir Anthony Knyvett. Gibson intended that all his property in Ratcliffe and in the City, near the Tower,

Accounts for 1571–72 depicting Astronomy, one of the liberal arts, which made up the mathematical quadrivium.

should form the endowment of a school and 14 almshouses which he and Avice had founded in Ratcliffe in 1536.

Gibson had inherited property from his father at Ratcliffe between the River Thames and the King's Highway. He purchased the Old Wool Quay in Lower Thames Street in 1511, presumably to develop his business as a grocer. We do not know his precise trade; he may have dealt in wool, timber or any number of different commodities. Clearly he was successful enough to acquire more property in Ratcliffe to the north of the Highway, where he eventually founded his school, and his wealth helped him prosper in his Company and in City politics. He bore one of the highest taxation assessments in 1535 and in May 1539 he rode with the Lord Mayor and his fellow Sheriff at the head of 15,000 citizen soldiers whom the King reviewed at Westminster. He died 18 months later in September 1540.

The provisions of his will reflect some of the uncertainties caused by the King's attack on church wealth. The dissolution of the monasteries was almost complete, raising doubts about a safe future for his charity, if he left it to the church's guardianship. The obvious alternative was to entrust it to a City livery company whose corporate status would ensure its perpetuity. Why Gibson did not choose his own company is obscure. He was content to leave matters in the hands of his widow to whom he left a life interest and a duty to maintain the school and almshouses in Ratcliffe. She was charged with making provision for a perpetual endowment on her death. (The Gibsons had no children.)

The link with the Coopers was most likely personal and professional. John Heath was a grocer by trade and Avice Gibson granted him the lease of the Old Wool Quay immediately after Nicholas' death. By deed of gift, in 1553, Dame Avice (her title after her second marriage) transferred the Old Wool Quay to John Charley, another grocer by trade and Master of the Coopers four times, on condition that, on his death, he bequeathed it to the Company. Heath and Charley were both wholesale merchants, both probably dealing in timber, and part of a small group of prosperous traders who dominated the Company in the 1530s and 1540s. Prominent in this group was Thomas à Wood, Master four times between 1530 and 1546 and almost certainly one of the witnesses to Nicholas Gibson's will. These existing links led to the Company's interest in taking a lease of the Ratcliffe garden in 1549 at a yearly rent of £3 6s 8d. It was neglected and in need of structural work as well as cultivation. Paths were cleared of rubbish and raked, new walls constructed, a bowling alley was paved and growing beds were enriched with four loads of top soil. In the first season it produced a good crop of strawberries which were picked by local women for eight pence a day.

By 1549, Dame Avice was widowed for a second time and had settled back in Ratcliffe probably in the Stone House, after a peripatetic life with Sir Anthony. She was actively considering ways of securing her first husband's charity after her own death and began negotiations with the Company. Complex legal arrangements began, with the Company paying the fees of two lawyers to help Dame Avice in her discussions with the lord of the manor of Stepney, who was Lord Wentworth. In the manner of the age, Dame Avice's status was recognised in the flow of gifts sent by the Company: 'a Capon, two rabbits for My Lady Knyvett'; three green geese, half a dozen rabbits and a potell (half a gallon) of sack on Whit Sunday, 1553; and in October, six gallons of muscadine, one rundlet (15 gallons) of wine and twelve gallons of vinegar.

During 1551 and 1552, the Wardens were kept busy dealing with the lawyers and Lord Wentworth's steward. The process they sought was a surrender of Dame Avice's lands to the lord of the manor so that she could continue to enjoy the use during her lifetime but ensure that the Coopers' Company would be allowed to enter into possession on her death.

When the surrender was complete, a great celebration was held at Ratcliffe. John Charley and other senior liverymen took a boat down the Thames laden with the feast. There were two breasts of veal, a shoulder of mutton, eight rabbits and a large salmon. Bread, beer and ale, a gallon of claret and a rundlet of sack, which seems to have been Dame Avice's favourite tipple, and a pudding of spicy pears made up the rest of the cargo. When the party reached the Stone House's quay, they found the table laid and decked with flowers. Three maids were waiting to receive the hampers of food and to dress it suitably for the table. The legal suit had proved an expensive affair and to help Dame Avice with the costs the Company collected £30 from its Livery. Even after the celebratory feast there was still much to-ing and fro-ing by boat to complete the paperwork. The scrivener was sent several times to Ratcliffe to copy documents. The Wardens were required there as witnesses. They had also to wait on Lord Wentworth and make a present to Lady Wentworth at Westminster.

Dame Avice's friends in the Company remained attentive and visited her during the last year of her life when she was probably about 60 years of age. They sent a potell of sack for the funeral wake in October 1554 and received, shortly after, a silver gilt basin and ewer with some damask linen. The maid who delivered these gifts received 12 pence 'for her pains'. It was the last courtesy in a relationship, notable for respect and friendship, between Gibson's widow and the Company.

The Company took possession immediately of its new properties even though it was struggling to pay its entry fine of £40 to Lord Wentworth in instalments. It suddenly had new responsibilities: a school with 40 scholars, a schoolmaster, Roger Hutchinson and his usher, John Watson and 14 almsmen and women. The Ratcliffe properties from whose rents the charity was supported, consisted of several cottages (seven are identified) several tenements with gardens, two crofts, one of which was the two-and-a-half acre site of the school and almshouses, three gardens, the Stone House, and some marshland pasture. The riverside tenements had wharves and storehouses and, although many residents were mariners, Ratcliffe still retained a rural aspect, dominated by mighty elm trees.

The school and almshouses were also beneficiaries of rents from a messuage and wharf, the Old Wool Quay, in the parish of All Saints, Barking (All Hallows by the Tower). This quay, situated a little upstream from the Tower, was destined shortly to be the site of a Custom House and had been held in trust until his death in 1553 by John Charley. His will clearly sets out the responsibility of the Master and Wardens. They were charged to maintain a schoolmaster 'mete and learned... in the letters of grammar to teach grammar and the knowledge of grammar and also instruct little children in the ABC and such learning as should be most convenient'. The schoolmaster was to be paid £10 a year and to have the assistance of an usher 'learned in Latin grammar'. His stipend was 26s 8d. The pensioners were to receive 6s 8d a quarter and the Master and Wardens were to inspect the premises twice a year, for which they were to receive 26s 8d. The first list of pensioners receiving their payment from the Company appeared in the 1554 accounts. It included three married couples. According to Dame Avice's wishes, seven almshouses were for the poor of the parish of Stepney and seven for the poor of the company or their wives.

The Wool Quay was leased to Richard Starr (Master in 1558, 1565 and 1570) who was related by marriage to John Heath. It yielded £22 in rent, while the Ratcliffe properties yielded £27 a year. However, the Crown saw the site as ideal for a Custom House to levy duties on goods coming into the many quays above London Bridge before the ships carrying them passed through the bridge. In 1558, Queen Mary compulsorily purchased the quay for £400, which passed into the safe keeping of John Heath, Richard Starr and Stephen Heath. They were the leaders of the Company and probably its wealthiest members, with secure premises to keep the money safe. From this sum, other property was bought to sustain the Ratcliffe charity. In 1560, two tenements in St Gabriel's parish, Fenchurch Street, were bought for £140 and ten tenements, a garden and stables in Billeter Lane for £220. Together these produced £23 rent a year. A third purchase of a house in Crooked Lane near London Bridge, for £50 completed the investment of the Wool Quay sale.

The Company's relatively simple existence had been transformed by these acquisitions. In order to take responsibility for the collection of rents, a new official was elected in 1563; Richard Bowland (Master 1588) became the first Renter Warden. Very soon, his successor had more rents to account for; the Company purchased the King's Head in Thames Street in 1566 for £40 and in Basinghall Street there were two properties leased out which were situated next to the Hall. At this time the total rental for the Company amounted to £68 a year.

For once the political activity, which spanned these years, impinged more directly than usual on not just the Company, but all Londoners. Mary Tudor's accession was challenged by the Duke of Northumberland's attempted rising and his proclamation of Lady Jane Grey as Queen instead.

His aim was a Protestant succession and the retention of the power he had enjoyed in Edward's reign. When his rebellion collapsed, Mary was formally received into London through Aldgate on 3 August 1553 by the Lord Mayor, Alderman and representatives of the livery companies. Whether their sympathies were Protestant or not, there was relief among Londoners that civil war had been avoided and the legitimate heir had claimed her crown. Even more alarming was the raising of rebellion the following January 1554, by Robert Wyatt at Maidstone. He championed the Protestant cause and gathered around him malcontents opposed to Mary's stubborn determination to marry Philip of Spain. Wyatt reached Southwark on 3 February, forcing his way towards London Bridge. Many cooperages there must have been caught up in the struggle from which Wyatt withdrew, to make a detour to cross the Thames at Kingston and eventually approach the City from Ludgate. The Company became embroiled in the City's panic decisions to provide troops to halt Wyatt's advance on London. Wyatt surrendered when he was trapped by Lord Pembroke's men at his rear at Temple Bar and the London citizen-soldiers at Ludgate.

When Mary asserted her hold on London, making a triumphal entry, on 1 May 1554 and progressing to Guildhall to receive a renewal of London's loyalty, the Company was present on its standing on Ludgate Hill, and again in August, this time in Gracechurch Street 'when the King came to land'. New white staves had been used for Mary's coronation, and yet more had to be purchased so that the Livery could be guided through the crowds to their places. Whatever were their private views, they cannot fail to have been impressed by the magnificence of Philip's retinue, the pageants, full of symbolism, the great crowds and the noise of the artillery.

With prudence, the Lord Mayor had earlier summoned all the livery company Masters and Prime Wardens to insist there must be no demonstration of xenophobia. A few days later, nimble apprentices, who briefly escaped their workshops, might have witnessed the ceremonial carting of 20 loads of Spanish gold through the streets. For their elders it would signal a period of relief from royal taxation. The following August, London again did its duty when Philip left for France. The City was crowded with people in from the country for Bartholomew Fair and they were rewarded with another royal spectacle. The Coopers' standing was once again transported to Gracechurch Street, this time with four gallons each of ale and wine. It was just as well that the carpenter had fixed railings around.

The views of individual members of the Company about the see-saw of religious change during the mid-century upheavals, are hard to discern. In general, Londoners accepted the Protestant changes made during Edward's reign but most sensible citizens knew it was safest not to challenge the government. The senior coopers knew their duty was to assist in the maintenance of orderly rule in London and this meant co-operating with the City authorities. When a man threw a knife at the preacher in St Paul's, just after Mary's accession, not only was the pulpit placed under guard on the following Sunday, but the Lord Mayor ordered liverymen to keep their eyes and ears open 'if any lewd or seditious persons' made rumours. Mary's persecution of Protestants, which gathered momentum in 1555, her unpopular marriage to Philip of Spain, and a war against France which led to the loss of Calais, England's last French possession, combined to damage her reputation in London. Elizabeth's accession on 17 November 1558 came as a relief.

There is scattered evidence that some members of the Company had embraced Protestantism in the 1530s. John Thompson's burial cost half the normal charge of 6s 8d 'because was had no torches or tapers', a sign of Protestant preference. In 1555, when Mary ordered 'rogations and processions' at Ascensiontide, several senior members of the Company left a St Paul's service early and avoided the procession. These ceremonies had been attacked by Protestants as superstitious and pagan. However, the Company's own service for Election Day was once more enhanced by the return of the singing men and children. Most members were best served by Elizabeth's moderate restoration of Protestant rites and uses and in particular by her determination not to 'make a window into men's souls'. Outward conformity and inward convictions were the safest compromise for most coopers. With the accession of a new monarch, the Company sought confirmation of its 1501 Charter by letters patent. It had other pressing matters which needed legislation, at best, or some kind of royal support. These included the re-grant of the Company's bye-laws, or ordinances and the strengthening of its position against brewers who ignored the ordinance restricting their use of coopers to the repair of casks, and against foreigners and strangers setting up shop without licence. Attempts at legislation had been made during the 1540s, pursued with much tenacity, at considerable cost to leading members in paying legal fees and making gifts to anyone at the Temple or Westminster who might be persuaded to use their influence. None had been successful.

Mark of Henry Gamble, c. 1550. Later assigned to William Staines.

New ordinances, granted in 1561, were enforced in 1563, effectively a re-grant by Elizabeth of the bye-laws approved by the Privy Council in 1507. They governed the size of vessels; the requirement of each having its maker's mark; the right to conduct searches; and the right to licence and levy quarterage from foreigners and strangers, who were charged to obey the rules of the Company and be under the authority of the Master and Wardens. Other ordinances dealt with apprentices, the levying of quarterage and what it could be used for, the conduct of Courts, elections, engrossing accounts annually and disciplining members. In 1562, led by Richard Starr, Henry Gamble and Richard Byrde, a campaign began to repeal that part of the 1531 Act which had fixed the prices of vessels. Inflation over the intervening years, caused in part by three debasements of the coinage, an increase in money in circulation and an increase in the population, had caused prices to double and, in the case of grain, to treble. Members contributed to a fighting fund which first allowed a successful suit in the Court of the Exchequer, followed by the repeal of the 1531 price list in 1565. In February 1566, new prices were issued by the Lord Mayor and the Company paid over £22 in legal fees, £5 15s for the Lord Mayor's reward of two hogsheads of wine and a similar amount for Gascon wine to the Speaker and other parliamentary officials. The new Act, passed in 1565, delegated the periodic fixing of prices to the Lord Mayor, mayors in towns and JPs in the country. Hence the importance of seeking the Lord Mayor's favour with a generous libation of wine.

During the campaign to amend the law governing the trade, London suffered one of its worst outbreaks of bubonic plague. It has been estimated that one quarter of the population died. Although there was no agreement on policy to limit the spread of infection, some effort was made to remove nuisances to public health. A huge dump of decaying rubbish was removed from Finsbury Court just north of Moorgate and the Company decided to clean out the privy. Its brickwork had to be dismantled, while 19 tons of night-soil were removed and the Beadle had to be night-watchman until the job was complete. Little business was transacted in July, August and September, usually the months when plague reached its climax, before declining as the weather cooled. Several senior members died, some leaving generous donations towards funeral costs. In September, a decision was taken to provide the Company with a new hearse, or pall cloth. Stephen Heath, one of the most senior and wealthy members, was made responsible for all the arrangements. The Broderers' Company was commissioned for the work, which took ten months, including night-work, for which nine shillings was paid to provide candles. The major cost was in materials; blue velvet, pearls,

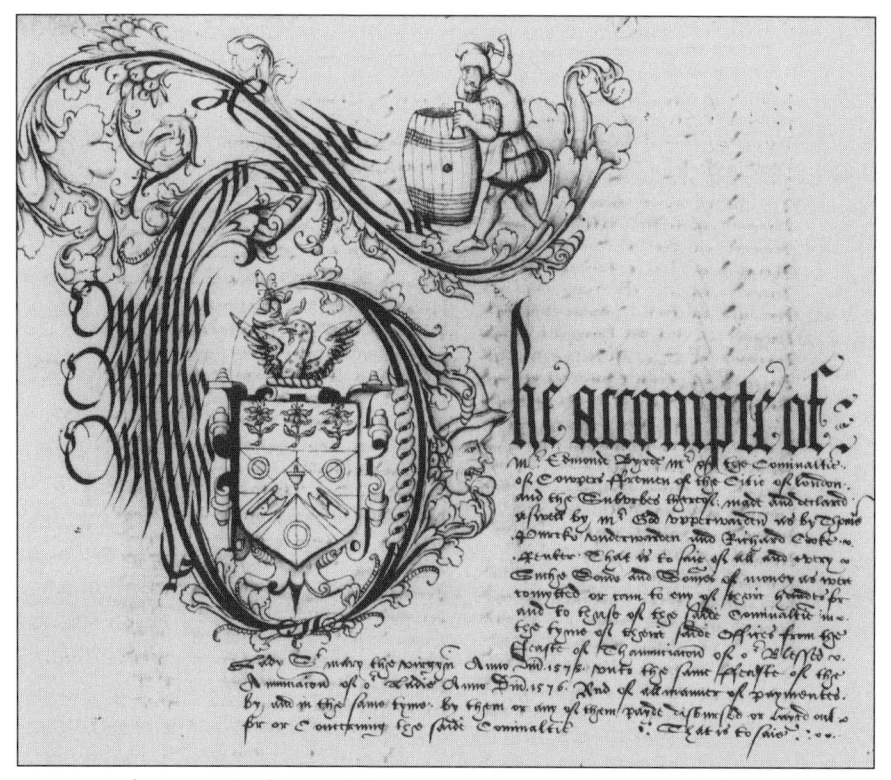

Accounts for 1575–76. The initial 'T' incorporates the Company's arms, first granted in 1509 and a cooper using a hammer and driver to hoop a cask.

embroidery silks and £42 for Venetian gold and silver thread. Many of the colours described in the accounts are strong and contrasting: purple and yellow; orange, pink and scarlet. By modern tastes the result must have been dazzling and gaudy. The total cost was over £70, enough to buy a house. It was the Company's most valuable, moveable possession.

Liverymen were expected to attend fellow members' funerals and were fined for not doing so. In 1574, three were fined for leaving before the sermon; and in 1575, one was fined for not wearing his gown at a funeral. The hearse cloth was entrusted to the Beadle's care and fees were set for its use: 2s 6d for a man; 2 shillings for a woman.

An occasional benefit for the living was the provision for supporting scholars at Oxford and Cambridge in cases where the young man was the son of a liveryman. The first recorded instance was an exhibition valued at 15 shillings, paid to Thomas, son of Peter Whitnall. This was increased to

40 shillings in 1577 and to £3 6s 4d in 1581. By 1584, Thomas was considered sufficiently advanced not to need his exhibition but 'on the earnest suit of Robert Molde', then Master, one more grant of 40 shillings was made. Another scholar, Benjamin Charier received £5 annually between 1590 and 1595.

Support for the Company's poor was for many years, haphazard, but by the 1580s there was a regular list of London pensions granted at £1 or 10 shillings (annually). Sometimes help came with a warning: John Homans was to have an increase from 10 shillings to £1 'on condition he shall not be found drunk'. The most frequent recipients were members' widows left to support a young family.

The doing of good works did not interfere with the pursuit of good fellowship in taverns, in the homes of wealthier members and at the Hall. Most meetings for a particular purpose, were an excuse for a few cups of ale or wine — 'a drynking'. In 1572, when new wainscot was viewed at the Hall there was supper and a drinking at Stephen Heath's house. When the assessors for wheat money met, they used Thomas Busby's house and had refreshments. Giving instructions to the carpenter, interviewing the bargeman, returning from Ratcliffe, carrying out a search, were all occasions for a drinking and a dinner. At the Hall, the dinner on Election Day had become a tradition after 1566 and so had the dinner on Lord Mayor's Day. These traditions probably encouraged a less spartan environment at the Hall. There seems to have been a time of affluence in the 1570s when more wainscot was installed to give greater comfort and a ceiling was put in to create a first floor room above the little parlour.

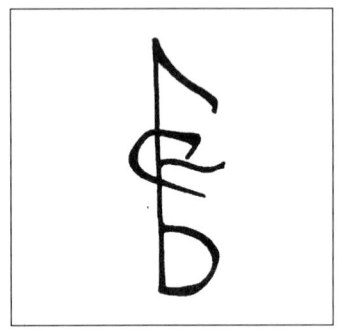

Mark of Edmund Byrde, Master 1571–72

An order in 1573 for the Queen's arms to be erected in the Hall may not have been carried out, or else the Company's arms were substituted. By 1589, the Queen's arms were displayed and a subscription list was opened to pay for their gilding. A painted cloth was given to hang in the Hall and new table linen at a cost of 30 shillings replaced what Warden George Dodson had 'negligently lost' during his term in office. The linen became finer, damask replacing plainly-woven draper for the best occasions and being given to a responsible liveryman's wife for washing. Gifts of plate came slowly. Stephen Gibson, probably a relative of Nicholas, died in the 1563 plague and left a silver gilt goblet. From 1547, newly-freed apprentices were encouraged to

THE FIRST HALL AND THE FIRST CHARITY

give a silver spoon. These were often used as cash, so few are accounted for in the inventories which survive.

As the Company's property became more extensive and valuable, and as the number of apprentices, freemen and foreigners grew, the responsibility of the Clerk was of crucial importance. It was a post which seems to have been filled by a member of the Livery in the early part of the sixteenth century. It required a good knowledge of the law and some training as a scrivener, although from 1570 the Company employed a scrivener to engross its accounts. The appointment of Thomas Brende as Clerk in 1569 was an opportunity for defining a job which had grown haphazardly since the acquisition of the Ratcliffe Charity and its endowments. Brende's regular task included making the quarterage book, keeping the rental, purchasing parchment, taking part in searches, drawing up and engrossing the accounts and attending the Master and Wardens twice a year at Ratcliffe when the salaries and pensions were paid. In addition, Brende earned fees for drawing up contracts and apprentices' indentures, for preparing legal cases, attending Court and Parliament. When this kind of business was brisk he could earn a comfortable living.

However, it seems that Brende lived beyond his means, became seriously indebted and needed to take so much time away from his duty to the Company, pursuing money-lenders to help with his debts, that he employed a locum to deputise. This man was himself imprisoned for debt in Ludgate. He had to be accompanied to the Hall by a keeper 'to our shame and discredit', complained the outraged Court when it discovered the truth. Brende was dismissed and his successor, appointed in 1585 was charged 'to well and honestly behave himself in the exercise of his office'. This new Clerk was Henry Foster who served the Company well until his death in 1595 and whose widow, Elizabeth, became a pensioner of the Company. His initial stipend of £6, plus fees, was raised to £8 and he was sufficiently trusted to be allowed to use the Company's seal to authenticate leases, purchases and loans.

The Company had varied fortunes with its schoolmasters at Ratcliffe. Their behaviour impinged less directly than the Clerk's but when the parishioners of Stepney complained of Thomas Warde's 'evil usage and demeanour' in February 1570, eight years after his appointment, the Company had to act. The complainants threatened to seek action from the manorial Court if the Coopers' did not respond promptly. Within days, a delegation of Master, Wardens and three 'Ancients' went to meet the complainants and three schoolmasters from London's leading schools, St Anthony's, St Paul's and Christ's Hospital. The latter gave a good report of

Warde declaring him to be diligent and to have a sufficiency in learning. Indeed, they declared, he might well have taught moral philosophy in any university. Two hours late, the complainants arrived and said their evidence was only hearsay that Warde neglected his pupils and was sometimes drunk. Warde responded by promising 'continuance of his diligence and reformation of anything in him remiss', and so the matter rested. It proved to be a case of 'no smoke without fire'. By Michaelmas (29 September), Warde was given his contractual half year's notice because of his 'evil demeanour... (and) want of diligence in work'.

A problem of a different kind occurred with his successor, John Petyt. He became a little too fond of the attractions of Westminster and its high-class brothels. He claimed he had visited Westminster for a cure but it seemed he was suffering from syphilis, a disease introduced earlier in the sixteenth century by soldiers who had served as mercenaries in Italy. So shocking was the disclosure of Petyt's plight that a capital P was used in the Court minutes to describe his illness. He too, was given notice to leave in June 1574. His successor was chosen on the recommendation of the inhabitants of Stepney, perhaps with the hope that he would be a safer choice than his two predecessors. It is only fair to note that Lancelot Andrewes, subsequently Bishop of Winchester, one of the most highly-regarded churchmen of his age, and an author of the King James Bible, was Thomas Warde's pupil and showed kindness and patronage to Warde's son to enable him to secure a living in the church.

CHAPTER THREE

Consolidation 1570–1630

Long-delayed war against Spain was preceded by Mary Stuart's execution in 1587 and culminated in the defeat of the Spanish Armada, 1588. In the 1590s, the Elizabethan glitter became tarnished. War, taxes, famine, plague, rebellion in Ireland and even in England, led by Essex, the Queen's favourite, all soured Elizabeth's last years. The succession of James VI of Scotland (the 1st of England) was smooth. He brought erudition and extravagance; he encouraged a new English Bible (1611) and discouraged extreme Protestants. Virginia became the first English colony. Shakespeare, Ben Johnson and Francis Bacon flourished. Intolerance of extreme Protestants caused some, including the Pilgrim Fathers, to emigrate.

AS LONDON INCREASED in population and prosperity during Elizabeth's reign, the challenges to the system of controlling the craft became more frequent and urgent. The Company had to be vigilant and ready to act in the law courts or to petition either Parliament, if in session, or otherwise the Privy Council. An obvious threat came from the influx of coopers from other parts of the British Isles and from overseas. Many of the latter 'strangers' were refugees from religious wars in France during the 1560s and 1570s. They came also from the war in the Low Countries, which began in 1572 as a war of independence against Spain and continued for the rest of the century. In the 1550s, 'Dutch' coopers in London who were householders, licensed to trade and liable to quarterage, numbered between 20 and 30; journeymen between 50 and 60. Twenty years later, the comparable numbers were 90 to 100 householders and 110 to 130 journeymen.

It was difficult to levy quarterage and to control the trade activities of these numbers. The task of seeking out and fining those who worked without licence or observation of the Company's ordinances fell to the Beadle, the Informer and the Sealers. The post of Sealer was split from 1589 between three senior members; George Swayne, Master in 1586, 1587 and 1598 taking responsibility for Southwark, Robert Tuttye, Master in 1592 and 1596, taking London and William Staines, Master in 1590 and 1591, taking St Katherine's liberty, which stretched from the Tower to Ratcliffe. Each, at first, paid a rent of £20 but St Katherine's made a loss and it was reduced to £16. Occasionally, 'dawn raids' were made on illegal cooperages and, from 1609, there was a short-lived attempt to organise monthly searches. Normally, the general search was held twice a year. The Beadle, John Pibble, and the Lord Mayor's Officer, Richard Foster to whom an annual fee was paid for his help to the Company, were effective investigators. They were frequently out and about in the City and able to warn the Sealers of illegal practices and suspect cooperages. Foster's successor, George Foster, who was probably his son, was given the official title of Informer.

The overseas coopers resisted the Company's claims in the courts. One major controversy was whether or not casks for export should be sealed. The foreigners would not pay the charge for sealing so the Company took them to court and won the case. Two years later, in 1595, the issue was raised again because of a claim that the Company's ordinances were contradictory and once again, the foreign coopers tried to exploit a legal point. After advice from the Aldermanic Court, the Company's ordinances were solemnly proclaimed at the Hall, in open Court, for the benefit of all freemen coopers, English, foreigners and strangers, to ensure 'none are ignorant' and to declare that there was 'need for reformation'. Among other deficiencies there had been a recent increase in the supply of oval and sappy vessels to Her Majesty's ships and to merchant ships. At sea, such careless work would endanger lives 'to the slander of the Company'. This was not the end of the controversy. A long, troublesome case ensued in the Privy Council, to prevent the attempted exemption from gauging of casks for the navy.

The right to gauge foreign, that is, imported casks was hard won, the result of a campaign pursued in Parliament and the Privy Council with great tenacity. The outstanding heroes were Adam Draper and Robert Vernon, whose lobbying took them as far afield as Windsor. In spite of their efforts, the Act of 1589 only gave authority until the end of the next Parliament. This explains the Company's efforts to have a Bill introduced when Parliament was called again in 1593. This Bill failed to become law because Parliament was prorogued. However, in practice, the gauging continued and in subsequent legislation, in 1627–28 and 1640–41, the 1589 Act was treated as though it remained in force. The grant of the gauge was made to Robert Shaw, Master in 1594 and 1600 and was administered as a separate activity from the usual sealing and gauging in London cooperages. There was a charge of two pence a cask and the income was split three ways between the Queen, the Company and the gauger. In 1590, the yield from 5,000 tons was almost £44.

These legal campaigns of the 1590s illustrate the tensions in the economy and how exacerbated they became during a time of dearth. The period from 1594–97 contained four successive bad harvests, which had been preceded by a severe outbreak of plague. The government wanted to retain and even to increase its controls over the economy but it also wanted to have the benefits of long-term rising trends and growing prosperity. The Company found itself caught in this dilemma; the mounting pressure for a freer market increased the resistance of traders, middlemen and manufacturers to the controls which the livery companies were obliged to maintain.

As the Company moved into a period when it had to fight harder to retain and apply its traditional functions, it continued for many decades to exercise a great deal of control over the lives of its members, freemen and their families. The inability of secular institutions to be as effective as governments would have wished in enforcing the law and maintaining social order gave livery companies an importance beyond their economic function. In London, the companies were a key strand in the web of communities formed by wards and parishes. It was at this level that central government had to rely on the maintenance of respect for authority and security for the rulers. Urban life could be volatile and violent. Those in authority were conscious of living near the edge of disorder and their very nervousness could provoke violence from a small incident. A xenophobic Easter sermon in 1517 led to rumours at the end of April that all foreigners in the City would be massacred. Cardinal Wolsey, the Lord Chancellor, ordered a curfew until 7am on May Day, but the apprentices came out on the streets, rallying hundreds to their familiar cry of 'Prentices and Clubs!' and set about hunting out foreigners. It took 1,300 troops commanded by the Duke of Norfolk and the Earls of Surrey and Shrewsbury to restore order. There were 13 summary executions and 400 prisoners, subsequently pardoned by the King in person. A century later, public order was just as fragile.

Hence the livery companies had an important role on the front line in the defence of public order, controlling their apprentices, damping down the inflammatory effects of quick tempers, bad language, and disdain for authority. They provided more positively a focus of loyalty and obedience for their members and dependents. The Company can, therefore, be likened to an extended family acting with parental care and severity, but because its members and their weaknesses were known, it could often afford to show leniency and compassion: lowering a fine, excusing arrears of quarterage when there was genuine hardship and true contrition. Because the Company was jealous of its corporate reputation and was ever-anxious not to lose face within the City community, it assumed authority over its members' appearance: there were fines for liverymen not wearing hoods in Court, at church and ceremonial occasions, and fines for appearing in working clothes at

Court. Drunkenness, loose tongues, boorishness and quarrelsome behaviour all came within the Company's jurisdiction.

There was mutual advantage to the Company and the individual cooper in these arrangements. Disputes could be settled more quickly, more cheaply and more privately than in the law courts and fines boosted the Company's income. Apart from routine fines for lateness or non-attendance at Court when summoned by the Beadle, there were fines for missing church services: six members were absent on the feast of the Circumcision (January 1) in 1567, and six missed the Queen's coronation procession in 1559. Absence on Lord Mayor's Day and at the election of Sheriffs merited fines.

Some of those most frequently fined for lateness or absence were also major offenders in either behaviour or repeated poor craftsmanship. George Dodson was one such multiple offender; often late, he was also often before the Court for careless work. In 1578, he was fined for using green willow for hooping wine casks, in spite of the fact that five years earlier, when this had been a widespread problem, he had been appointed to advise other coopers. He was also in trouble for 'rebuking Mr Warden Thelloe in front of certain journeymen'. Jasper Cromwell was a householder who appeared at the Court frequently for poor workmanship. When he and his wife became pensioners in the almshouses at Ratcliffe, they were reported to the Court 'for living very unquietly ... to the slander of the Company and the disquiet of the other poor people there'. They were warned, in June 1573, to behave well or they would be turned out at Michaelmas.

William Hamlet was another liveryman seldom out of trouble. In 1574, he was reported by other liverymen for trying to entice away their customers. This led to a fight. Hamlet's work was often defective and he was often fined for being late. Even when quite senior in the Company in 1589, his apprentice accused him in Court of teaching him nothing and the lad asked to be 'set over' to another master. The matter enraged Hamlet; he abused all and sundry, appealed to the City Chamberlain, who kept the register of City apprentices and as a result, was threatened with expulsion from the Livery. He survived until well into his sixties and when he died, in 1611, left his widow and two children well provided for with rents from leases on property adjoining St Paul's.

Sometimes the disorder was so out of hand that a matter went to the Aldermanic Court and the offender was imprisoned in one of the Lord Mayor's Compters. Thomas Nicholas was so committed in July 1589 for 'violent and irreverent speeches openly cursing and willing a purge of god on all the Company' and for other unspecified misdeeds. Peter

Cooper's hammer and driver. The hammer can be as heavy as eight pounds and is used against the driver to hammer hoops into place around a cask.

Whitnall, who was Renter Warden in 1582, was seldom long out of the records. He was probably disorganised and he was often short of money and in debt. Several times he failed to present an apprentice on time, and he tried to take one too many in 1582. One son, William, was described in 1597 as a 'disordered brother' and sent to the Lord Mayor's Court.

The other son, Thomas, was the long-time scholar, supported at Cambridge by the Company.

Arbitration was often a civilised and swift method of damping down tempers and reaching a settlement between disputants. A memorandum of one such solution in 1574, records that it took place at the Master's house where Thomas Busby and the Wardens were able 'to pacify, control and persuade [Thomas Wilson and Thomas Wheeler] to be friends, whereupon they shook hands and were friends'. Wheeler's name appears again in several episodes involving Gilbert Sapcote, (whether he was provoker or victim is impossible to know,) who was heavily fined for going into Wheeler's home 'and doing unto him certain hurts and injuries and giving evil words'. A more tricky arbitration took place in 1597 before eight senior members to settle a dispute between William Doane, Master that year for the second time and Thomas Perkins, who eventually became Master in 1602 and 1607. Perkins had 'behaved very obstinately and contentiously demeaned himself not only to some private members but most injuriously spoke against the Principal members [of the Company]…' He had behaved badly on Election Day before all the Livery. The outcome was a fine, Perkins' submission and apology and a cooling off period, when he was to have no summons to Court meetings 'to avoid contention'.

Dismissal from the Livery was the ultimate weapon: it was a loss of face and status, possibly a loss of custom, too, because of the disgrace. In 1593, John Peede was found guilty for disclosing secrets, was dismissed from the Livery, continued to be stubborn and unrepentant but nevertheless the Court was prepared to re-admit him with sureties of £40 for his good behaviour. When Thomas Bedwolff was dismissed from the Livery in 1565, his hood, the symbol of membership, was ordered to be left in the Hall. He was 'not to have or wear his hood again if he do not become a new man, fit for the fellowship in conditions and deeds, sober and quiet'. A year later, he was re-admitted and 'his hood delivered to him'.

Outrageous behaviour, which led to imprisonment in the Lord Mayor's Compter, was not a barrier to promotion to the Livery. In May 1593, George Wrenne was imprisoned for 'divers sundry abuses'; a month later, having paid 40 shillings as a fine, he secured his release, then slandered the Company to the Lord Mayor and was fined £5. It was remitted on his humble petition on behalf of his wife and children and, from the Court's point of view, 'in hope of his better obedience'. In November, he was admitted to the Livery. When he was Upper Warden, in 1608, he also became the gauger but was sacked a year later for 'inexperience and negligence'. Worse followed; during his term of office, he was responsible for supervising rebuilding work at Ratcliffe, but spent his time in a tavern, lost the Company money, failed to appear at the audit, where his accounts were challenged, and then refused to pay £8 he owed the Company. He was taken to the Lord Mayor's Court within weeks and ordered to pay. Perhaps his earlier experience of prison was sufficient for him to offer to go with the Master and Wardens that night to retrieve most of what he owed.

The community at Ratcliffe provided as varied disorders and contentious issues as the members of the Company. In addition, its property had to be kept in repair, and leases of the tenements, wharves and gardens managed. The case of George Wrenne illustrates how the Warden was expected to assume personal responsibility, acting as a clerk of works. The pensioners were often troublesome; there were occasions when expulsion was the only solution. It was resorted to in 1574, when two couples were removed for drunkenness and having strangers in their apartments. Twenty years on, it appears that policy had swung against admitting married couples and when an almsman and an almswoman brought in their partners, in April 1593, each pair was given notice to move by Whitsuntide or lose the pension.

A close watch was kept on almspeople introducing lodgers, or relatives into their house. One pensioner wanted to keep a journeyman there, perhaps hoping to get some business. Another, a widow, badgered the Court for permission to marry a young man, who was very poor and just 'out of his time' which probably meant he would be 21 or 22 years old. She was advised it was an unequal match and she would lose her pension. A few years later, in 1611, one did marry and created a vacancy. Often the filling of a vacancy caused trouble because conflicting patrons nominated their own candidates. In 1581, the Court had to issue a decree that only the Master and Wardens could authorise a new almsperson; although in practice they took advice from the churchwardens of Stepney and Lady Wentworth. She recommended a widow in 1611. In spite of assurances, the lady proved very troublesome, a drunkard, who abused the other inhabitants, setting one against the other, who knew how to submit meekly when threatened with expulsion and who survived until May 1620, when the Wardens had had enough. She was ordered out with her goods 'before Wednesday next'.

The antics of the almspeople were often an irritation to the Court, necessitating a visit by the Beadle or even by a delegation of Wardens and senior members but they were easily over-shadowed by legal disputes in which the Company's fundamental rights to the estate were challenged. One such challenge came from a member of the Gibson family, disputing the bequest of

Dame Avice to the Company. It was quite quickly settled in the Company's favour. A more serious threat occurred in 1574 when the lord of the manor of Stepney, Lord Wentworth, challenged the legality of Dame Avice's surrender. The Court acted speedily to petition the Queen and collect a fighting fund for legal expenses from among the wealthier liverymen. Documents had to be copied, including parts of the Company's books. The surrender document was translated from Latin into English and many meetings were held at Ratcliffe and the Master's house. The usual gifts were made to secure attention and favour. The Lord Keeper received a hogshead of wine from Stephen Heath; Lord Wentworth's steward was entertained to dinner by Thomas Busby; the clerk of the Queen's bench, his man, a porter and the intermediary 'who helped us speak to his master' the Lord Chief Justice, were all rewarded. In the Clerk's words, 'expedition and effort' were applied to gain, after 18 anxious months, a favourable decision, taken by the Lord Chief Justice in chambers in February 1576. The Company had to acknowledge Lord Wentworth's right to levy an annual quit-rent of 6s 8d, a small charge which recognised his ancient right to services in kind, while he dropped his case. A new agreement cost the Company £20, and a further £6 in claret and 13s 4d for a purse, as presents for Lord Wentworth.

A later legal case, which arose from a disputed lease, was more tortuous, lengthy and disappointing for the Company. It arose from a 41-year lease for one of the more substantial properties at Ratcliffe, assigned in 1557 to Richard Starr, who was Master in 1565 and 1570. His son, Baptist, inherited the lease on his father's death in 1571, when he was just out of his apprenticeship. He proved a poor tenant, soon behind with his rent, taken to court by the Company to secure £40 he owed in 1576, still owing three years' rent in 1578 and having to borrow to pay an instalment of his debt in 1580. The Company was remarkably forbearing even though Starr failed to fulfil the repairing covenants in his lease, and absented himself from attending the Court as a liveryman, when summoned during the following four years. There was, perhaps, some lingering respect and affection for his father and a desire among older members to prevent bringing humiliation and even penury on the Starr family. At length, in 1589, the lease was bought from Baptist Starr and granted to Edward Elliot, who thus became the major leaseholder at Ratcliffe, holding the Swan, its orchard and three other tenements. In 1596, Baptist Starr took a suit to the Court of Chancery against the Company, alleging that the settlement made by his father, conveying the Ratcliffe leases to him and his son Richard, had been contravened by the Company's action in 1589. The case turned on a dispute about repairs to the

CONSOLIDATION 1570–1630

Map view of the hamlet of Ratcliffe, 1658, from the Faithorne map. The fine row of elms described by John Stow still stands although a great number of buildings, including large warehouses by the river, has sprung up since Gibson's time.
Ratcliffe Cross is at the river steps which lead to Butcher's Row, the main north-south road. Broad Street (the highway) runs between the built-up area by the river and the row of tenements which border the gardens, orchard and vineyard. The Charity building is probably the building at right-angles to the tenements north of Broad Street and seventh from the left.

properties and new building on the land undertaken since 1589 by the Company, for which it sought compensation from Starr.

The advice the Company received from Tobias (Toby) Wood, its standing Counsellor, was prudent in the circumstances. It seemed that the case could as easily be lost as won; that because it was finely balanced, it could be a long and costly one to pursue and with the Company involved in other legal battles and 'forced to hard extremities for money and lately greatly taxed', arbitration would be sensible. Wood advised the Company to offer Starr compensation in the form of an annuity. In July 1597, the matter was settled out of court; Starr was awarded an annuity of £8 a year for life and 28s 8d for his eldest son after his father's death, if he were still under 21 years of age.

The end of Starr's tenancy, in 1589, coincided with the Ratcliffe estate being divided into 26 tenements in preparation for re-development. During the next decade, there was a spate of rebuilding, improving and adding new houses, wharves and warehouses. In 1593, one of the ruinous wharves was rebuilt in stone, creating the Stone Stairs which became a feature of the Ratcliffe waterfront. It cost £140 and its builders were paid, not by the usual day rate, but at one shilling a tide, since they had to contend with the tidal flow of the Thames. Three new tenements were built by the Company itself against the school house in 1595. A loan of £100 from Alderman Gurney made this possible. It was judged worth paying interest at 10 per cent as the new rents brought in £15 a year. One of the leaseholders pulled down two old cottages and replaced them with three new ones. The best of the timber frames were sold at reasonable prices, 40 shillings and £6 (new ones cost £40) to two senior Coopers, Robert Tuttye and Robert Shaw, who held leases of other cottages at Ratcliffe. Tuttye supplied tiles and bricks for improvements to the schoolyard, so he may have been in the construction trade.

Another major tenant was Mr Nottingham, who paid over £17 a year in rent and who was also busy adding new tenements. By 1607, he had built over the orchard which formed part of his largest messuage. These activities confirm the impression of John Stow, historian and topographer of sixteenth century London, who wrote in 1598, 'There hath been of late, in place of elm-trees, many small tenements raised towards Ratcliffe…' In 1597, the Company granted a 50-year building lease on 6 cottages, one known as the Green Dragon, to Thomas Manning, carpenter, to build 16 new houses on the site. His rent was £27, which was so satisfactory to him that he gave the Company £5 for a 'repast'. Manning's work was kept under review by a rota of the 'Ancients', visiting the site. For about 20 years the whole area was given over to improvements and new buildings. Tenants were allowed to build new chimneys, even jutting two or three feet into the street, water pipes were laid to the larger new houses, warehouses were replaced, using oak timbers and wharves were extended. It all reflected the increase in mercantile activity, and the stimulus of the protracted war with Spain (1585–1604). Senior Coopers were not slow to make a profit from the growth at Ratcliffe. Thomas Perkins took a lease in 1611 and Arthur Bray, Upper Warden in 1617, Master in 1621 and 1625, first had a warehouse, which he gave up as too expensive, and then, in 1612, he took a 51-year building lease on a house at an annual rent of £4. He covenanted to rebuild four houses on the plot, two storeys high, at least half the construction to be brick, with adequate oak timbers. In inflationary times he had secured a fixed rent for half a century and opportunity to profit from sub-letting.

The school building was not neglected. In 1598, its roofs were repaired with new lead, 2,000 tiles and ridges. Windows were repaired in the almshouses and the plasterer was employed for four days to make good decaying wall sections between the timber framework. The chapel windows had new glass and, with paving and gravel laid around the courtyard, the whole complex looked better and was more comfortable for its inhabitants.

All of this was not achieved without controversy, in which clashes of personality heightened the differences of opinion on policy; and whether or not expansion and improvement was a wise course of action. In 1590, there was 'contention' about the Company's government, complaints about how decisions were reached and about the 'mis-spending of Company stock'. The contention was an episode in a five-year argument between Robert Shaw, a young liveryman who presented the Court with a series of articles in 1585, alleging 'disorder' in the way the Wardens were conducting the Company's affairs. Such a challenge to authority and seniority was rare and Shaw was not believed. He did not give up easily and began searching the Company's records for evidence to substantiate his articles. In May 1586, he was reprimanded for 'following his cause in an unbrotherly fashion'. Somewhat perversely, his seniors condemned his behaviour as intolerable; he must prove his allegations — precisely what his researches had been intended to do — or he would be excluded from the fellowship. Shaw was wise enough to know he had gone far enough for the moment, and he let matters ride.

The Upper Warden, whom Shaw had accused of mismanaging the Company's affairs in 1585, was George Swayne, son of Robert Swayne, Master in 1552 and 1553. Like his father, George Swayne served as Master for two successive years in 1586 and 1587. During these years there was peace between him and Shaw, but in 1589 more 'discords, strife, contentions and debates' were noted in the minutes between the two men. Shaw was Under Warden at the time and therefore in possession of more facts and evidence than when, earlier, he had been a junior member of the Livery. The majority of members, however, wanted no more trouble and at a Court meeting insisted that these differences 'concerning the Company…shall not be spoken of in future'. Shaw and Swayne signed their assent followed by 14 other senior liverymen.

When the issue of the Company's expenditure was raised in 1590, it seems to have had broader support than Shaw's earlier complaints. It was taken seriously enough for a panel of six arbitrators to be appointed to hold hearings into the complaints and to make recommendations for improvements. Prudent members may have been alarmed at the prospect of taking risks at Ratcliffe in the programme of re-development and borrowing to do so. Demands on Company resources would continue to be high from war-time taxation as long as the war against Spain continued. Equipping soldiers continued to be a charge; ship money, a tax on London to equip ships for the navy, was levied in 1591 and 1594.

Other expenditure under consideration at the time, was the cost of rebuilding the other tenements on the Basinghall Street site next to the Hall. Some costs were immediately re-couped from a £50 entry fine paid by the new lessee, John Stonarde, who was also a liveryman. The new building was built partly of brick, in the newer and more hygienic fashion, providing fewer refuges for rats. At the same time the Hall was also improved and repaired. Ceilings were inserted in smaller rooms to make them more comfortable, and green wall hangings were bought to set off the newly-gilded royal arms. These improvements and some more wainscoting may have been regarded by some as unnecessary expenditure. A number of other items, bought between autumn 1588 and 1591, probably came into the same category. They can be explained as part of understandable relief and celebrations after the victory over the Armada. They include the carving of the Queen's Arms for Ratcliffe; the gilding of the Company's set of royal arms; a new ensign of green, watchett (pale blue) and crimson silk for the victory celebrations at St Paul's and a new pall chest to take the ensign as well as the pall cloth. To the more conservative members all this may have represented too much eagerness to spend money when economy would have been a wiser alternative.

The view which eventually prevailed was that the Company had to borrow in order to invest in development which would increase its rental income, both for its own corporate spending and for the support of the Ratcliffe charity. The original endowments were not yielding enough income by the end of the sixteenth century to support the pensioners, the schoolmaster and the usher. The schoolmaster and usher received a 'benevolence' from time to time but the payment was uncertain and the system unsatisfactory. In 1596, the almspeople's pensions were increased from 26s 8d to £2 each a year.

Two timely bequests to benefit Ratcliffe eased this situation but did not solve it and did not make the drive to improve income from other sources unnecessary. The first bequest was that of Henry Cloker, a grocer and possibly the son and heir of John Cloker, Master on several occasions between 1517 and 1534. Henry may have been a freeman of the Company briefly between 1545 and 1548 when 'Hary Cloker' is listed in the quarterage book. But he cannot be certainly identified as the same Henry Cloker who gained his freedom in the Grocers' Company in 1537, unless he translated to his father's Company and then back again, when he failed to be elected quickly to the Livery. Whatever were his youthful manoeuvres, Henry Cloker fulfilled the intentions of his father, John Cloker, who appears to have intended to bequeath property in Crooked Lane, later known as Miles Lane, in the parish of St Michael's, near London Bridge. For a number of years during the 1540s and 1550s, there was litigation over 'Mr Cloker's matter' and legal fees as well as the cost of a conveyance and the writing out of deeds and Mr Cloker's will were paid by the Company in 1553. When Henry Cloker died in March 1574, he made a bequest of two tenements, known as the Ship, to the Company, specifying in detail how the income from rents was to be dispersed annually to augment the income of the Ratcliffe charity. To ensure his wishes were fulfiled, he appointed the Grocers' Company to supervise. Annually, the Master of the Coopers was enjoined to pay the Master of the Grocers 40 shillings to purchase eventually, 12 silver pots each costing £6, to be engraved with Cloker's name. The Master of the Grocers was to ensure, with the advice of a carpenter, that the houses were in good repair. As a further insurance, the relevant branch (or section) of Cloker's will was to be read out on New Year's Day (March 25) after the Master and Wardens had provided, from the rents, for a sermon to be preached in St Michael's church. All these provisions came into effect after the death of Cloker's wife. If the Coopers defaulted, the Grocers were to assume ownership of the property.

The first appearance of rents from the Ship is in the accounts for 1593–94, and the first payment of augmentation to the schoolmaster and usher of £3 6s 8d and £1 13s 4d respectively, was made in 1594–95. With inflation having caused prices and wages to double since the 1550s, the increases were very welcome. The first tenant of the Company's to hold the lease of the Ship was Robert Shaw, under a covenant to pull down the upper storey and rebuild. He paid a rent of £6 for one house, while the other yielded £5. A few years later, Peter Thelloe, a draper and most probably the son of Thomas Thelloe, Renter Warden in 1569, bequeathed half a property in Birchin Lane to the Company. The validity of the will was questioned by the Company's standing Counsel, Toby Wood and, to avoid the costs of an action in the Court of Chancery, he advised the purchase of the other half of the property from Thelloe's sister. It cost £70. Slowly the Company was acquiring a useful portfolio of property in the City.

In October 1611, Toby Wood died and, in a codicil to his will made after the death of his only daughter, he left £600 to provide six more almshouses at Ratcliffe for poor coopers, and to purchase property to yield income for their pensions, which he stipulated should be £4 a year. No time was lost by the Company in buying up a lease on land in School House Lane at Ratcliffe in order to clear the eastern boundary of the Charity's site for the new almshouses. A small committee was empowered to make the arrangements and the contracts with the builders. By April 1612, work had progressed so well that the Upper Warden was owed £160 for land purchased and building costs. Some licence was used to ease the Company's indebtedness the following month, when £83 of Wood's money was used towards the cost of a new wharf at Ratcliffe. It was later repaid as part of the purchase of three tenements in Garlickhythe to support Wood's almshouse. As a result of the new provision for poor coopers, the practice began of using seven of the old almshouses for coopers' widows.

Although the Cloker and Wood bequests eased the situation at Ratcliffe, the Company continued to survive by borrowing and was thus able to finance the improvements to its Ratcliffe properties. With the return of peace after 1604, interest rates began to fall from the peak of ten per cent in 1596. Loans taken out in 1604 were charged at eight per cent and by 1620, at seven per cent. At any one time during the first 30 years of the seventeenth century, the Company had between £300 and £360 in loans, amounting to almost half its other income. Many who lent money to the Company were its own senior members; William Doane, Stephen Hosier, John Elletson and Hamlet Rochdale, all of whom were Master at least twice during these years. It is puzzling that during the same period many leases were renewed with no rise in the annual rent, only an increase in the entry fine. In some cases it was doubled.

The Company's financial problems were shown up in its involvement in the City Corporation's venture to take part in the colonisation of Ireland. The Irish wars of the 1590s had failed to destroy the power of the Irish

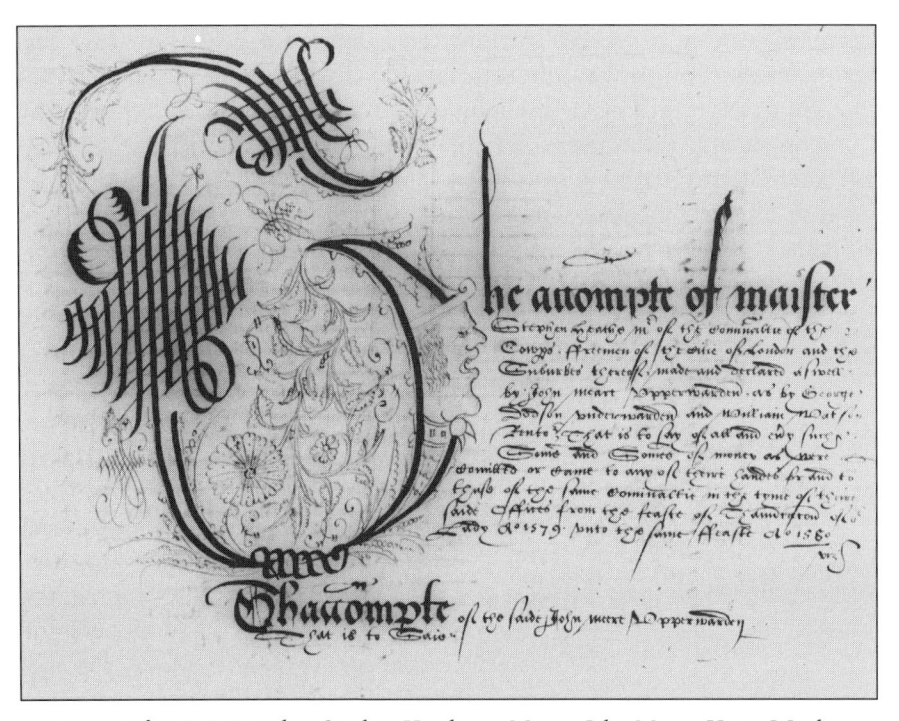

Accounts for 1579–80, when Stephen Heath was Master, John Meare, Upper Warden, George Dodson, Under Warden, and William Watson, Renter Warden.

chieftains, but James I was more fortunate than Elizabeth had been. The flight, to Europe, of the two main leaders of resistance, the Earls of Tyrone and Tyrconnell, gave a breathing space for a more pacific approach to Irish affairs. From 1608, James and his government promoted schemes to control Ireland by setting up a framework of military command, an infrastructure of garrisons and roads and then invited joint-stock venture companies to build towns and attract Protestant settlers. Most came from Scotland. The City Corporation's joint-stock company set out to take control of Coleraine and the county and town of Derry and to raise £20,000 to pay for the operation. In time-honoured fashion, the livery companies were invited to contribute towards this investment. The Coopers were assessed at £140 and paid by instalments, borrowing from members to do so. By 1610, three instalments of £35 each had been raised mainly by borrowing from members. The Company was then unable to repay these small loans and had to borrow £100 from Richard Callow of Hammersmith. Once members had been reimbursed, a little remained over towards the fourth instalment, which was due in May 1611. The City then launched a further precept to raise £10,000, the

Company's share being £70. In July, the agonising decision was taken to surrender the Company's option to take up the extra £70 worth of shares even though it meant losing the initial stake of £140. The Clerk wrote, 'This Company is very poor and could not [raise] ... in the whole Company £80 but were forced to take up money at use being already in debt'.

Such financial embarrassment did not inhibit either the traditional dinners on Court days, after general searches or after the twice yearly 'view' of Ratcliffe. In 1597, when the Company was paying ten per cent on loans of £230, the dinner on Lord Mayor's day consisted of 15 stones of beef, 6 legs and 2 loins of mutton, 2 loins and 2 breasts of veal, 2 gallons of cream, a quart of 'barberries' (bilberries) and 3 pounds of oranges, as well as prunes, dates, ginger and large quantities of bread, beer, ale and wine. This was to feed 37 liverymen. A dinner at the Dolphin, after a search, cost 49s 6d, almost double the amount allowed under Dame Avice's will for the view dinner when Ratcliffe was inspected.

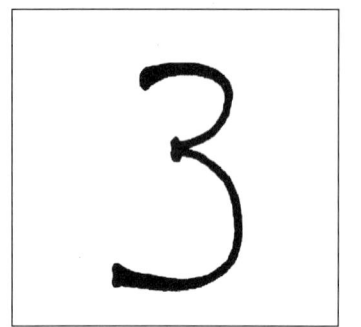

Mark of Thomas Gybson, 1593, later assigned to John Read.

In 1598, the Lord Mayor's dinner was more sumptuous, with ten capons, 6 geese, biscuits, caraways, currants, saffron and cakes (for consumption on the barge during the river procession), added to the previous years' ingredients. Beef cost 18 shillings a stone, and a luxury such as ginger, 13 shillings a pound. As a comparison, a labourer would earn 12 pence a day in London.

In an economy where inflation had increased uncertainty and contributed to a wider gap between the wealthiest in the Company and ordinary, young coopers, there was need for assistance to those starting out to build their own business. Several small bequests, beginning with that of John Meare, Master in 1582, recognised this need. He left £20 to be awarded annually on sureties being provided, as a loan. Edward Stileragge left £10 to be loaned to two poor men in the Company, and George Swayne, during his lifetime gave £10 in 1591 to be used as two £5 loans to worthy young coopers who were each to pay five shillings annually on Election Day, to the churchwardens of St Martin's Vintry and St Olave's Southwark, for the use of the poor in the two parishes. Swayne also gave the Company a set of the works of St Augustine, probably not the first choice of reading matter for members, but valued by some of their sons who were studying for university or the Inns of Court. Like John Heath, a contemporary of his father, George Swayne was generous in the manner the Company best enjoyed; he provided good hospitality. In 1586, he entertained several of the Livery to a venison dinner at the Rose in Barking.

The accession of James VI of Scotland as King James I in 1603 was the occasion for great rejoicing as the King made a slow, expensive and triumphant journey south. Although his coronation procession was delayed by an outbreak of plague in London, the Company ordered 50 shillings-worth of sarcenet (silk tissue) for two new streamers to be used in ceremonial river processions and to decorate the standing for royal processions through the City. A further £5 was paid for painting the streamers and for two more in watchett and yellow silk. A silk banner with buckram stiffening was painted with the King's arms and, together with new staves, fringes, other banners, and the painter's charge, £6 more was spent. For the coronation procession the City Corporation ordered splendid allegorical pageants and tableaux for which the livery companies had to pay a share. As the plans became more grandiose, the original charge was twice increased until it totalled almost £12. The Company's standing in Fleet Street needed lengthening and its ironwork and railings painting. It had probably not been used since the Thanksgiving service at St Paul's following the defeat of the Spanish Armada.

The spirit of celebration continued into 1605 and 1606, coinciding with years of good weather, bumper harvests and peaceful conditions. Trade and industry flourished, prices steadied and the justification for pressing ahead at Ratcliffe with improving the wharves and warehouses was vindicated. In 1605, more coloured silk banners with fringes were purchased, painted and gilded. On the barge, flutes and trumpets replaced the old entertainment on Lord Mayor's Day of drums and fifes. The waterman was also given a retainer fee of 30 shillings to reserve and prepare a barge for the Company's use. When James I's brother-in-law, Christian IV of Denmark visited England in July 1606, there was another splendid royal show in the City. The Company was again assigned a place in Fleet Street only to be told it had to be moved to another position, after the carpenter had spent two days on its construction.

Within the Livery there were various frictions, partly a result of incompatible temperaments among leading members and a growing tendency of a few to treat the majority with disdain. A gap was opening between the majority of modestly comfortable liverymen and a few quite wealthy men, those capable of providing £100 loans. John Fullwood created tensions during and after his year as Master in 1604. He questioned the previous year's accounts of Stephen Hosier, the Upper Warden in 1603 and said they had been altered since the audit. There followed an argument about the 'foot' (balance) of Fullwood's own accounts as Upper Warden in 1602, accounts which Hosier had inherited. The matter was eventually resolved with Hosier paying over £6 to the new Upper Warden in 1604, Richard Harrison.

It seems that Harrison then examined the two years' accounts carefully: in the circumstances, a very sensible action. He found there was a debt still owing to Hosier for barge hire. This may have annoyed Fullwood, for it became a matter of contention between him and Harrison, coloured most likely by some personal animosity. Harrison made a complaint against Fullwood, that on Lord Mayor's Day, 1604, the Master had abused him and his wife 'with very opprobrious and indecent speeches, very unfit for a man in his place to speak'. The matter went to arbitration and it was agreed that both parties, their wives and others of the Livery should meet at an agreed place for dinner and 'by mediation of the Company to become friends'. Fullwood failed to keep the appointment and after further arbitration he was warned he was setting 'a dangerous example to the younger sort' and he was fined 20 shillings for calling the Company 'Jacks'. He was further charged with 20 shillings towards the cost of the dinner. Harrison had not been able to control his anger through these proceedings and he, too, was fined 6s 8d for bad language.

Harrison went on, unusually, to serve twice more as Upper Warden. In March 1607, John Stamp, the Upper Warden, died and Harrison was elected to serve the rest of the term and to continue for another year. He was Master twice, in 1610 and 1614. Fullwood was soon involved in trying to pull rank, having been Master, by persuading the Clerk to register the presentation of an apprentice outside a Court meeting, saying that the Under Warden had given permission. The Under Warden denied this, the poor Clerk was acutely embarrassed and Fullwood was fined 6s 8d for his 'extraordinary dealing'.

Another sign of wealth among a few members was having a residence outside London. One such was Henry Roades, who made it clear, when his turn came to be elected Master in 1601, that he would not be able to attend Court meetings. His absence was no barrier to his election and re-election in 1611. On both occasions, Robert Shaw acted for him. For different reasons, Robert Newland and John Lufton had to withdraw as Wardens for several months. In 1591, Newland was accused of 'committing folly with a certain person' and sought to clear his name by presenting the Court with a copy of a declaration made on oath before the Archdeacon of London and five other witnesses that the slanderous stories circulating about him were untrue. This seems to have satisfied the Court for a time but it failed to quell the rumours and Newland was suspended from April 1592 to clear his name.

Again, Robert Shaw stood in for him. John Lufton, Upper Warden in 1615, declared he was so busy with law suits, whether as plaintiff or defendant, was not made clear, that he had to withdraw from his duties from October until February 1616.

It was fortunate that Shaw had a clear resolution authorising him to act for Roades in 1611. After peaceful government at the Ratcliffe school since 1580, the schoolmaster, John Turk, appointed in 1594, and commended by 'divers noblemen and others of good credit', was accused of 'negligence and encouraging the almspeople by his unadvised speeches many times to disquietness'. Turk was warned and in June 1613 given notice to leave by Christmas. Parents complained that their children 'profit very little'. While Turk taught 10, his usher taught 40, who learned better. The Court became alarmed at the decline in the school's reputation, as local parents refused to send their children.

In January 1614, a replacement was found for Turk, in Thomas Hudson, a Cambridge Master of Arts who had letters of approval from the Archbishop of Canterbury. Hudson, however, did not gain the necessary licence to teach from the Bishop of London, but in good faith, the Court had already agreed his lease of accommodation. He remained for at least a year and was paid his salary. Meanwhile, Turk intruded himself into the school and began teaching, and claimed not only his salary but also two rooms, which, he said, the Company had agreed he should have, together with a pension of £10 yearly, before Hudson's appointment. The Court took the matter to Chancery, hoping for a quick decision. In June 1615, the annual accounts could not be completed because of the dispute as to which schoolmaster should be paid.

When the legal decision was issued in January 1616, Turk was allowed his pension of £10 and the Company was ordered to pay him two years of arrears and a further £6 13s 4d because of his poverty. Turk was to surrender his post, which he did the following month. The Master and Wardens took care with the next appointment to report their choice of Samuel Wilson of Brasenose College, Oxford, to the Bishop. After two brief appointments, Richard Edwards MA petitioned in May 1620 for the next vacancy and was appointed within three months. He was successful in persuading one of the Wardens to purchase books for the school, and came to the City with his usher, Richard Baker, to guide the Warden round the booksellers in St Paul's churchyard, Aldersgate and finally Mr Hill's shop in Duke Lane. In 1625, an outbreak of plague took the lives of Edwards, two almspeople, the Master, Arthur Bray, who still had business interests in Ratcliffe, and the Upper Warden, John Halden.

CHAPTER FOUR
Rebels, Radicals and Civil War 1630–1660

> *Charles I asserted royal authority in taxation, the law, and religion and was challenged by Parliament. His ministers and advisers, Buckingham, Archbishop Laud and Thomas Wentworth roused more opposition. Rebellion in Scotland and Ireland forced the King to call Parliament to raise taxes and led to Civil War in 1642. Defeats in the field at Marston Moor, 1644 and Naseby, 1645, brought about Charles' surrender, trial and execution in 1649. The re-modelled army, led by Oliver Cromwell, dominated Parliament by 1647, and then suppressed extreme radicalism — Levellers, Diggers — and the Irish. Cromwell was made Lord Protector in 1653. On his death (1658), his son succeeded briefly, then resigned; General Monck presided over a Convention Parliament which invited Charles II to return from exile. Pepys began his diary.*

IN JUNE 1614, William Checkett was summoned to a Court meeting to explain his absence on Election Day. He replied that 'he holdeth the election, being on a Sunday, the thing itself unlawful' and he went on to say he refused to attend until 'his conscience be further satisfied'. His view was supported by another liveryman, Anthony Kem, but from the senior members of the Court he received an unsympathetic, somewhat brisk response: he could take his ease and he would not be summoned as a liveryman until such time as his conscience could be satisfied. If not widely supported, Checkett and Kem were highly respected. In a somewhat intemperate outburst a few months later, William Bray, a member of a long-established coopering family, declared that the only two honest men among them were Checkett and Kem.

Such adherence to strict observance of the Sabbath was one indicator of puritan views, represented at all levels in the Anglican church and ranging from moderate to radical. All who came within the definition of puritan were agreed that the church needed further reform, purifying of lingering traces of superstition and idolatry, but they disagreed on how far such reform should be taken. Checkett and Kem were part of this tendency in the Coopers' Company.

There is, however, an accumulation of evidence to suggest that the Company contained several groups of members who held radical religious views and may well have given support to John Pym, the Parliamentary leader of the opposition to the King in 1640. One manifestation of allegiance to a purer form of Protestantism, without the dominance of bishops or the tyranny of the 1559 Prayer Book, was the appointment, with or without the permission of parish vestries, of preachers or lecturers.

Supported by the faithful, these Protestant ministers provided extra sermons and mid-week lectures which satisfied the craving of large numbers of London parishioners for more biblical teaching than they experienced from the official incumbents. William Laud, as Bishop of London, and from 1633 as Archbishop of Canterbury, had used steely methods to discipline the churches into stricter conformity to the 1559 Church Settlement. For him, an altar at which the priest interceded with God on behalf of the laity was not a mere table at which the faithful stood to receive Communion. The liturgy, Laud argued, should be enhanced by beautiful surroundings, stained glass, statues, the priests' robes and the music of organs. The radicals had resisted this for almost a century. When Laud ordered the restoration of organs, that of St Michael, Crooked Lane, had to be rescued from disuse which had lasted since 1559. Altar rails seemed vulnerable; when they were erected they were frequently vandalised and removed. Sometimes the motives for such actions were mixed: religious conviction and the opportunity for free firewood.

At times, the leadership of the Company was inclined to favour and support the radical, puritan line. Among charitable gifts, there was support given to a poor minister, Lewis Highes, in 1637, and to the wife of a poor preacher in 1633. A new liveryman in 1637, bore the imprint of religious radicalism in his name: Humiliacion Hynde. This was no obstacle to his taking his turn as Warden in 1650 and 1651. Among the wine-coopers, there was the Venner family, one of whose members, Thomas, raised the last truly radical rebellion of the Fifth Monarchists in 1660. The soap cask-makers included in their number several families who, by the 1650s, can be identified as Quakers. Among them were several Allens — George, William, James, Richard and Henry — who became freemen during the 1630s and 1640s. A younger member of the family was Robert, whose upright, but awkward, uncompromising attitude caused himself and the Company much grief in the 1660s and 1670s. There was a Stutzberry family which included Richard, John, Thomas, Daniel and Giles, and by the 1660s, others joined this close-knit group of Quakers: Gerard Roberts, Hezekiah Kitchen, William Powell, Thomas Nelson, Jonas Smith and William Thompson.

Even without evidence of a Quaker presence in the Company, its members can scarcely have avoided being touched in some way by the religious ferment in London. Laud's strenuous government of the Church stiffened resistance in the City, where there was support at all levels of society for the radical movement. St Stephen's, Coleman Street, one of the four largest parishes in the City, also contained some of the wealthiest radicals. They included founders of the New England Company, subscribers to the Massachusetts Bay Company and founders of the Feoffees for Impropriations.

The parish had a history of dissent: Lollards had been active there in the 1520s and it had been a centre for distributing Lutheran books. Since the 1620s, parishioners supported joint venture schemes to establish settlements in North America for religious exiles, while the Feoffees purchased tithes owned by laymen so that they could influence the appointment of suitably Protestant and anti-Laudian incumbents. St Lawrence Jewry, another immediate neighbour of the Company's Hall, possessed one of the most lucrative preacher-ships in London. By contrast, St Botolph Aldgate was a fast-growing parish occupied mainly by poor craftsmen. It had a number of cooperages because rents were lower than those within the City walls. But it, too, shared the puritan spirit of St Stephen's and St Lawrence. There were other centres where coopers were concentrated; there is still a Coopers' Row off Fenchurch Street and the Company owned property in the neighbouring parishes of St Katherine Coleman, All Hallows Staining and St Olave's Hart Street. All three had puritan curates in 1628/9. There were many in the Company and practising the trade who were influenced by radical ideas in both religion and politics by the time of the crisis which turned into the Civil War in 1642.

After Charles I's accession there was an increase in criticism of royal policy in pamphlets and from pulpits in the more radical parishes of the City. From 1629 to 1640, no Parliament was called, so political issues, resentments and grievances were denied a legitimate outlet. Protesters were treated savagely. Brave MPs, who had criticised the King's policy and methods in 1628 were imprisoned and left to rot without trial. Taxation, never popular, was resented because it was deemed illegal in the way it was levied and was used for a foreign policy which seemed to fly crazily in the face of traditional national, Protestant interests. All these grievances came to focus on the King's favourite and chief adviser, the Duke of Buckingham, who in turn was very dependent for advice on his astrologer, Dr John Lambe.

In June 1628, Lambe was attacked by a group of apprentices when he left the theatre in Finsbury Fields. He was taunted as the 'Duke's devil', chased through Moorgate, and along Coleman Street, the crowd growing as more apprentices joined the mob. The local constables were helpless against the numbers. He was eventually rescued in Cheapside, but so kicked and wounded in the head that he died the next day. Within weeks, the Duke too was dead, at the hands of an assassin in Portsmouth.

The King's anger was so great that he sent for the Lord Mayor, threatened to revoke the City's charter of liberties and ordered the miscreants be brought to justice. As in so many apprentice affrays, it was impossible. The lads simply melted away to their workshops, foundries, cooperages as if nothing had happened. The City was therefore fined a swingeing £6,000, but eventually it was reduced to £1,000 and apportioned among the livery companies. Not until January 1633, did the matter come to the Coopers' Court. The Company's share was a mere £7 but the majority refused to agree to its payment. The surviving evidence for the period is very sketchy and the reasons are not given, but the existence of religious radicalism among the Livery and resentment of royal interference in a number of City matters were probably decisive factors.

The payment caused 'much argument and differences' among the Company. It was left to the generosity of Robert Cheslyn, next in line for office as Under Warden, to give the fine on condition he could be relieved of the burden of office.

Worry about solvency was a recurring topic for the Court, especially as a severe trade depression closed in on the City and the country in the late 1630s. In the coopering trade, however, the underlying trend was buoyant, as was evident from the increase in cooperages and their volume of work in Southwark. There the Sealer, Joseph Knapp, paid £16 in rent until 1635, when it was raised to £20 and in 1642 to £25. Southwark probably benefited from war-time conditions. A review of rents for the seal made in 1642 concluded that about £65 a year could be produced from the great activity of cooperages, breweries and soap-boiling in Southwark. In spite of this, the trade depression on the eve of the civil war made it more difficult for the Company to collect quarterage from members and rents from its tenants. Both were important sources of income. Another source, which the Court began to exploit, was to call up to the Livery more frequently and in larger numbers, some of the householders able to afford a fee of £10 or, if they refused, £5. A 'call' to the Livery was stronger than an invitation; it was more akin to a summons: the freeman had to show very good reasons why he could not accept, such as poverty, illness, or old-age.

In October 1637, seven promised to come on to the Livery at the next Lord Mayor's Day and a further call to the Livery was made in 1640. By then the financial situation was more desperate and the Court explained its difficulty 'prosecuting and defending great suits in law ... and likewise for the great taxation already imposed on them which, with much ado they have paid ... they are now so far necessitated for monies that it is thought fit a new livery shall be forthwith called and taken in for a present supply of money'. The legal fees had arisen from a challenge to the Vintners' Company over its attempt to monopolise the retail trade in wine. The outcome, apart from heavy fees, was to restrict coopers to retailing wine only for christenings, weddings and funerals. It was probably a decision designed to close off a loophole exploited by wine-coopers, some of whom carried on not only a retail trade in wine, but also kept illegal presses in their cellars. The other great expense was a demand by the King for money from the City to enable him to stop a Scottish invasion. He had called Parliament in April 1640, in order to raise money to deal with the Scots but the MPs had argued that, first, the grievances of the past 11 years should be considered. Rather than give ground, the King dissolved the 'Short' Parliament within three weeks. The Coopers' share of the City precept was £500. With great difficulty they raised a little over £300 with promises of loans from the senior liverymen.

The policy of increasing the Livery solved the immediate financial problem but created another: shortage of space at the Hall to accommodate the Livery at Court meetings. Two lists were, therefore, drawn up, each including the Master and Wardens and dividing the new members between the lists. In future, it was declared, Courts would be kept by each list in turn 'in respect of [the Livery's] great assembling and our want of room to contain them'. The two lists numbered 25 and 23 respectively. The Hall needed to be extended but such plans were put aside as the City and the country at large braced itself for war between the King and Parliament.

The City Corporation refused any further loans to the King and, with the Scottish forces undefeated and encamped in Durham at the King's charge, Charles was compelled to call Parliament again in 1640. It met in November and its programme of reform, debated and put into action during 1641, created tensions which spread beyond Westminster and added extra drama to the London scene.

For apprentices seeking excitement on Sundays and holidays, rowdy diversions were not difficult to find. Disorder could erupt easily and little provocation was needed to bring out the London militia regiments to keep or restore order to the crowds of young men and teenagers. Without doubt, some coopers' apprentices, journeymen and masters were among tens of thousands of demonstrators at Whitehall Palace and Westminster during the winter of 1641. The twelve days of Christmas, which were kept as holidays, were particularly tense. The tumult contributed largely to the King's concern for the Queen's safety: her Catholic loyalties made her an obvious target for both moderate and radical, Protestant Londoners. The Court retired to Hampton Court, marking the first stage in the King's withdrawal from his capital.

On 21 December, 1641, elections to the Common Council of the City returned enough radicals — supporters of the Parliamentary opposition to the King — to swing the balance of power in London. The Aldermanic body and the Lord Mayor, Sir Richard Gurney, remained loyal, in spite of the King's mistakes and repeated bad faith. A struggle for power ensued in London. The outcome was influenced by massive support for Parliament from crowds gathering daily outside Westminster Hall, and from the petitions which they signed in their tens of thousands. Two petitions were presented from apprentices and recent freemen, with 30,000 signatures. Not all the issues were political. With the City in the grip of a deep recession, 15,000 'poor labouring men' had protested at the decay of trade, which added to the accumulation of grievances. In spite of the ferment of excitement and expectation, there was, surprisingly, little violence. The crowds were composed of all classes and were well-informed. They cannot be dismissed as a mere mob.

During these weeks of feverish activity, Coopers' Hall was not far from the centre of action in the City. Adjoining the Hall to the west was Guildhall, where a civic revolution took place, causing the dismissal of the Lord Mayor and his replacement by Alderman Isaac Pennington, a radical and an MP for the City in the Long Parliament. The street immediately to the east of the Hall was Coleman Street, where Pennington lived among the highly influential radicals of St Stephen's parish. When King Charles precipitated a deeper crisis on 4 January, 1642, by his attempt at storming Parliament to arrest five MPs, those five were already safe in the City, most probably in Pennington's house. It is tantalising that the Court minutes for these weeks are so inadequate. The Clerk, Peter Hodgson, was so neglectful of his work that he was dismissed a month later.

Opportunities to absorb the ideas which informed the vigorous debates in London during the months which preceded war were to be found everywhere. For the more serious, cerebral men in the Company — with minds eager and open — London was a centre of intellectual excitement. The relaxation of censorship by the Long Parliament resulted in a great outpouring of pamphlets and newspapers. Exiles from Laudian persecution returned from the Netherlands. European intellectuals, such as Comenius, were attracted to London. He remarked on the high level of literacy, the large number of bookshops, the flood of pamphlets and the packed churches. Congregations, he noted, including young and old, sat attentively through sermons lasting two, three or even four hours. Some took shorthand notes.

There was, however, more than a war of words raging in and around London in 1642. In the summer, the King moved north, first to York and then to Nottingham. The raising of his Standard to summon military support on 22 August was the symbolic event which marked the beginning of war between the King and his Parliament.

London's government was, by this stage, firmly in the hands of Parliament's allies. Almost unnoticed, the most important royal arsenal in the whole country, the Tower of London, also slipped into Parliamentary control. It was an event with less accompanying drama, but with no less significance than the fall of the Bastille in 1789. The closure of the theatres in September 1642 was more likely to have had an impact on lively young coopers and to bring home to them the fact that normal life was about to be suspended.

Without doubt, London was a city full of nervous tension. The King's aim was certain to be the recapture of his capital city and the humiliation of the Parliamentary rebels and traitors. Londoners of royalist sympathies kept their counsel. All were united in fear of the consequences of failure. The besieging, storming and sacking of cities was a major feature of seventeenth century warfare. Since 1618, war had raged across central Europe and many officers who took charge of London's preparations for its defence had learned their skills as career soldiers in Protestant armies on the continent. They knew from direct experience, but most ordinary citizens were aware, of the terrible fate suffered by besieged cities. The sacking of Magdeburg in 1631 was widely known in England. Its pillage, arson and the indiscriminate torture, rape and murder of its citizens, was a chilling reminder of the horrors of warfare. All of this was recent enough to concentrate the minds of Londoners of whatever persuasion on the vital matter of preserving self, family and wealth.

Londoners were convinced that their city was under serious threat and would be almost impossible to defend. In this latter view they were correct; with over half the population of the metropolis living outside the ancient walls and a built-up area stretching five miles from the Strand to Stepney, London would defeat any preparations against siege. In the autumn of 1642, Prince Rupert's force was advancing south and east along the Thames valley. Rumours were spread that the King had hired mercenaries from Europe and Ireland. There was, therefore, a high level of alarm in the capital.

The City's preparations for the inevitable clash of forces focused first on the citizen militia, a volunteer force of trained bands for which the Society of the Artillery Garden (the Honourable Artillery Company) provided officers. In 1642, the trained bands numbered 8,000 men in six regiments. By

1643, there were 20,000 under arms; 18 regiments of foot and two of horse. For recruitment and organisation, London had the advantage of the livery companies, which together with the wards and parishes provided the necessary administrative network. In August, the Lord Mayor issued a precept to the companies for arms. The Coopers responded early in September, recording that they had delivered to Mr Swayne at Guildhall for 'Parliament's use ... six muskets, six rests, six bandoliers, six corslettes and six pikes'. The speed of the Company's reaction, repeated a year later, in raising money for the Parliamentary war effort, reinforces the evidence of a balance of support within the Company for Parliament. It certainly contrasts with the delays and wrangling in 1633 over the Company's share of the fine for Dr Lambe's murder.

As the Royalist army approached the capital in November 1642, the trained bands somewhat nervously agreed to add their number and fire power to that of the Earl of Essex and his Parliamentary army. Whatever views were held on the morality of taking up arms against the sovereign, ordinary Londoners were concerned to defend their homes and families against attack. Four companies of trained bands were badly savaged by Prince Rupert's forces at Brentford, which was sacked on 12 November. Nevertheless, the main force of trained bands, skilfully led and encouraged by Philip Skippon (later to become one of Cromwell's Major-Generals), stood its ground at Turnham Green. In the event, the royal army did not attack and the City breathed more easily again and left the citizen soldiers in a better state of morale and confidence. Later, several regiments were persuaded to join the Parliamentary armies in the field, but the results were mixed. Londoners were unaccustomed to 'roughing it', to the skirmishing in hedgerows, ditches and fields to which they were subjected. The bleak cold of January, experienced during the siege of Basing House, drove most of them back to their homes. They left the field to the professionals.

London concentrated its efforts at self-defence in creating a quite astounding ring of fortifications which at some distance encircled the City, Westminster and Southwark. These so-called 'lines of communication' were not intended as a means of withstanding a siege but they formed a cordon around a 'safe' area. They were far enough from heavily populated out-parishes to protect the population from royalist artillery. Typically, the fortifications consisted of an earthen bank, thrown up from a ditch, with added turfs, revetted with wattles and palisaded with sharp stakes. Accounts for payments to stonemasons and bricklayers suggest there were also more permanent structures. The lines ran from Wapping to Shoreditch, then to

Islington, west to Hyde Park Corner, Tothill Fields and then south of the river, they enclosed Lambeth and Southwark.

The master plan originated in Guildhall, with Coopers' Hall becoming the nerve centre of activity during the building period, late summer 1642 to May 1643. By then, the 24 main forts had been completed. During this time, the 'Committee for the Outworks', which was set up to direct operations, met daily at Coopers' Hall. While the Company continued, with some difficulty, its routines of admissions, freedoms, rent collecting and imposing and collecting fines, the committee brought out thousands of citizens and set them to work, even on Sundays, digging ditches, carting earth and timber, stone and bricks, clearing hedges and trees which blocked sight lines and erecting sharp, stout palisades. The Venetian ambassador reckoned that 20,000 worked daily without pay and that among them were many leading citizens, rich merchants, common councillors and liverymen. For a time, in October 1642, Parliament ordered the closure of shops and markets so that the people 'may with greater diligence attend the defence' of London.

Some activities of the Company were curtailed by the daily presence of the Outworks Committee and the comings and goings between the Hall and the work sites on the lines of communication. Some liverymen clearly felt inhibited at attempting to carry on business as usual in consideration of 'great distraction and sadness of the times'. To take time discussing such matters as stewards' fines, always a subject of contention, feasts and monthly Court dinners seemed quite inappropriate. In June, the liverymen decided that the stewards should contribute £12, but failed to agree on whether or not the Lord Mayor's Day dinner should take place. However, they were more decisive on the subject of the monthly Court dinner. Dishes were to be reduced in number to two or three and attendance by the Livery was to be restricted.

The election and swearing-in of the new Master and Wardens took place as usual in 1643, but against a background of renewed alarm. There was disorder in Parliament and a royalist plot within London, master-minded by the court poet, Edmund Waller. The constant threat of trade being cut off by royal forces who remained in control of the Thames valley, added to uncertainty. The trade in goods also provided opportunity for communication between the enemy within and the enemy without. It was, for instance, rumoured that soap casks were used to send out gold to the King in Oxford.

Parliament tried to calm the unease by declaring a day of Thanksgiving; the foiling of Waller's plot and the completion of the defensive lines were thought cause enough. But the news from the west country was not good. On the same day as the Thanksgiving, 13 July 1643, there was a royal victory at Roundway Down, near Devizes, and Prince Rupert captured and sacked Bristol.

The nerves of Londoners were not steadied by these events and there is evidence of rising tension in August. A special meeting was called at Coopers' Hall, when the only business was how the Company could meet the urgent levy by the Lord Mayor for prosecuting the defence of London. The demand for £350 from the Coopers out of a total of £5,000 levied on the livery companies was a massive charge. On this occasion there was action rather than debate. The Company's plate was promptly valued at between £150 and £200 and within the day was sold to a goldsmith. To the Court's pleasure and surprise it raised £259, of which £150 was taken the following day to the Treasurer at Guildhall. The Coopers' new Clerk, John Looker, had by this time put most of the Company's affairs in order. He began to deal with business more systematically than his predecessors and introduced an annual numbering of freemen's spoons, as though he expected to be called upon again at short notice to account for the Company's liquid assets in response to a war emergency.

The raising of taxes was one of the least popular aspects of Parliamentary rule in the 1640s. In spite of the City's overwhelming loyalty to the parliamentary cause, the acid test was taxation. By 1647, London was virtually on a tax strike and popular anger over taxes played a part in rousing the support of crowds for counter-revolution, an attempt to back Parliamentary moderates against the triumphant New Model Army. Many apprentices who were encouraged to join the throng at Westminster, felt aggrieved with the more extreme reforms of the radical Protestants. The abolition of holidays, which were traditional Christian feasts, was badly received. By way of amelioration after the July tumults, one Tuesday in each month was declared a holiday. There was, however, no relief from the amount of taxation, and Sir Thomas Fairfax's collectors were insistent on the assessment. A regular payment of £5 was being levied on Coopers' Hall in 1647. After the New Model Army occupied London as a result of the failed counter-revolution of 1647, the demands came more frequently, and payments were levied of £12, half-yearly in advance, and five shillings a month.

The effects of the war on trade are not simple to unravel. As in all wars, there were winners and losers. Where craftsmen and traders were directly concerned with supplying the needs of the armies, war offered opportunities to many and rich pickings to the few. Victualling and munitions required casks of all sizes, for they were the all-purpose form of packaging, for salt beef, beer or gunpowder. The flight of the Court and its circle was a disaster for the luxury end of the market and caused some hardship but probably was of no consequence to coopers. However, there is little doubt that the years from 1642 to 1644 were difficult for London as a whole. All trades would have felt some effect from the uncertainty of the markets and general slowing-down of trade.

It is difficult to disentangle those aspects of a city at war and under threat of attack from the deep recession in trade which existed at the time the crisis began in 1640. Overall, the recovery from the recession was delayed by war conditions and came about only slowly. This may be reflected in the steady rents and entry fines on Company leases re-let in 1642 and 1646. Until 1644, the rent from the Company's Sealers remained constant. Then in 1645, there was a complaint from Mr Rayner that the small St Katherine-side seal yielded no more that £8 a year. The Southwark Sealer's profits rose steadily in 1642, but then dipped. Although a concession was made to the Sealer, the Court was confident that the seal's value would recover quickly.

Conditions in London were certainly not the harsh ones of a city under siege. But there were shortages and the most obvious was the lack of coal. This persisted until the royalists were driven from Newcastle and the coastal trade in coal was able to resume. The shortage of coal must have made for considerable discomfort in the particularly cold winter of 1643, as well as interrupting trades dependent on coal, such as brewing, soap-boiling, glass-making and smithying.

The uncertainty of some supplies may explain the outbreak of illegal wine-making and retailing among coopers. After several offences, Thomas Rawlinson was at length told to 'take his ease' until the full court decided otherwise, for having sold Widow Bridger three casks of 'sophisticated', that is, adulterated, sack. His fine for this was a hefty one of £30 and the reimbursement of Mrs Bridger. For some time he was in disgrace for behaving to the 'great disparagement of the Company'. Eventually, in 1651, his translation to the Vintners' Company was agreed. During the hard winter of 1642–43, seven coopers appeared at the Court charged with having illegal presses, retailing wine and putting unwholesome ingredients into it. Stiff fines of £20 were imposed and the wine presses were destroyed. One of the offenders challenged the Court's ruling a year later and on receiving no satisfaction, demanded translation to the Vintners for 'divers weighty reasons'. He was refused.

Other persistent offenders in retailing wine were the Flamsteds, Francis and George. They too were defiant and challenged the Company to take them to court. The Company's Informer, attempted to stir up more trouble by trying to involve the Vintners' Company. The Vintners declined to be at any charge for legal fees. It was a problem for the Company to control and curb defiant and determined members; and though the illegal wine-making may have been a response to wartime conditions, the underlying issues of trade demarcation and the engrossing of trade persisted into peacetime.

As a consequence of the war, the Master and Wardens had extra duties. There were the emergency demands for money to prosecute the war, there was more regular and heavier taxation than ever experienced, even during King Charles's so-called 'Eleven Years' Tyranny', and there were the demands for arms. Another call on the senior officers was to see to the more efficient management of greater quantities of grain stored in the Company's granary. The Company also had a duty to recruit its members, journeymen and apprentices to help the war effort. The daily meetings of the Committee of the Outworks at the Hall must have raised expectations that the Company would respond with plentiful volunteers for the digging, building and carriage of supplies. During the war, several liverymen acquired military rank. Joseph Knapp, the Sealer, became a Major in 1646; John Milton, Master in 1653 also became a Major in 1647. Others who gained Parliamentary commissions were Captain Wildey, 1646 and Captain Brookhaven, 1647. Several apprentices were recruited or volunteered to fight. Their masters, aggrieved at the loss of the apprentices' labour, took their complaints to the Court. The adjudication usually granted at least a quarter of the young man's army pay as compensation.

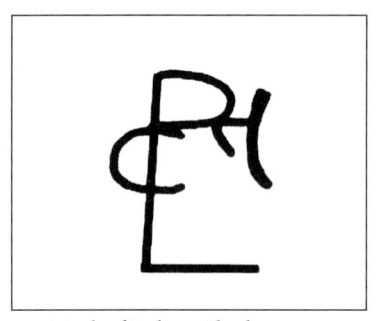

Mark of Robert Cheslyn, 1612

By the end of 1649, more settled times had arrived. The scatter of revolts across the country in 1648 which constituted the Second Civil War had been suppressed, the King had been put on trial and executed and the country was becoming adjusted to being a republic.

The Company had emerged from the turmoil of war in fairly good shape, even daring to begin thinking about how to achieve suitable accommodation for the much enlarged number of Livery. It was a long-awaited improvement. Further new calls to the Livery were made in 1644 when there was a list of 22, and 10 more were listed in 1647. It became a circular problem; increasing the Livery put more pressure on the space at the Hall and the only way of finding money for expanding the Hall was to increase the Livery. Other ways of fund-raising were considered at a Court meeting early in 1650, when a further call to the Livery was agreed, and the sale of 20 dozen spoons presented by new freemen was authorised. The sale was disappointing and raised only £91, while the call to the Livery yielded £131.

Enlargement was so much desired that, in spite of the scarcity of capital, a committee of the Master, Wardens and six senior liverymen was set up to obtain estimates and report back. More delays followed, probably because of a lack of funds, and yet another call to the Livery was made in June 1653. A scheme was then confirmed for an extension to the parlour and a model of it was presented by the Company's carpenter, Figgins, and approved. A committee of 20, which included younger liverymen, was empowered to manage the work, to agree contracts, to employ workmen and approve all necessary costs. It seemed a cumbersome way of handling a building programme, particularly when compared with the more streamlined approach to rebuilding after the 1666 fire. One of the younger committee members in 1653 was Roger Morris, who clearly learned from his experience. No quarterly Court was held in October 1653 because building was in progress. When new windows were designed, there was an opportunity for the Master, Wardens and past holders of these offices as well as members who were Aldermen to have their arms incorporated. They presumably paid for the privilege. Robert Cheslyn, who had been a wise influence during the troubled war years, did not live to see the extended Hall completed. In his will, dated July 1651, he left £40 towards the building costs.

There was one final outburst of frenzied religious radicalism in January 1661, which embarrassed the Company. One of the wine-coopers, Thomas Venner, had practised the craft in the 1630s and others of his family were householders, freemen of the Company. By 1660, Thomas was regarded as an 'ancient', probably in his fifties and had already served a term in the Tower for his violent words, if not his deeds. Oliver Cromwell's secretary, Thurloe, described him in 1657 as a 'fellow of desperate and bloody spirit… to have designs to blow up the Tower with powder… He had also spake at the same time very desperate words concerning the murdring of His Highness [Cromwell]'. Venner was a Fifth Monarchist, one of the most extreme of the fundamentalist, radical religious sects which the Civil War and the republican revolution which followed, brought to the surface of English life. He preached in a conventicle, a clandestine religious meeting house, in Swan Alley off Coleman Street, and with his followers, believed that the Fifth Monarchy, that is, the rule of Christ on earth, prophesied by Daniel (chapter II verse 44; chapter VII verses 18, 19, 27) was imminent.

After preaching to his congregation on the feast of the Epiphany 1661, he attempted to move matters along with a little more speed. With 20 followers, whom he promised would soon be increased tenfold, he arranged a rendezvous at St Paul's. A sentry was shot, the alarm raised and the Lord Mayor called out the trained bands. About 100 joined Venner's rising. They proved difficult to catch because they split into two groups and for a day and a night withdrew to Ken Wood, north of the City, to await a sign from heaven. None came, but the King was sufficiently alarmed to call out the forces of General Monck, Duke of Albemarle. On the third day of the rising, the rebels were rounded up, Venner was wounded, and in all about 20 were wounded or killed on each side. The inevitable end was a trial at the Old Bailey of 20 of the rebels of whom 16 were found guilty of treason. Venner and his chief lieutenant were hanged, drawn and quartered and by royal clemency, the rest were hanged. It was a sad little episode; no doubt the Company did all it could to distance itself from Venner. It had, however, one wider outcome. The King ended the process of disbanding the army and Monck's force, which had restored order in the City, became the Coldstream Guards.

CHAPTER FIVE
Restoration, Plague and Fire 1660–1680

Charles II returned to an uneasy political balance: he could dispense with Parliament but needed it to vote him taxes so that he could govern. He found a solution by becoming a pensioner of France. With no legitimate children, his likely heir was his Catholic brother, James, Duke of York. The Earl of Shaftesbury and his 'Whig' followers tried to exclude James from the succession but failed just before Charles died. Pepys, Evelyn and Defoe described the great plague and great fire and Christopher Wren, a member of the newly founded Royal Society, transformed the face of London.

THE UNCERTAINTY OF POLITICS and the lack of stability which infected government after the death of Oliver Cromwell in 1658, hastened the decision to invite the King to return from exile in Holland. Charles II's journey from the Hague to London was a right royal triumph which culminated in an ecstatic welcome to the City on 29 May 1660. There was a keen desire to return to what was, by then, a half-remembered state of normality. Among chartered organisations, this took the form of securing a re-grant of their privileges from the new King. The Company acted promptly and by February 1661 a committee had been formed to discuss with counsel what revision was needed. Some ideas had already been debated about enlarging the powers of the Company to control the trade, possibly by Act of Parliament. This was rejected in favour of revising the Charter.

The main change in the new Charter was the formal recognition of Assistants. Their number was fixed at 17 and, with the Master and Wardens, they constituted the Court, or governing committee, of the Company. They held office for life, but might be removed for 'just and reasonable cause'. The term Assistant had occasionally been used as early as 1560 to describe the senior members of the Livery, the 'Ancients', who were most frequently consulted by the Master and Wardens because of their experience as 'those which have borne the several places of Master and Wardens'.

The Master was to be chosen annually from the Court and the Wardens from the Court or from the Livery. The opportunity for the Wardens to be chosen from the Livery was seldom taken. One early exception was that of Roger Morris, who was not on the Court when he was elected Under Warden in 1665, nor was he promoted to the Court when a vacancy occurred during his term of office. The majority view was that it was 'very improper to choose him as Assistant whilst he remaineth Warden besides the losse in such case of an Assistant for the time being'. Having served successively as Under then Upper Warden, Morris returned to the Livery until the next vacancy on the Court occurred in 1669.

The new Charter confirmed the practice, established since 1658, of holding Election Day on the Monday before Pentecost, rather than Sunday. Elections under the new Charter were held in June 1661, although the letters patent were not issued until 30 August. The delay may have been caused by careless drafting and mistakes in copying. The Company's solicitor, Mr Floyd, twice had to amend the text to incorporate corrections. All the office-holders — that is, the Master, the Wardens, the Clerk and the Beadle — had to take oaths to serve dutifully and honestly. Finally, the Charter re-granted the powers held under the first Charter of 1501 to draw up 'reasonable orders and ordinances' for governing the Company and for their enforcement 'by fines or other reasonable pains, penaltyes and punishments'. The ordinances of 1741, which remain as the Company's fundamental rules, were framed by the authority of this clause.

The costs associated with obtaining the new Charter were a convenient but real excuse for resisting payment for the full amount of the Lord Mayor's precept for the King's coronation. The Company paid £42 by April 1661, but declared its inability to pay more. Privately, it was agreed to avoid or at least delay payment 'as long as may be'. The sum of £21 had already been paid in the previous summer as part of the celebrations of the King's return. This may also have encouraged the Court's reluctance to spend more on royal pageantry.

The return of the monarchy brought little relief for the City companies from taxation. In that aspect of government, there seemed little to choose between republican and monarchical regimes. War and the threat of war with The Netherlands over trade and colonies added to the government's problems of securing adequate income. In 1664, a demand for £100,000 from the City of London resulted in the Coopers' share being fixed at £1,000. After vehement protest, it was reduced to £600. Once again, plate had to be sold, but it fetched only £142. In all 29 dozen spoons and 4 wine cups were sold to Humphrey Stoakes, a goldsmith in Lombard Street. The Company made up the sum to £200 and the deficit of £400 came from loans from the Clerk and eight Assistants, repayable in a year's time with six per cent interest.

Further demands were made in 1665, for a contribution towards fitting out a warship and a precept for the poor. The Company gave £3 to the poor and invited subscriptions, which amounted to £75, for the ship. For many coopers, the naval building programme brought additional income, providing barrels for the victuallers appointed by the Navy Board Commissioners. There was also disadvantage to some. Early in 1664, the Company was alerted by liveryman Captain Wildey and Assistant Younger to a serious threat to its property and tenants in Ratcliffe. In this thickly populated district, a powder house had been built for the manufacture of gunpowder. It was a source of great alarm. The Court agreed with the tenants' representative that the powder house must be removed. A grant of £10 was made towards the cost. But this was an inadequate response and on further pressing, it was agreed to take the matter to the Attorney General. The Master and Wardens were present at the swearing of evidence and declared what had already been done to remove the danger. The fact that no further reference was made at subsequent Court meetings suggests that the timely action and persistence of Captain Wildey was successful in removing this unwelcome piece of private enterprise. On Audit Day, 1665, a complaint was made by William Bell's wife that their apprentice had been seized by Josias Dewey, the King's powder master, to make gunpowder barrels. The Court approved paying the apprentice's master compensation for the loss of work while his apprentice was detained on royal service.

The rapid development of more far-flung trade with India and the East Indies brought pressure on London's economy to loosen and remove the restrictive practices which were at the heart of its existence. There were great temptations to craftsmen and retail traders to exploit new opportunities to create more wealth, although to do so would be to challenge the protective rules which had kept livery companies in London and trade guilds in other cities in existence.

The Company found itself involved in just such a conflict in 1663. It was brought into the open by an uncompromising householder, Robert Allen, who was also a Quaker. He had been fined by one of the Sealers but on appearing at the monthly Court he refused to pay and accused the Sealer of incompetence, because he sealed only two or three casks in every last or cartload. Allen's accusation was repeated a little later by another householder, George Burbidge, about another Sealer, Daniel Ireland. Both coopers were confirmed in the accuracy of their story by a senior member of the Court, and by the experience of a third householder in his dealings with Ireland. Ireland, however, called a spokesman for the Soapboilers, who used the casks supplied by Allen and Burbidge, and who gave a good account of Ireland's work as Sealer.

Allen did not let matters rest. He appeared at the November 1663 Court meeting and formally accused the two Sealers of being involved in a 'combination' between a group of Soapboilers and soap-coopers, an agreement which Allen said was supported by a bond. The Court demanded written documents from the Sealers to clear their names. Suspicion had probably been increased by Ireland's arrears in paying his rent for the Seal. The Court waited three months for the evidence and then asked the Clerk to investigate, by meeting the Clerk to the Soapboilers. At the same time the Sealers were ordered to pay their debts or some part of them on pain of legal action against their sureties.

The imminence of a general search planned for March 1664, flushed out the group of coopers whom Allen had accused. Seventeen, including some respected senior liverymen were summoned before the May Court to answer the charge that they had been making 'untight' casks, that is suitable for dry goods, and supplying them to the soap-boilers. The implication, although unstated, was that the casks could be made suitable for semi-liquid soap by putting clay on the joints. The coopers were reprimanded and warned for the future.

Robert Allen had not finished his mission to bring the conspiracy into the open. His story soon received corroboration from Richard Winch, Ireland's successor as Sealer. He had been drawn into the conspiracy on his appointment but decided that sufficient information had come into the open to undermine his role, which was to connive in deceitfully sealing unsound casks. He gave evidence at a special Court meeting and as a result the matter was referred to the Lord Mayor's Court. This was enough to bring a full confession from one of the most respected Coopers, Ambrose Cleeve, who 'submitted and acknowledged his weakness'. He told the Court that the boilers had persuaded him that the arrangement was lawful. He was, he said 'very sorry he had so done', and he promised 'never more to make any such covenants'. He produced the agreement which the Court had been trying to obtain for a year since Allen's first accusation and so the proceedings in the Lord Mayor's Court were stayed. A number of private arrangements were subsequently uncovered but the fines were very modest. Perhaps the Court was uncomfortable because many senior Coopers were involved, including Caleb Scott, Master in 1656.

Mark of Richard Winch

The issue was difficult to settle and re-appeared in the next decade, as soap-coopers continued to feel their livelihoods were under threat from competition from soap-boilers. As in brewhouses, they could keep up to two coopers to trim and repair casks but not to make them from new. It became harder to regulate, as the soapboiling industry expanded and as larger quantities of imports into London made available more casks for re-use. One feature of the illegal agreement between the soap-coopers and the soap-boilers was that the coopers would make slack (or dry) casks for the soap-boilers instead of the tighter casks needed for semi-liquid soap. The Sealers were easily persuaded to seal a few token casks, which were sound ones, in each last and to ignore the rest. The soap-boilers then daubed the joints between the staves with clay to seal the container, and, in doing so, they increased the total weight to their advantage. The agreement assured the soap-boilers of cheap casks, and for the time being, the soap-coopers stayed in business. The customer was the only loser.

The Company responded to a petition for assistance to the soap-coopers. It was drawn up by Thomas Firman, who became, for a time, the spokesman for the soap-coopers. In response to the petition, the Court appointed a committee, which drew up a new table of cask sizes and weights for soap. The Sealers accepted it and agreed to use special care in its application. Their intentions were probably good, but they proved unreliable and vulnerable to bribes because of their debts.

Richard Winch's career as Sealer for St Katherine's from 1669 illustrates the problems of regulating the trade against the increasing pressures to allow greater freedom and competition. The fact that he was promoted from deputy after confessing his involvement in the soap-coopers affair and then re-appointed after getting into debt with the Company as well as being found inaccurate in his work, shows either that the Company was slack in its standards, or it had great difficulty in finding an alternative to Winch. He became a target of complaint for the Quaker coopers. They argued that he brought the Company into disrepute with victuallers who received short measure from brewers when Winch sealed barrels as correct at 36 gallons when they contained only 33 gallons. He could also be bribed to seal barrels which were unfinished. In October 1674, he was dismissed 'for his ill behaviour' after many warnings. The other two Sealers were equally incompetent or corrupt and were also dismissed, followed by one of their replacements within a year. The office failed to attract suitable candidates; it was onerous, uncertain as a source of income and becoming an impossible job. The difficulties signal the steep decline of the Company's ability to control and regulate the craft.

During the period of peace which followed the Second Civil War in 1648–49, the Court turned its attention to reforming some aspects of the government of the Ratcliffe charity. It may have been an awareness of having held this responsibility for a century that prompted a review of the admission of pupils and the pensions of the almspeople in 1654. The schoolmaster, Tobias Randall, was asked to gather information on the number of pupils, the charges made on their entry to the school, how they were selected and what subjects they were taught. The Court made clear that the number of pupils must be limited to 30 who were to be appointed by the authority of the Master and Wardens. Once the school was full, the schoolmaster and usher were permitted to take private, that is, fee-paying pupils. To keep a check on this, a register had to be kept and new admissions, were, for a time, recorded in the Court minutes. The majority came from Ratcliffe or nearby within the parish of Stepney and were sons of tradesmen or mariners. Fees, even for the free scholars, were confirmed as legitimate to provide writing materials and for subjects such as arithmetic and writing which were judged outside the provisions made in Dame Avice's deed of gift and Nicholas Gibson's will. Such an interpretation was probably not what the founders intended but was necessary at a time when the charity's income, which was a little over £62 a year from rents, had not kept pace with inflation.

This view was confirmed from the frequent applications made by the pensioners for extra help. In October 1659, the Court decided to increase all the Ratcliffe pensions, by an extra five shillings a quarter for the men, that is those on the Toby Wood foundation, and three shillings for the women who were supported on the original Gibson foundation. This meant the men received £5 a year and the women £2 12s. The Company's relations with Ratcliffe were considerably enlivened by the arrival of William Speed, appointed schoolmaster in March 1663. He was probably the most scholarly of all the appointments made up to that date and the author of a widely-used book of Latin wit and skill, *Epigrammata Juvenalia*. As well as being a scholar of some note, Speed was devious, contentious and irascible. He could not get along with his ushers and spent a good deal of energy quarrelling with them and writing papers for the Court's benefit to defend his position. After one particularly trying incident when Speed and the usher had each read a paper to the Court denouncing the other but failed to answer any of the points raised against them, the Court ordered them to answer the charges and sent them away to prepare their responses. On their return they had obviously decided it would be to mutual advantage to patch up their quarrel, which was all about the sharing out of pupil fees; so they expressed sorrow to the Court for the trouble they had given and 'prayed pardon and oblivion of what was past'.

One morning in June 1665, Speed and Webb, the usher, arrived quite unexpectedly at a Court meeting and 'prayed direction as to their continuing or discontinuing with learning in the said school during this sad time of the pestilential visitation'. Who, one wonders, was minding the school? Speed was told to go back to his post and to 'continue there for so long as it might be safe so for him to do'. As a man of some independence of mind, he probably did not delay long. Many pupils had already left and others were preparing to go with their parents to friends or relatives in the Essex countryside. The last major and best-known outbreak of bubonic plague had begun a few weeks before Speed's visit to the Hall in the newly-developed and fashionable suburbs around Whitehall, Westminster and Covent Garden. By the second week of June, the weekly mortality bill, a publication of City parish burials, rose sharply to over 100. Samuel Pepys reported in his diary the flight of the royal household from Whitehall, which he described as 'full of waggons and people ready to go out of town'.

Plague deaths rose steeply early in July and Pepys noticed its spread into the City with seven or eight houses in Basinghall Street 'shut up of the plague' and more along his way by Long Lane and London Wall. The quarterly Court for July was cancelled, the Clerk merely noting the list of charitable disbursements which he and the Beadle would be responsible for delivering. The same happened again in October, and monthly courts remained closed until November. This meeting, attended by the Master, Wardens and two Assistants, kept the essential work of the Company ticking over. Six marks were registered for new coopers and the rent from the Sealers was collected. The hard frosts of November helped to reduce recorded plague deaths from almost 7,000 a week in September, to under 400. London began to return to something like normality, having been for months a place derelict and deserted. 'What a sad time it is to see no boats on the river; and grass grows all up and down Whitehall Court ... how empty the streets are and melancholy, so many poor, sick people ... everybody talking of this dead and that sick man ... in Westminster there is never a physician and but one apothecary left, all being dead.' So Pepys sketched the capital in that early autumn.

From November, there was a steady return of citizens. One sign of normal life was the re-starting of the coach service to York. The January quarterly Court had a good attendance of 31 liveryman. Three Assistants had died since July 1665, but with no information about the causes, their deaths were just as likely to be from old age as from plague. However, there is strong evidence that the plague victims were likely to be most numerous among the old, the very young and the poor. There were three vacancies to be filled at the Ratcliffe almshouses and an unusually long list of petitioners to fill them.

The plague brought much personal misery, but the fire which engulfed the city in September 1666 was a corporate disaster, as well as a personal one. Pepys' maid, Jane, alerted him at three in the morning of 2 September, to a blaze south-east of his house in Seething Lane. But even quite extensive fires were not uncommon — a large part of Cheapside had been destroyed in August 1664 — and the Pepys household returned to bed. By that time some of the Coopers' property was probably already on fire in Thames Street.

The morning's news, though, was that 300 houses had been burned around Fish Street, near London Bridge. From the vantage point of the Tower, Pepys saw the huge scale of the fire, which was being swept along by strong easterly winds. The houses and shops on London Bridge were ablaze '… People almost distracted and no means to quench the fire …' wrote the diarist.

The great spire of St Lawrence Pountney, which dominated the riverside between London Bridge and Blackfriars, was a dramatic sight, ablaze from the top, where the fire first caught hold, until the whole collapsed. It was the church where Pepys' schoolfriend, Thomas Elborough, was rector. Many cooperages in the tiny, tightly-packed riverside parishes were destroyed on the first day of the great fire. In this area, where wines and brandy were stored by wharves in the Vintry, the fire raged particularly fiercely. Everywhere, it was easily fed by timber-framed buildings dried out during the long, hot summer.

Early attempts were made to check the passage of the fire by pulling down houses in its path, but they failed in spite of the efforts of the King and the Duke of York giving directions from a river barge. For a time there was hope of halting the fire at Three Cranes' Wharf, well known to members of the Company as their rendezvous on Lord Mayor's Day; but in vain. As darkness fell, Pepys watched the scene from Bankside, across the Thames from the Three Cranes '… It appeared more and more; and in corners and upon steeples and between churches and houses as far as we could see up the hill of the city, in a most horrid, malicious bloody flame, not like the flame of an ordinary fire'.

By Tuesday, 5 September, the fire was spreading both westward and northward, towards Cheapside, Guildhall and St Paul's. Basinghall Street was in imminent danger when the Wardens arrived for what would normally have been the monthly Court. They were met by an agitated and anxious Clerk, and together, the three men set about saving the Company's valuables.

Plate, linen, pewter and other movables, including the pictures, were loaded on carts and stored at Warden Morris's home. He was the organiser of the evacuation. The Clerk took care of the documents '… assisting in the collecting and conveying away of the Register books and other writings and papers… in his custody and closett' at the Hall. They were just in time. Later that day, the Hall was consumed by 'the dreadful devouring fire'. It is not recorded whether they had time, like Pepys, to dig a deep and large enough hole in the courtyard to hold the best wine.

Cellars were no protection from the fire, as the booksellers of St Paul's Churchyard discovered. They used the cathedral vaults for their stock, but as Richard Baxter explained, the weight of the stones of the collapsing cathedral broke the vaults. 'I saw the half-burnt leaves of books near my dwelling at Acton, six miles from London… but others found them near Windsor'.

Matters began to improve the next day. Dockyard workers from Deptford, brought in at Pepys' suggestion, used gunpowder effectively to break the progress of the fire, while in parts near Coopers' Hall, it burned itself out on reaching London Wall. There were secondary blazes; one in Bishopsgate was quickly dealt with by the Deptford men, but not before rumours spread that it was part of a Papist plot. The Duke of York came under suspicion as a Roman Catholic and it was claimed that he was lenient with people accused of 'casting fire balls'.

The immediate aftermath filled Richard Baxter with horror at the scale of the destruction '… What a ruinous, confused place the city was… chimneys and steeples only standing in the midst of cellars and heaps of rubbish'. People were stunned 'and wandered the street with scarce sense left in them to lament their own calamity'. Those without means of transport away from the City, and without relatives who could shelter them, camped out with their remaining possessions in Moorfields. As soon as the ground was cool enough, a watch was placed on the City ruins to prevent looting. Pepys and some companions walked through the town 'our feet ready to burn'. By the end of the dreadful week it began to rain, dampening the smouldering timbers, but bringing more misery to the Moorfields campers. It took several more days and royal intervention to supply tents.

Exactly one week after the aborted monthly Court, the Master of the Company summoned a special meeting at the Queen's Head, in Bishopsgate. The Wardens and nine Assistants were present. Orders were approved for Warden Morris to continue to house the Company's plate and 'to have like regard as to his own'. The Clerk was to look after the books and to collect them all together. Urgent action was agreed to find accommodation at some other

Company's hall. This was achieved by the end of September and subsequent Courts were held at the Bricklayers' Hall in Leadenhall Street. Other special meetings took place at Roger Morris's house. The Beadle was given £3 to find himself other lodgings and was enjoined 'to be very industrious in inquiring and taking names of such freemen who have lost their house in London by the said fire, together with the places where they now reside or can be found'. The Wardens required the Sealers to 'diligently entreat the duty of their several places'. Finally, they arranged to meet at Mr Denis's cooperage just outside Aldgate, for the journey to Ratcliffe on 26 September to pay the pensioners.

The Company had suffered a bitter blow. Never wealthy, usually struggling to meet its commitments, it had recently made Herculean efforts to improve the Hall and increase the Livery. The losses in the fire were all the more desperate. None of the Company's properties from which it drew its rental income had survived. Some of the Ratcliffe properties were safe, it is true, but their income supported the Charity and at times failed to do so entirely, so that some charges fell on the Company. It was estimated that in the City as a whole, an annual rental income of £600,000 was lost by the fire.

Drastic measures were needed. For the time being, quarterly pension payments were suspended. The Company's plate was sold to discharge debts on several bonds, probably the renewals on the money borrowed to meet the King's 'loan' in 1664. It was agreed that 'special gifts of worthy members' should be exempt from the general sale. The Lord Mayor's Day feast was cancelled and the Stewards discharged their duty by payments to the Company of £8 each. Two apprentices had to be disciplined. One had been absent for a fortnight and another, 'very vicious', was accused of theft. Perhaps it was a case of looting.

Courageously, the Court gathered its collective strength to continue exercising its authority over the craft in London. It acted with vigour, and perhaps in doing so gave its members confidence that they could face the future and prepare for rebuilding. Many members had lost everything in the fire, homes as well as businesses. It says much for their resilience that planning was undertaken with such speed.

Rebuilding the Hall and securing its claim to the ground area of all its properties was the Court's main concern at its second meeting after the fire. Encouraged by the energy and optimism of Roger Morris, the decision was taken to terminate the leases on the tenements adjacent to the Hall. Morris urged that a larger, more convenient Hall was necessary, and the old site was 'very straight (narrow) and not capacious enough'. He even tried to hasten matters and privately offered £100 to the tenants to give up their claims. The offer was refused.

The Company had to wait for the outcome of arbitration which was concluded in its favour in November 1668, awarding only £50 compensation for the lessees. Meanwhile it complied with the requirements of the City Corporation to clear its sites of rubbish and submit to the general survey of the whole area of destruction carried out by the Surveyor to the City, Peter Mills and two new assistants, John Oliver, a common councillor, and Robert Hooke, Reader in Mathematics at Gresham College. The standard charge for a survey was 18 pence a site. These surveyors had powers to enforce new building regulations issued in a series of mayoral and royal proclamations during spring 1667. The new rules created a safer, more spacious city. Brick or stone was to be used for main walls, wooden floors and roofs were to be sound structures; there was street-widening and no encroachments allowed on either streets or alleys. A new duty levied on coal helped to pay for these improvements.

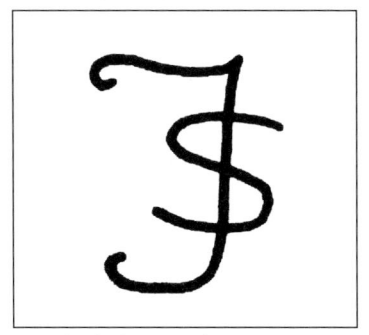

Mark of John Stutzberry, 1669, one of a number of Quaker members.

During the two-year wait for permission to rebuild, the Company set up its own fire court, its members drawn from among the Assistants. It met on Tuesdays, except on the regular Court day, which was the first in the month and its task was to hear representations from its tenants and then to determine a settlement of their claims. Some were prepared to take up a new building lease, usually at the old rent but with an extended term, others surrendered their lease in return for compensation. Usually these were tenants who could not afford to rebuild. One was a small trader in Garlickhythe, facing ruin after the fire, who wanted £50 in compensation. He was offered £25 and settled for £29. A neighbouring leaseholder wanted a reduction in rent as well as help with rebuilding costs and refused all the Company's offers. After nine months of dispute, he agreed that his case should go to the City's Fire Court, which arbitrated an agreement. He surrendered his lease in August 1668. In Fenchurch Street, the opportunity was taken to exchange land with the Drapers' Company to achieve a better shaped plot for rebuilding. In Crooked Lane, Edward Palmer, Master, was granted a favourable 51-year rebuilding lease at the old rent of £6.

This example implies that there was less speculation driving up the price of land than Pepys suggested. However, the diarist was a shrewd observer as well as a careful investor, and recognised that land and property would rise

*Cooper's Hall 1831–32 by Thomas Hosmer Shepherd (1793–1864).
This shows the Hall rebuilt after the Great Fire of 1666.*

in value once reconstruction began. When he viewed the newly-widened King Street in November 1667, he wrote: 'Ground which was at four pence a foot will be worth fifteen shillings once houses are built'. By 1670, the Company had reason to feel quite satisfied with its work in settling all its new leases. It had managed to devolve all rebuilding on to its tenants and it was assured of almost £200 a year income from rents, an increase of 50 per cent since the Civil War.

Roger Morris once again used his initiative to put in motion preparations for rebuilding the Hall, while the arbitration of the leased portions of the site was still awaited. He secured the Court's approval of Deputy John Wildgoose, a past Master of the Carpenters' Company and a common councillor, as architect. The design model Wildgoose produced was received with such enthusiasm by the Court that it earned him five gold pieces. It was, some said, 'beyond any hitherto made'. Wildgoose was also helpful in securing the issue of the official surveyor's certificate, which permitted building to begin. Supervision of the work was delegated to a committee of Master, Wardens and three Assistants of whom any two could act and make payments to the craftsmen. This arrangement and the appointment of a clerk of works 'to prevent as much as maybe deceit and idleness of workmen and labourers', speeded the work. Wages were two shillings a day for skilled craftsmen and one shilling for labourers. During the period of short days in January and February 1670, work was suspended. It was both an economy and a welcome breathing space to consider the vexed question of raising more money to pay the bills.

The Clerk wrote proudly 'at Coopers' Hall' above his minutes for the Court meeting held on 1 March 1670, 'it being the first day of holding a Court there since the rebuilding thereof'. It must have been a cold, uncomfortable occasion in an unfinished building without wainscot, plaster or water and with very little furniture. The rawness of the experience probably gave some urgency to the task of raising money to complete the interior. The members of the Court set an example by subscribing £120 but progress during the rest of the year was slow because of unpaid bills, and unreliable workmen who failed to appear or came in the wrong sequence. In September, the joiner making the wainscot could not continue until the mason and plasterer returned to finish a job. With so much reconstruction taking place in the City, skilled labour was at a premium. Older members were shocked at the expense of having piped water from Sir Hugh Middleton's New River Company, which brought fresh water from Hertfordshire into the City. At a charge of 45 shillings a year, they felt it was an unaffordable luxury, but they were outvoted. There was a two-year delay because the original pipes supplied by the Company's plumber were too large.

There seems to have been a similar debate about upholstery. The outcome was an order for 18 chairs upholstered in fabric costing 10 shillings each and 18 in another pattern costing 13 shillings. The contract for this went to Samual Vernier, a liveryman who was an upholsterer by trade. Other furniture purchased for the Court Room included 2 long tables, 2 carpets, 10 cushions and a pair of andirons. The Hall contained 13 forms, 3 long tables and 6 Spanish tables, which were elaborately carved side tables. There was a little parlour, as in the old Hall, used by the Master, Wardens and small committees, furnished simply with a table, two forms and a green carpet. Thomas Mason, Master 1670, gave 'a hammer or knocker tipped at the end with silver on which the Company's arms are quartered, for the use of the Court' and he also paid for the King's arms to be carved in wood and placed between the two great windows at the east end of the Hall, looking out into Basinghall Street. The old pewter and six silver spoons were sold to pay for newer pewter and larger plates. The pictures, which included the portrait of Dame Avice and Sir Anthony Knyvett, her second husband, had been rescued from the fire and were cleaned before being re-hung in the Court Room.

The ground plan of the Hall was an awkward polygon with the Livery Hall running east to west from Basinghall Street, the kitchen set at angle westwards and separated from the Hall by screens, as in an Oxford or Cambridge college hall. It had a cupola painted with the four seasons and Ganymede with the eagle. There was a long gallery at first-floor level opening on to the hall, used to accommodate extra tables when all the Livery were present for dinner. At the screens (west) end of the Livery Hall a desk and a shelf fixed to the wainscot were used for large folio volumes with the shelf probably holding the Company's Bible. The Court Room was at the north side of the Livery Hall and overlooked St Michael's churchyard. The small parlour occupied a space south of the Livery Hall and next to an archway gate surmounted by the Company's arms and leading from the street to a courtyard. The Clerk had rooms above the Court Room and above, on the second floor, were probably the Beadle's quarters, the gown room and secure storage for the increasing stock of Company plate. There were cellars below, entered separately from the Hall and providing a useful rental.

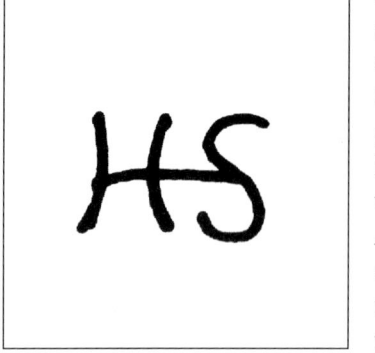

Mark of Henry Strode, snr, 1644. He was the father of Henry Strode, the benefactor of the Egham Charity.

The new Hall was a much larger building than the one destroyed by the fire. It had an extra storey and it occupied the whole site where formerly there had been the Hall, a yard, a cottage and a tenement. Although the Company used the new Hall from March 1670, it was not completed until 1678. Paying for such a large undertaking was a struggle, but somehow the Company managed to keep money flowing to pay the bills during the building phase. Some larger and wealthier companies had to rebuild in stages because they ran out of funds. The Merchant Taylors had to stop in 1673 and could not resume building until 1681. The Grocers and the Goldsmiths were so heavily burdened by their rebuilding that it took until the 1740s to return to their former levels of prosperity.

The initial capital for rebuilding came from the gifts and loans of wealthier members. The Assistants' gift of £120 was matched by a similar sum from the Livery. Edward Palmer's widow, Judith, lent £371 at six per cent. The Master and Under Warden each lent £200 in 1670. Even the apprentices made involuntary contributions when Warden Emms began fining them sixpence for appearing in Court with long hair. Such collections were too small to be of help in the building but they boosted the poorbox.

The Company had already set itself a precedent in the 1650s when it used the expansion of numbers in the Livery as a way of funding the extension of the old Hall. In 1659, an important decision was taken about the method of determining when a new 'call' should be made and who should be called to the Livery. Both matters were to be decided democratically by a vote of all the Livery after a general warning had been issued about the time and purpose of the meeting. The 1659 decision also included raising the entry fine to the Livery to £15. The 'calls' to the Livery from 1668 were more ambitious. the five calls made between 1668 and 1676, raised £2,040 from 136 new liverymen. It was almost double the total rental income for the period.

Some of those who refused and whose excuses were genuine, were encouraged, to pay a subscription in instalments, towards the cost of the Hall, with the option of having the amount deducted from their Livery fine when they could afford to pay. The excuses illustrate the varied kinds of poverty among the freemen: 'sayth not able— old and sickly; is but a journeyman and worketh for his mother; too young; no house but lodgings; having lost all by fire; sayth 'tis hard with him; sayth but a small trade'. Stubborn refusers, who were known to be well able to pay the Livery fine, were at length referred to the Lord Mayor's Court. One such was Henry Strode senior who refused in 1653, in 1669 and in 1671 when he even refused the minimum £5 subscription, 'whereupon it was resolved...that the Recorder of London's warrant be obtained for the apprehending of the said Strode'. He was saved from arrest by his son who paid £10, as fine money for the refusals of 1669 and 1671.

Stick and carrot methods were used to secure payments from existing liverymen who had not made a voluntary subscription to the Hall. In 1670, only the subscribers among the Livery were allowed on the Company's barge on Lord Mayor's Day. John Goodman saved himself from being summoned to the Lord Mayor's Court for failing to guard his unwise speech, by producing £10 towards the Hall. One of the wealthier Quakers in the Company was Gerard Roberts. He secured the concession of not wearing his gown at meetings as the price for agreeing to pay his Livery fine. He set a precedent which was followed by other Quakers in the Company.

During the difficult times since the Restoration of the monarchy, the Company was fortunate to be led by several able men who proved their leadership qualities in the aftermath of the fire in 1666. They persuaded the whole Company that ambitious targets were achievable if everyone contributed what he was able. They did not evade difficult decisions and to their credit, at a time when there was a strong reaction against religious dissenters, a few wise Assistants, led by Roger Morris, accepted and accommodated the Quaker members of the Company. By 1680, the company was financially secure. The Hall and its new furnishings were paid for, rental income was steady, the barge was no longer hired but was the Company's own, also paid for by members' subscriptions and the annual audit showed a modest surplus year by year. It was a rare moment of calm prosperity.

CHAPTER SIX
Fighting for the Charter 1680–1700

> *The attempt to stop the succession of James II stimulated the formation of the first political parties, Whigs and Tories. James subverted the law, even more than Charles II had done, to restore Catholics to political influence. In so doing, he provoked the revolution of 1688. Whig and Tory leaders jointly invited William of Orange, James' son-in-law, to bring an army to England. James fled; William and Mary became joint sovereigns. James was defeated in Ireland. The constitutional settlement included a Toleration Act, a Bill of Rights, triennial Parliaments and a Protestant succession. The Bank of England was founded in 1694 to help pay for William's wars against France.*

DURING THE YEARS of the Civil War and the period of rebuilding the Hall, the Company was fortunate in having two knowledgeable and efficient clerks. They were John Looker, Clerk from 1642 to 1665, and his son, also John. Both were attorneys-at-law who were able to protect the Company's interests and defend its statutory rights to control the craft and coopers in London. The elder Looker had to resign, in 1665, probably because of blindness. From 1653, he had been assisted by an amanuensis and needed two senior members of the Court to sit with him on Election Day to help him count the votes. The younger man died suddenly in 1673, leaving his widow with two small sons. She did not become a charge on the Company, though, because she was well-connected in the City as the daughter of the Keeper of Ludgate, and probably received help from John Fleet, a liveryman and future Lord Mayor.

The new Clerk, Joseph Browne, was also an attorney, chosen from among 13 applicants. In the next four years he busied himself with taking action against hawkers, who tried to evade the Company's regulations, and against the Vintners and Brewers with whom there were continuing demarcation disputes. Suddenly, in March 1677, Browne was arrested, locked in the Tower and charged with publishing a seditious pamphlet *The Long Parliament Dissolved*. It urged Parliament to uphold popular liberties and it revived memories of the heady days of revolution in 1640 and 1641. This was dangerous ground. Browne argued he was merely sending a copy of the pamphlet to his brother in the East India Company. The Privy Council nevertheless thought he was dangerous; he may already have been known as a political radical, and so he received a severe sentence; a fine of 1,000 marks (£666). As he could not possibly pay, he was sent to the debtors' prisons, first the Marshalsea and then the Fleet. He was struck off the roll of attorneys with the additional proviso that he must find sureties for his good behaviour for seven years after his release. The Court reacted with panic, fearful of the repercussions on the Company, but also afflicted with some compassion for the Clerk. At first there were orders to change the locks at the Hall. It is not clear whether this was to keep Browne out if he managed to pay his fine and secure his release, or to prevent informers finding more incriminating material in his rooms. By November, it was evident that Browne had no means of release, other than a royal pardon, so the Company settled its debts to him and paid him a sum of £82 one year later in settlement of all claims. A replacement was appointed in the summer of 1677, one Peter Stepkin, who proved not very diligent in keeping the Company's records accurately and who left his post without warning in October 1681. His employment was formally ended in February 1682.

Browne's harsh treatment was the result of a volatile political struggle within the government led by Lord Danby, Lord Treasurer, and a judiciary which was compliant with royal policy. One month before Browne's offence, the King had sent a group of peers to cool their heels for a time in the Tower. They opposed his pro-French foreign policy and his support for his brother and heir, the Duke of York, an overt Roman Catholic. Danby wanted to strike a balance; to restrain the opposition but persuade the King to be a little more compromising and 'fall into the humour of the people'. A foolish clerk circulating a document which raked over old political embers could expect little compassion or leniency.

The dangerous programme which the opposition peers intended to promote, when a suitable opportunity occurred, was to panic Parliament into passing a Bill to exclude the Duke of York from the throne. Their first opportunity came in 1679 when the country was gripped by anti-Catholic fever caused by the fabrications of two Protestant fanatics, Titus Oates and Isaac Tonge. These two alleged there was a plot to kill the King, raise rebellion in Ireland and Scotland and then overthrow the Protestant religion in England. It was nonsense, but it was believed for a time, particularly as the King's secret arrangement of receiving payment from France came into the open, leaked by a disgruntled civil servant. The King was thrown on to the defensive to save his brother's inheritance and regain his own popularity. He sacrificed Danby to appease the opposition and ordered a review of recent Court cases which had been blatant miscarriages of justice. Browne's case was one. He was released in December 1679, personally received by the King at Whitehall, recommended for return of his former posts and his restitution to the roll of attorneys. In the early part of 1680, the Privy Council issued a document releasing him from the consequences of his sentence.

The Company hesitated for over two years before agreeing to restore Browne to his clerkship. The political ferment, which lasted throughout 1680 until the King prorogued Parliament at Oxford in March 1681, was a convenient excuse for doing nothing. Just as the political nation divided into the first recognisable political parties, the Court also showed partisanship, some members favouring the Whig opposition, which tried to have the Duke of York excluded from the succession and others, the Tories, favouring the government and the King. The Whigs, skilfully led as a loose confederation of opposition by Lord Shaftesbury, kept up a frenzy of anti-Catholic fears, rumours and demonstrations. They orchestrated country-wide bonfires and pope-burnings on 5 and 17 November (the anniversaries of the Gunpowder Plot and Queen Elizabeth's accession) and kept up pressure on the King to call Parliament with frequent petitions. Unlike his father, Charles I in 1641, Charles II controlled the military forces in London. Nor was Shaftesbury as able an opponent as John Pym had been. The popular mood was also less fervent. Although there was alarm, tension and genuine fear of a Catholic triumph, the populace did not have quite the enthusiastic determination it displayed in 1641 and 1642. King Charles judged correctly that the memory of civil war was fresh enough to be a strong antidote to renewed civil violence. By calling Parliament to meet in Oxford, he removed it from any possible interference from London radicals.

Against this background, caution or inertia prevailed in Basinghall Street. The Court waited for the political climate to become calmer, as it did during 1681, and then, in the autumn, it permitted Browne to assist its standing Counsel, Luke Astrey, in a difficult Chancery case brought by the parish of Stepney. Browne was re-appointed in March 1682 and began putting the Company's neglected accounts, registers, minutes and records into order. His accounts for 1683 were given rare praise by the auditors, being 'found very exact and methodical'.

There was still some element of doubt about Browne's judgement, if not his politics. Before his arrest he had been mildly rebuked for becoming too involved with the petitioners for places in the Ratcliffe almshouses. 'He was often drawn into prejudice of the worthiest that may be found'. Then in 1683 his failure to attend a service, on 30 January, was reported and recorded: 'The anti-monarchical clerk: non-attendance at St Mary-le-Bow for commemoration of the execution of King Charles I'. Clearly he had enemies in high places. The secretary to the Privy Council accused him of acting improperly when he took the poll at the election of the Lord Mayor. His integrity was vouched for by the Sheriff, Thomas Pilkington, '…as a person well known to us [the two sheriffs] and in whom we could put our trust and confidence'.

The Company was soon caught up in a new crisis which threatened its independence and the freedom of the City Corporation. Once the uproar of the Exclusion crisis died away, the King set about to purge public life of the influence of the Whigs, the exclusionists. His aim was to replace the charters by which London and other cities and boroughs were governed with new charters. Under them, many of their traditional rights and privileges would be removed and the Crown would assume the power of appointing officers. From December 1681 to June 1683, the City Corporation resisted the King's attempt to declare its charter of liberties forfeit. The device which was eventually successful was a writ of *Quo Warranto* ('by what right') which challenged the City and subsequently all boroughs, to show by what right or warrant they held the privileges granted in their charters. London had the financial resources to resist the King's challenge in the courts but gave up the battle when it was clear that the judges were all biassed in the King's favour. When London admitted defeat, other boroughs also gave up the legal fight and surrendered their charters. New charters were then issued under which the Crown had the right to appoint officers: the Lord Mayor, Sheriffs and Aldermen. All became royal nominees and safe Tories were placed in office.

Other city institutions, including the livery companies, were then issued with writs. The Court met on 11 April 1684, with Luke Astrey in attendance, to consider what response to make. Preparations were made to answer the charges in court, but there was little stomach for an expensive legal hearing in which the Company would certainly be the loser. At the June Court, having held no elections, the surrender of the 1661 Charter was accepted as inevitable and the discussion turned to the best means of protecting the welfare of the Company, the charity and their other possessions. From 24 June 1684, the minutes were in a new hand, beginning with the King's instructions. Thereafter, the record was brief, but routine business, paying the pensioners, admitting apprentices, granting marks to new householders, continued as before.

The waiting period ended in February 1685, when the new Charter was ready. New officers, Master, Wardens and a Court of 14 Assistants, instead of 17, were to hold office until the next year's elections. A new Clerk,

William Kempe, replaced Joseph Browne. The Company lost its right of self-government. In future, the Aldermanic Court, which had been purged of Whigs, was charged with accepting or rejecting the Company's nominees for office and for admission to the Livery. The nominees, presumably of Tory persuasion, were William Wimberry as Master (he had already served in 1677) and two newcomers, Edward Booker and James Hudson, as Wardens. Nine Assistants, all past Masters, were removed from the Court and promoted members were nominated in their place. The Livery was newly constituted by the Court and had to have the Lord Mayor's approval. Of 34 names submitted, only 17 were accepted. All had to take oaths of allegiance and supremacy, a requirement which allowed none but Anglicans into membership. The King retained the right to dismiss members at will and to order new elections for Master and Wardens.

These arrangements left the Company as a 'rump' of its former self. Its main concern was to increase the number on the Livery but it was a slow process with only two or three names approved at a time and the procedure taking four to six months.

After Charles II's death in January 1685, James II continued his brother's methods but used them to achieve a different purpose. He wanted to remove the penal legislation which excluded Catholics from political life. Dissenters were also excluded by the same legislation so the King sought to enlist their support by using the powers of the Crown, contained in the new charters, to remove the Tory and Anglican incumbents. In October 1687, the Company received an order to remove their Master, Wardens and several Assistants and liverymen.

After this purge, only one Assistant remained: John Fleet. It was on his authority that nine of the Assistants deprived of office in 1685 were recalled. They then elected Richard Devon, Warden in 1684 when Charles II cancelled elections, as the Master and began the process of recalling members of the Livery who had been deprived of their membership since 1684. The King issued letters patent in November, giving the Court power to administer oaths of office and dispensing with the recent requirement to take oaths of allegiance and supremacy. This indicated James' determination to open public life to non-Anglicans. However relieved the Company might have been that deprived members were restored, everyone was aware that the Crown was still able to intervene in the Company's affairs. The see-saw of politics was causing division in the fellowship.

In February 1688, there was a further royal intervention. Twelve recently-restored liverymen were again evicted, three others who had not been restored by the new Court were ordered to be reinstated and the Under Warden and newly-appointed Assistants were removed. It was an example of how intrusive royal power was under the 1685 Charter. The Clerk made an attempt to produce a definitive list of the Livery and managed 82 names but he commented a little despairingly, 'Many of these have for many years withdrawn themselves from London some beyond seas and in places unknown to us'.

Normality returned in stages in the autumn months of 1688. James' pro-Catholic policy led to a Whig-Tory alliance to remove him with the help of an invading force led by his son-in-law William, Prince of Orange.

The first Parliament called by William and Mary as joint sovereigns, annulled the 1683 judgement against the Corporation of London. From that followed the restoration of the City's charter and the charters of the other livery companies and boroughs. The Company's deed of surrender which had allowed Charles II to replace the 1661 Charter was delivered back to the Company in November 1688 by Lord Jeffreys, the Lord Chancellor. This action cancelled the 1685 Charter. The intruded Clerk was given notice to leave his lodgings at the Hall by 1 February 1689 and once more Joseph Browne returned.

Throughout the turbulent half century since 1640, the Company's routines were little affected. Even in the times of disaster, the fire, and the loss of the Charter, there was determination to continue, as far as possible, with business as usual. The good reputation and effectiveness of the Company rested with the diligence, efficiency and probity of the Wardens. They determined the standards by which a freeman's proof-work was judged. They set the test, the conditions in which it was to be carried out and decided whether the result was worthy of the man being granted his mark and the consequent right to set up his own business. The Wardens were expected to control the Sealers and ensure they behaved honestly; a task which became increasingly difficult as the Company doubled the size of its Livery. They had to take responsibility for the Company's finances and maintain good standards of general behaviour among the members.

When a Warden's own behaviour fell short of the expectations of the Court, he was answerable to the Company and often fined more severely than ordinary liverymen. Richard Mills, Under Warden in 1640 was fined 20 shillings for being 'very negligent and remiss in attendance' and putting the Company 'at trouble almost continuously for someone to supply his place'. William Coultman, Master in 1654, was overheard, in 1664, revealing details of the Court's business in an ale house. Perhaps his age and seniority were in his favour. He withdrew from a Court meeting while the matter was discussed and was excused a fine since it was his first offence.

For a time, during the 1640s and 1650s, the arbitration of disputes between members concluded with the Livery being invited to vote on several alternative levels of punishment, usually a fine. After the Restoration of the monarchy, the method dropped out of favour. Its use suggests that the radical politics of the New Model Army and the democratic ideas boldly debated by the Army in Putney parish church in 1647, found an echo in Coopers' Hall. Certainly the tender puritan consciences, which had led some to question the holding of elections on a Sunday, eventually succeeded first in moving the Livery dinner to Audit Day in July but it took until 1658 before the elections themselves were moved from Sunday to the Monday before Pentecost.

It is impossible to tell whether Edward Sandiloe's outburst after a Quarterly Court in 1657 was partly influenced by the freedom of expression and radical political ideas of the age or wholly caused by the beer he had been drinking. Addressing the senior members of the Livery he called out 'What have they to do more than me? Let us go up and sit with them. Why should they have wine with them and we have beer?' Once sober, he was sufficiently contrite to be let off with a warning and a fine instead of being summoned to the Lord Mayor's Court. A few months later, also at a Quarterly Court, Sandiloe three times called Warden Bray a knave 'and a cheating knave'. He continued in an egalitarian mode, 'although Mr Bray [is] one of the great ones of Coopers' Hall and when they were in Court [I] must stand before them hat under arm, but out of Court [I] am as good a man as Mr Bray'. Many present probably shared the general sentiment but wisely would utter such words only in private. On this occasion, Sandiloe's fine was 20 shillings for the three times he had called the Warden 'knave'.

The Company's social life suffered interruptions on account of the Civil War, and the great fire. The Election dinner was cancelled in 1643 because of the disruption caused by the presence in the Hall of the Outworks Committee, and after the fire it was not resumed until 1675 when the cost was shared between the retiring and newly elected officers. In 1688, on the eve of revolution, it was saved from cancellation by the flight of James II, whose action averted a civil war. Occasional cancellations were a consequence of the Company's penury and the need to economise. These were unpopular decisions and not good for the morale of the Livery. When a cancellation was reversed in 1692, the Clerk noted with approval that the Livery dinner 'contributed so much to the peace, tranquillity and reputation of this Company'.

The Company bore the main cost of these dinners but that on Lord

Mayor's Day was by custom provided for from three senior liverymen, chosen by turn each year, to act as Stewards for the feast. The alternative to serving in the office as Steward was to pay a fine, calculated as roughly equivalent to what would have been spent on providing a share of the food and drink. It was a duty generally regarded as onerous, for in addition to providing the dishes and quantities stipulated by the Court, the Stewards were responsible for making good losses of napkins, stolen spoons and missing silver plate.

The Stewards in 1675 proved very troublesome, perhaps because the fine had been increased to £16, an indication of the Company's difficulty in paying for the completion of the new Hall. The arguments between the Court and the Stewards resulted in the Stewards being summoned to the Lord Mayor's Court. All three were excluded from the 1676 feast 'because of the great trouble they have occasioned and the slighting they have offered this Court'. From 1677, the Company eased the demands made on the Stewards by contributing to the dinner from corporate funds or in kind. In 1677, it allowed £15, from which 18 pence each was to be given to the almspeople at Ratcliffe. In 1682, it provided 3 hogsheads and 12 gallons of claret. In 1685, the allowance was £5, three meat dishes, three dozen bottles of wine and the cost of musicians.

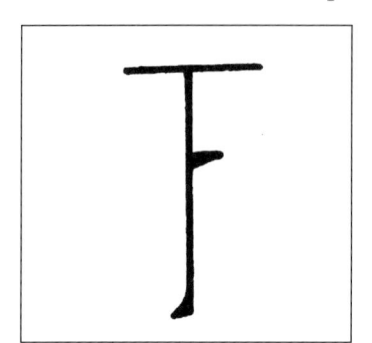

Mark of John Fleet, 1666, and formerly the mark of Thomas Firman

When the cost of the dinner in 1697 came to £112, the Stewards resorted to the law. They were prepared to pay £20 each and the Judge agreed that their stance was reasonable. Some of the problems of the dinner were solved when Mrs Hobhouse, the Beadle's wife, and Mrs Byfield, the usher's wife from Ratcliffe, undertook to be butlers, taking care of pewter, plate, glasses and napery. They had the good sense to stitch the napkins to the table-cloths. With porters to guard the gate against intruders and a limit on guests and personal servants, the end-of-century dinners became more orderly. They were certainly a little grander after the sale of the old pall cloth for £8 in 1678. Corporate funerals had gone out of fashion so the cloth's sale allowed the purchase of 2 silver salts, 4 dozen napkins and 4 large tablecloths. With gifts of silver plate becoming a normal bequest in the wills of the wealthier Officers and Assistants, the Company could at last boast a well-furnished table.

Although the fraternal support of the corporate funeral had disappeared, the Company's charitable giving remained a fundamental purpose of its existence. Whereas there were 12 pensioners receiving annual payments from the Company in the 1590s, that number had risen to 21 in the 1690s. The widows and children of Company servants, the usher, schoolmaster, Beadle and Clerk, were always treated courteously and considerately. They were given time to find accommodation and a pension if they were in need. A new category of supplicant appeared in the seventeenth century: captive coopers held hostage for a ransom in Constantinople or Tangier, wherever Barbary pirates had landed with booty from a captured ship. The Company continued to help with bursaries or exhibitions to 'hopeful scholars' at the universities when the parent was a needy liveryman. Two of the old charities were neglected and for a time forgotten. George Swayne's loan charity had not been used between 1626 and 1648 but it was revived and supporting a six-year loan in 1686. The Rector of St Michael's Bassishaw was able to restore the payment for coals to help the poor of the parish as a result of his research into John Baker's will.

The Ratcliffe foundation was the main recipient of the Company's charitable gifts. Its income was not sufficient for its needs by the 1680s, so it was given additional support from the corporate funds. Rather boldly, the Company enlarged its commitment in 1687 by adding two more pensioners to the Ratcliffe list. They were non-resident; one was intended for a Stepney widow, the other for a company nominee. The Court declared that although it was 'in great straights [sic] ... it is thankful to Almighty God for its preservation'. Such optimism was a little premature; it probably was a response to the partial restoration to the Court and the Livery of some of the members deprived of their places by the 1685 Charter.

The sentiments may also have some connection with a case in Chancery brought against the Company by the parish of Stepney in 1681 but which was beginning to run into the sands by 1687. The issue was whether Dame Avice's bequest had made the Company the trustee of the estate and charity at Ratcliffe or whether the Company was the absolute owner. The parish sought to prove the Company the trustee. As such it would have to run the charity exclusively from the foundation's income. If the Company owned the estate, there was nothing to prevent it benefiting from any surplus. This was the case in which Joseph Browne, continued to assist the Company's Standing Counsel, Luke Astrey, even during the period of his dismissal by the 1685 charter. It proved to be a very laborious case, with Stepney insisting on a thorough search of all the documents, which had to be copied, as had all the accounts and vouchers for payments. In three years, the Company spent £500 on legal fees. By 1688, the parish was using delaying tactics, objecting to the price of four pence a sheet for copying and refusing to return documents lent by the Company. The Company recorded no decision in the case; the parish may be presumed to have given up the fight. The new pensions of 1687 may have been a sign that the Company was confident of victory.

The success of the Glorious Revolution of 1688, which re-established Protestant rule, and the defeat of James II's attempt to regain his throne at the battle of the Boyne in 1690, led to a new wave of optimism, investment and prosperity. It was felt in Ratcliffe, which had benefited from the revival of coastal trade after the end of the Civil War and from the spectacular growth of London. The demand for coal, timber, brick, foodstuffs and luxury goods created the need for more wharfage, warehouses and shipping.

The Company took advantage of these conditions, when the lease of a substantial part of the Ratcliffe estate was renewed in 1692, to increase the entry fine and double the rent. The lessee, Captain Wildey, was granted a term of 61 years and the opportunity to rebuild. In 1694, the original almshouses which dated from 1536, were pulled down and a new, two-storied range was built on the northern side of the charity site. The open ground behind was fenced and divided into 14 plots so that the widows could keep hens and grow some of their own food.

During these changes, the schoolmaster had died and the Company sought a replacement. The year was 1689 and a young graduate of Trinity College, Dublin was a penniless refugee in London, having escaped from the temporary Catholic ascendancy in Ireland where King James' authority still survived. He was Alexander Jephson, the second son of a Protestant landowner of modest estate in County Neath. He had managed to secure a job as usher at the parish school of All Hallows, Barking (by the Tower) at four shillings a week and had to wait until he could be ordained by the Bishop of London before he could enter the curacy of the same parish.

From the schoolmaster of the parish, Jephson heard of the Ratcliffe vacancy and set about making the acquaintances of the Warden of the Company, who lived in Barking, in order to secure an introduction to other members of the Court. In an autobiographical essay, Jephson related a coffee house meeting with the Court. The introduction of Jephson and his expression of interest in the vacant post turned the conversation to listing his knowledge in arithmetic, astronomy, algebra and handwriting. The party moved on to the King's Head tavern where Jephson continued to impress, this time with his 'merry stories'.

At the end of this convivial evening, they all promised him their vote. However, Warden Fowler advised the young man to secure the goodwill of Sir John Fleet, the Sheriff of London, and a senior member of the Court. Jephson was told that if Fleet 'should patronise any other's cause, he'd draw off every one of us, for he bears so great a sway, that nobody dares disoblige him'.

The enterprising and persistent Jephson secured an introduction to Sir John and by the end of the evening he had not only been promised that Sir John 'and all his interest was at [his] disposal' but had been invited to call at his country home in Battersea on the morning of the next Court meeting and accompany him to Coopers' Hall. Jephson was duly appointed schoolmaster, invited to remain and dine after the Court meeting and on every Court day and act as chaplain. His Irish charm, accomplishments, which included playing the spinet, and references to the 'misfortunes and calamities of poor Ireland, which drew tears from some of the old gentlemen's eyes', recommended him to the Court. The news he was able to bring from Ireland of some particularly barbarous murders stirred the Court to horror and indignation 'that like men amazed clapped their hands upon their breasts and cried out, "God deliver us from Popery, God grant King James and his bloody crew may never return into this nation"'.

Jephson brought back a more disciplined regime to the school and soon increased its numbers to 150 day boys, of whom a large number must have been private pupils, and 11 boarders, who were certainly private. Some of these were sons of the leading merchants in Ratcliffe and All Hallows. Several went on to have successful careers in the East India Company, some became enterprising manufacturers in Ratcliffe and Wapping and a few went into the professions. Jephson was obviously very proud of their achievements and seems to have kept in touch and followed their careers. He found, however, that life in the little Ratcliffe community was poisoned by the usher's wife, Mrs Byfield, she who was so useful and helpful to the Company in bringing order to their feasts. First Jephson discovered her to be a thief, defrauding him of his groceries. Then she used her influence with the Court to damage his reputation which became easier as the older members who had appointed him died and were replaced. Worst of all, he discovered she kept 'a bawdy house in her part of the School House and wenches for some of these old Coopers and other Town Sparks'. Jephson made his position very uncomfortable by speaking out, unwittingly, to the very members of the Court who were Mrs Byfield's customers. He found a new position in 1700 as Master of the Free School in Camberwell.

The postscript of the Byfield saga is brief. Byfield himself was promoted to be schoolmaster but proved so inadequate he was beaten by his own usher and left in 1702. The usher was also dismissed. His wife remained, resident in the next usher's house and was paid £4 a quarter when he became schoolmaster. She, too, soon fell out of favour with the majority on the Court and was ordered to leave, with her children, within months of the new arrangement. The Company continued to have difficulty in maintaining its control at Ratcliffe and ensuring its rules were kept. Jephson's claim to have 150 scholars may have been an exaggeration, but his successors were able to maintain 60 or more boys for years at a time, breaking the Court's rule that the maximum number of free scholars was 30. In 1716, the Court chose the 30 boys it deemed to be the deserving scholars, and dismissed the rest.

Jephson's patron, Sir John Fleet, was the first member of the Company to become Lord Mayor. His father, Richard, was a cooper in Bourton, Buckinghamshire and had connections with the Company. When he died in 1659, young John was sent to be apprenticed in London, eventually becoming a liveryman in 1674. He made a fortune from trade with the American colonies and he continued to take apprentices, one of whom was the orphaned son of John Looker, late Clerk to the Company. He would have had some sympathy with the family's predicament and may have had reason to be grateful to the Clerk when he first came to London as a 14-year-old.

Fleet's rise to prominence in the City was rapid, aided by his fortune and his skill in avoiding political entrapments during the feverish controversies at the end of Charles II reign and under James II. It was probably his lack of political commitment, allied to great ability, which resulted in his being the only member of the Court who was not purged by one side or the other when the 1685 Charter was in force. In 1688, he was elected Renter Warden but he declined to serve and paid his fine for refusing. He pleaded his numerous other commitments which included being Sheriff from October 1688. He was elected Alderman for the Ward of Langbourn and knighted on becoming Sheriff. When his turn came, in 1689, to be elected Master of the Company he refused once again because there would be an overlap of his duties as Sheriff, but he was persuaded to change his mind and oblige the Company when Peter Baldwin, Master 1689, died in October, just as the Sheriff's year of office ended. As Jephson made clear in his encounter with Sir John, he relied heavily on a deputy and kept in touch with Company matters by dining with the Court after each monthly meeting.

Sir John's wealth, position and personality made him a powerful force in the Company and in the City. He was made a director of the East India Company in 1691, and rose rapidly to become its Deputy Governor and

Governor during the years when the Company fought to keep its historic privileges against the challenge of the New East India Company. He played a key role in the amalgamation of the two companies in 1702.

When he was elected Lord Mayor in 1692, a traditional requirement was that the office must be held by a member of one of the Twelve Great Companies. Sir John had to translate to the Grocers' Company, with great regrets, which even in the minutes sound genuine. He was given a pipe of Canary wine as a parting gift from the Company and in his speech he promised he 'would always be willing to serve [the Company] upon all occasions'. His easy manner, good-humour and kindness seem not to have been destroyed by success. When the Court members quarrelled over whether his portrait for Coopers' Hall should be painted by Zachary Alberston or Sarah Leader, wife of a liveryman who was also the City Gauger, Sir John was open-minded and tactful. 'If the [Coopers'] Company thought fit and made choice of a woman to do it, he would sit and he had as lief be drawn by a woman as any another person'. The outcome of the quarrel was that Alberston received the commission.

An exact contemporary of Sir John's was Henry Strode, junior. He was the son of the householder who had resisted several calls to the Livery in the 1660s and who had been saved from appearing at the Lord Mayor's Court for his wilfulness, by the younger man paying his fine. Henry Strode senior had claimed he had no estate and could not afford the Livery fine. In fact, he had an interest in at least two properties, one in Southwark and one in Lambeth from where he diversified his coopering business. He arranged a good marriage for his daughter to a Lambeth timber merchant and in 1654 he inherited a copyhold estate in and around Egham from his father. His son had served an apprenticeship but probably did not practice as a cooper and was as reluctant as his father to take up the livery. His action suggests that his business interests lay elsewhere and freedom of a livery company was all he needed to trade in the City. In middle age, however, he became a respected member of Livery, serving for many years as one of the Company's auditors. He served neither as Renter nor Under Warden, another indication of pre-occupation with other business matters. From 1683, when his father died he also had the responsibility of the Egham lands, which his sister supervised on his behalf.

From 1692, his personal account book reveals he was a flourishing wine wholesaler operating from a house and warehouse near Coldharbour, by the river between the Fishmongers' Hall and the Steelyard. He took his elder nephew, John Herring, into partnership, lending the young man most of his share capital in a firm worth £10,000. A younger nephew, Harry, joined a year later in 1693, with some capital from his mother but the chief part loaned by his uncle. Within three years, the firm's capital had risen from £10,000 to £16,000. It had over 100 accounts and in some months a turnover exceeding £4,000. It dealt in sherry, 'Red Lisbon, Red Alicanti, Old Barcelona, Mallaga and Galetian wines'. Customers, apart from wine retailers, included Aldermen, Assistants of the Company and wealthy merchants buying in bulk for their households. There was very exact accounting for sherry butts so it is possible that both Strode and his father had begun their business with exporting casks to southern Spain and Portugal. There are instances of members of the Company moving to Portugal to develop this trade in the late seventeenth century. It would fit easily into the connections between the Strode family building up their business in Lambeth and John Herring senior, the timber merchant, supplying their raw material. The partnership with the Herring boys was dissolved in 1697, each of them assigning their share of the firm's debts to their uncle as partial repayment of the capital he had lent them.

Mark of Arthur Bray, jnr, 1678.

Henry Strode became Upper Warden in 1701 at a time when the Company was in financial trouble. It had over-stretched its resources in rebuilding the Ratcliffe almshouses, repairing the Master's house and building a new one for the usher. At the same time it suffered a rent strike in Ratcliffe because it mishandled the collection of the newly-imposed land tax. Strode brought order to the Company's accounts and overhauled the records of quarterage, ensuring it was easier for the Company to collect its dues from members. Like many other London merchants, he had his country retreat but for Strode, a man of very tender Christian conscience, his time in Egham was spent walking the fields, supervising, organising, improving and building another house on the edge of Windsor Great Park. He took a great and active interest in the plight of the poor both in Egham, where during his periods of residence he attended the monthly Sunday evening meeting of the churchwardens and overseers of the poor, and in his London parish, St Lawrence Pountney, where he also regularly attended vestry meetings and had served his turn as overseer and churchwarden.

During his year as Master, 1703, he was taken ill and did not appear at a Court meeting after February 1704. He died suddenly in May. It was with considerable astonishment that the June Court meeting learned of the terms of his will. He left £6,000 to build and endow a new charitable foundation in Egham with accommodation for 12 almspeople and a free school for 40 poor children. (The will did not state they must be boys.) All the beneficiaries were to be from the parish. It was his wish that the Company, acting with his heir and sole executor, Henry Herring would become trustee. Strode left £500 to Christ's Hospital of which he had been a governor, and £500 to augment the Ratcliffe pensions. As an expression of its gratitude, the Company placed an order with the limner, Mr James, for a full length portrait of Strode, for which 20 guineas was paid, without frame. It has long since disappeared. Maybe it suffered a fate similar to Sir John Fleet's portrait which his relatives were told, in 1728, they were at liberty to take away for 20 guineas. It is difficult to know whether memory and gratitude are short-lived or whether the painter's style had gone out of fashion.

CHAPTER SEVEN
A New Direction 1700–1750

> *Queen Anne, the last Stuart ruler, continued the war against France (the War of the Spanish Succession). It brought a series of victories for the Duke of Marlborough and by the Peace of Utrecht colonial gains at the expense of France and Spain. George I, of Hanover (1714) was the Protestant heir, challenged in the Jacobite rising (1715) by James II's son, James Edward. A more serious Jacobite rising in 1745, led by Charles Edward, was suppressed brutally by the Duke of Cumberland in Scotland. Robert Walpole as 'prime minister' developed cabinet government and a prosperous, stable economy.*

AT THE BEGINNING of a new century, the Company could look back with some pride and satisfaction on its achievements since the great fire in 1666. It had built and paid for a new, larger and grander Hall than the one the fire destroyed. It had doubled and then re-doubled the size of the Livery. It had built a second, larger, more ornate ceremonial barge in 1687, and in 1692, it had witnessed the inauguration, as Lord Mayor, of Sir John Fleet.

There was, however, a more pessimistic prospect for the Company's position as the governing authority over the craft in London and the suburbs. In 1684, the Company's regulatory powers were struck a serious blow when the Navy victuallers refused to allow the Company's Sealer, Thomas Rowe, to gauge and seal casks for the Navy. There was an indignant reaction from the Court which sought, at first, to meet with the Commissioners for the Navy. This approach failed but the Court continued to campaign to have the Company's rights restored, 'as by law and time out of mind hath been accustomed'. In October 1691, an unsuccessful attempt was made to petition Parliament. Ten years later, the Clerk had the matter raised in the House of Lords. Within a few months the Company was faced with allegations from the Lord High Admiral that it was exceeding its legal powers. A Committee of the Master, Wardens and the immediate past Warden, Henry Strode, presented the Company's case again to the House of Lords and answered the allegations, but without any success. An 18-year campaign came to an end. The Company's Sealers had to become reconciled to a considerable loss in revenue and the Court had to accept a defeat which proved irreversible. If the Naval Commissioners could by-pass the Company's statutory authority, then there was little chance the Company could control foreigner householders and journeymen. Foreign coopers had, for at least two centuries, resisted attempts to subject them to Company control. As they became more numerous and widely spread in new London suburbs, the task of policing them became more difficult.

The decline in the value of the rent which the Sealers could afford was steady. In the 1690s, the St Katherine's seal dropped to £12 and then to £8. The London and Southwark seals dropped to £18 each and then Southwark fell to £10 and London to £16. This decline can also be traced in debts which the Sealers accumulated as they struggled to pay the rent on their office. Once the seal lost its value, there was no objection to widows taking over the duties of Sealer. Frances Delabarr held the London seal for six years from 1697 to 1703; in the 1720s two of the three Sealers were widows. After 1729, there was only one Sealer. No more income from sealing was entered in the accounts. The coup de grâce was struck in 1733. The Court sued a soap cooper, Caleb Blake, for persistently not having his casks sealed. The defendant won the case on the grounds that the Act of 1531, which gave the Company its powers to search and seal, had been made virtually obsolete by subsequent legislation.

In spite of these set-backs, the Company did not give up easily in attempts to maintain its powers. The general search continued to be carried out at least twice yearly and at the major fairs, St Bartholomew's in August and Lady Fair in Southwark at the beginning of September. Between these general searches there were private ones, that is a search of a particular cooperage or brewhouse on the strength of information usually from the Beadle or Informer. The surviving 'Default Books' indicate the diligence with which these attempts at policing the craft were carried out. Occasionally there was trouble, as in October 1701 when some brewers resisted the search party and then assaulted it.

The Company also remained vigilant in legal matters and was ever-ready to challenge encroachments on its monopoly from Brewers and Vintners, and to take legal action. It brought a case in 1728 against a brewer who had flouted the law limiting the number of coopers who could be employed in a brewhouse. It was regarded as a test case when it came to be heard at the Assizes at Kingston-on-Thames in July 1729 and it was important for the Company to make a stand against the growing resistance among larger breweries which defied the law with apparent impunity.

As well as being active in defending its powers through the courts, the Company took a key part in resisting attempts by Parliament to raise revenue by imposing duty on the import of wine. In 1693, a duty of £12 a tun was proposed. There was already a duty on wine, and a prohibition on the import of French wine (a war-time measure) which the Coopers claimed had halved imports. The Company's particular interest was the trade in casks which coopers exported to Spain and Portugal 'for bringing in of wines that country (Portugal) being not able to supply them with casks for the same'. The Company argued its case well in a broadsheet which concluded that 'passing this bill tends to the ruin of the coopers' trade, with many hundred families, and utterly destructive of a Company so useful and necessary at land and to their Majesties' navy at sea'. There was concerted resistance to the proposal and the particular clause dealing with duty on wine was removed after the second reading.

The broadsheet was republished and another petition was presented to the Commons in 1697 when the wine duty proposal re-appeared. The government urgently needed to raise taxes to prosecute the war against Louis XIV. Once again the extent of the opposition was effective and the Bill was lost. Using similar arguments about the damaging effects on the home economy, the Company campaigned successfully using evidence it collected from soap coopers, to persuade the government to abandon an attempt at raising a duty on soap.

While these last-ditch battles were being fought, the Company was assuming new responsibilities which in the next decades gave it new purpose. The first of these responsibilities was the implementation of the terms of Henry Strode's will. In practice, the Company itself did little and left the purchase of a site in Egham, the commissioning of the building of twelve almshouses, a school and master's house to Henry Herring, Strode's nephew, heir and executor. As joint trustee with the Company, Herring also purchased land in Egham and Staines, which yielded £80 a year in rent, and the manor of New Barnes in Plaistow. This cost just over £3,000 and was let in two parcels for farming and market gardening at rents amounting to £185 a year. Herring engaged the first schoolmaster, Francis Phillipps, a choice endorsed by the Court. A standing committee of the Court was set up in April 1706 to meet with Herring, to purchase the estate and to 'advise and consult ... in all matters relating to Strode's charity'. No further meetings or activities of the committee were recorded in the Company's minutes.

Launching the new charity was not without difficulty. There was keen interest in Egham on the part of the churchwardens, overseers of the poor and the leading townspeople, who paid the bulk of the poor rates. The new charity promised to ease some of the local problems with poor relief, so there was impatience to have the school and almshouses built. The churchwarden, George Cotterell, began an action in the Court of Chancery to have an inquiry made by the Lord Chancellor into the execution of Strode's will. It is just possible that Cotterell was motivated a little by dislike of the Strode family, and perhaps resentment of very rich, metropolitan neighbours who had returned to live part-time in Egham. There was certainly friction annually, at ploughing time, because the Strode and Cotterell strips in the large open fields were frequently adjacent. In November 1699, Strode wrote in his diary, 'Cotterell is such a knave he plows upon me every where where I ly next him'.

The Lord Chancellor investigated the accounts of purchases made by Herring and ordered that £98 surplus be conveyed to the Company, that surplus income from rents was to be invested in stocks and that Herring and the Master and Wardens were to visit Egham annually to ensure the charity was properly run. In practice, Herring ran the charity, kept the accounts, made investments, appointed two successive schoolmasters and a lady to teach the little boys their letters and just occasionally invited the Master and Wardens to visit. In many respects, though the arrangements flouted the Lord Chancellor's judgement, they worked admirably for the charity.

Herring was a shrewd and very successful businessman who became one of the wealthiest men in London. In 1707, for example, he had investments in three ships, one sailing to India, one to St Louis in West Africa and one to Vera Cruz in Central America. By 1722, he was a director of the Bank of England and became its largest share-holder with investments of £27,000. Yet he kept track of the twopenny payments made to the reading teacher for each child, purchased a house in Old Jewry in 1727 with surplus income, supervised the repair and maintenance of the buildings and worked with the parish authorities to appoint the pensioners and children. When he felt it was time to retire from active management, he was in his seventies. He handed over a well-managed charity, whose income he had increased by £60 a year from invested surpluses and which looked set to continue to show a small annual surplus.

Mark of William Alexander, 1697, who bequeathed his estate at Woodham Mortimer to the Company. Formerly the mark of William Allington, 1669.

The transfer of management was conducted in stages during 1744 and 1745. Herring must have been astonished to receive a letter from the Clerk accusing him of neglecting the requirements of the Chancery judgement in 1707. He had not handed over the surplus of £98 to the Company; he had received rents, and made payments without the Court of Chancery's consent 'which that Court hath particularly ordered'. He had also made investments (£1,000) in government annuities and bought property without consent. The only indication of compliance with the Chancery order had been his 'sometimes asking the Master, Wardens and Assistants to go ... or meet [him] at Egham to view'.

The letter concluded with a somewhat self-righteous statement of the Company's desire to 'execute with the utmost exactness the trust reposed in them by Mr Strode' and the decision to lay 'before my Lord Chancellor the naked truth'. The Clerk was concerned that the recent transactions between Herring and the Company might be invalid.

In a more conciliatory tone, a joint approach to the Lord Chancellor was suggested. Herring was not inclined to co-operate; he was no stranger to the Court of Chancery, having successfully fought off claims by one of his in-laws for nine years. He doubtless thought that the Company was equally at fault in ignoring the 1707 Court order and more culpable than he in withdrawing from all management of the charity during the following years. Even while memories were still fresh about the Court order, the Company had not asked to audit the accounts or visit Egham between the issue of the order in 1707 and 1710 when invited by Herring.

After a flurry of special committee meetings led by Robert Scott, one of the Assistants, the Company claimed that Herring owed a further sum of £1,469. It was proved to be wide of the mark but Herring eventually negotiated a compromise: he took the Old Jewry house back to his own account and gave the Company £585, representing the purchase price of the property. The Company dropped all charges.

The Company acquired another charitable trust in 1725. William Alexander, a member of the Court since 1722, left his manor house and over 300 acres of land at Woodham Mortimer, near Maldon in Essex, to the Company to provide pensions for needy coopers. It was a welcome source of income to support the pensioners list on which there was always pressure to add new names. In 1712, the Court agreed to extend the number to 30, each receiving a maximum grant of five shillings a quarter. It was a pitifully small pension, about half a journeyman's wages for a week. As a result of William Alexander's generosity the pensions were doubled in 1727.

Alexander was a Londoner by birth, served an apprenticeship in the Company and became a liveryman in 1697. He was a wine cooper but probably became a wine merchant; his name occurs in Henry Strode's account book. Although he prospered sufficiently to purchase an estate outside London in 1714, Woodham Mortimer appears to have been leased and not used by Alexander as a home in the country. The Company inherited a number of problems from unsatisfactory tenants and some agreements had to be challenged in the courts. In 1729, the main tenant, Mrs Carver, was evicted for persistently breaking the terms of her lease and being in arrears with her rent. The house, a mediaeval structure with additions made in the seventeenth century and an imposing late seventeenth century four-gabled facade, was put in order and a Dutch barn and threshing floor were provided. A local land agent was employed to find a reliable tenant. The estate became a possession of which the Court was proud and on special occasions, the house was used for entertaining, as in 1727 when Sir John Grosvenor became Sheriff of London and was host at Woodham Mortimer Hall to the judges.

The Company had shown unusual courage in taking the risk of rebuilding most of the charity's buildings at Ratcliffe in the 1690s. The country was at war, harvests were bad for several years and taxes were high. The imposition of a land tax by the government led to a dispute in 1697 between tenants and Company of rare bitterness. The Court appointed a Lands Committee to treat with the newly-established Land Commissioners whose task was the assessment of the new tax. The tenants refused to pay the tax in addition to their agreed rents and claimed that the rents included all taxes so the matter was the Company's responsibility. The rent strike provoked the Company to threaten the tenants with arrest for debt. Fortunately for all concerned, the Company renewed negotiations with the leading tenants, Richard Wildey and John Gorum; the Commissioners and its own legal adviser, Luke Astrey. A compromise was reached by which, for the time being, the Company paid the taxes of two recent leases, while the rest were to be re-negotiated to include a new condition, that tenants were responsible for the payment of land tax. Without this change, the charity would have suffered a loss of income just at a time when it was heavily indebted to the Company for rebuilding. The Commissioners made a concession, too. It was not government policy to penalise charities: they therefore allowed a refund of £27 to be distributed among the tenants. Presumably this was the sweetener to get agreement to the new leases. The Company still felt dissatisfied with the outcome and as late as 1707 it threatened to appeal against the Commissioners.

The Company's own accounts gave cause for concern. Between 1699 and 1701 there were frequent references to its impecunious condition: 'out of cash...stock very low...stock is greatly decreased and very low'. The main cause of this financial crisis was the rebuilding at Ratcliffe which continued in 1698 with the replacement of Toby Wood's almshouses. By 1706, the seriousness of the situation was recognised by an order cancelling all Court day dinners and placing the affairs of the Company into the hands of the Master, Wardens, Clerk and Beadle. The Court was to be summoned only when essential. So many workmen's bills remained unpaid, most of them for repairs to the wharves and Stone Stairs at Ratcliffe, that an order was made for payments to 'be put into some better method...and more narrowly inspected'. Recovery came about slowly and was the result of calling up more liverymen, collecting rents more assiduously, dealing promptly with tenants who got into arrears, and practising sensible economy in the Company's own spending on dinners, cakes and ale. The Livery was increased from 126 in 1699 to 150 in 1706 and by 1724 to 203.

By 1713, recovery had been accomplished. The Company was out of debt and had a sufficient surplus to purchase East India Company bonds. The Land Committee turned its attention to acquiring new property, and bought several small houses in Hatfield Street, just off Goswell Road. In 1718, it invested £690 in buying several new buildings in Blackman Street (the southern part of Borough High Street) in Southwark, and then after arranging surveys in Islington and near Temple Bar it finally bought two properties in Little Tower Street (part of Eastcheap) for £2,000.

All this activity merited a new rental. It marks the point at which the Company turned in a new direction, away from hopeless attempts to restore the past and control the craft of coopering and towards managing a balance of investments in government stock and equities and in property. Its three charities, which ought to have provided a new purpose to replace the old regulatory one, failed to rouse the old men of the Court from complacency. Until one or other presented a crisis, Ratcliffe, Egham and Woodham Mortimer were left very much to themselves.

The Company's financial recovery coincided with several members following in the footsteps of Sir John Fleet and playing a leading part in City political affairs. Peter Eaton was a Deputy on Common Council before he became an Assistant in 1710. He was Upper Warden in 1715 and was knighted in August that year, probably because he had shown loyalty to King George during the Jacobite rebellion. His City duties may explain his irregular attendance at Court meetings even when Upper Warden but it did not prevent his election as Master in 1716. Like Sir John Fleet, he probably behaved as many did at the time, and employed a deputy. John Grosvenor was a much younger contemporary, entering the Livery after being apprenticed to his father in the same year, 1718, as his father became Master. He had ambitions in City politics but he failed to gain election as Alderman for Bridge Ward in 1727. However, that same year, he was elected Sheriff and was knighted after presenting an address of congratulations to George II on his accession. Such distinction was promptly rewarded in the Company by his being elected to the Court in May 1728 and immediately being elected Master. During his term as Sheriff, the Hall was made available for his use for City functions, as was the custom before there was an official residence for the Lord Mayor.

George Champion was another liveryman attracted by the world of politics. He began his career as a deputy on Common Council in 1726 and was elected Alderman for Bridge Ward, where Grosvenor had failed, in 1729. Perhaps his advantage lay in being a strong supporter of the Whig interest. In 1734, he stood for election to Parliament and became the member for Aylesbury, and a loyal supporter of Sir Robert Walpole. He served as Sheriff in 1737 and expected to be elected Lord Mayor in 1739. In preparation for this he translated to the Haberdashers' Company but he had reckoned without the storm of protest which erupted in Parliament and beyond when Walpole introduced a plan to raise taxes from excise duty. Champion's close links to Walpole destroyed his chance of becoming Lord Mayor; he was not elected. His consolation prize was becoming Master of the Haberdashers' Company in 1740.

Champion's exact contemporary in the Coopers' Livery was Daniel Lambert, who was most probably in trade as a Vintner. He prospered sufficiently to follow a career in City politics and, between 1732 and 1737, advanced from deputy on Common Council, to Sheriff, to Alderman. When he became Sheriff, he was elected to the Court but he was soon in trouble. He failed to attend a Court meeting, as did another Assistant and the pair were astonished at being removed in 1735. Both took the matter to the Court of King's Bench on the grounds that their dismissal was invalid, as they had received no due warning. They won the case and were reinstated. The episode suggests political rancour at work and a minimum of brotherly love abroad among the Assistants. Lambert took his turn as Upper Warden in 1739 at the height of the excise crisis. In mid-term, the Lord Mayor died and Lambert was elected in his stead. The consequence was a hasty translation to the Vintners' Company of which he subsequently became Master and then one of the MPs for the City.

One other cooper succeeded in becoming Lord Mayor shortly after Lambert. He was Robert Willimott, an orphan of the parish of Stepney who had been apprenticed in 1708. There is no evidence to connect him to the school at Ratcliffe but as an orphan he would have been just the right kind of candidate for a place at the free school. If the conjecture is true, it would be very natural for the parish to seek an apprenticeship for him in the Coopers' Company. In common with many apprentices at the time, he did not seek his trademark to practise as a cooper and he delayed some years before claiming his freedom in 1726. Both facts suggest he was making his living in some other way, perhaps as a supplier to ships, perhaps investing, as Henry Herring did, as stockholder in the voyages of merchant ships. He was later described as a merchant and insurer of Mincing Lane and so would have been a neighbour of Herring's. His political career followed a familiar progression: Common Councillor in 1729, City MP in 1734, Alderman for Lime Street Ward in 1736, Sheriff in 1741 and Lord Mayor in 1742. But the story had a twist.

As Lord Mayor-elect, Willimott encountered some annoyance after his translation to a major company. His choice was the Clothworkers, but they elected him by a very small majority and then refused him the use of their Hall for his official functions. This was a bitter blow to Willimott. George Dance's Mansion House, planned as the Lord Mayor's official residence was already under construction but was a long way from being finished. Willimott needed the use of a Livery Hall for entertaining and the Coopers were ready to oblige him as they had all their members who had served as Sheriff.

Thus it came about that Willimott found a solution to his problem. He decided that if it was so troublesome to translate to another company it might be acceptable in law for him to remain in his own. The matter was duly tested in court and found to have no more authority than the force of tradition perhaps based on the practicality of having a large and dignified Livery hall suitable for the City's chief magistrate. No further objections were raised at the time of Willimott's election and so an ancient custom was ended. There was great rejoicing in the Company, marked by remitting Willimott's fine for not having served as Warden before being elected Master in May 1743. On Willimott's part, he presented the Company with two silver waiters (trays) lengthily inscribed with the circumstances of his election as Lord Mayor and a description of the splendid show the Company provided 'both by land and water' on Lord Mayor's Day. In February 1745, when the country was threatened with invasion by Prince Charles Edward, Willimott and Lambert were both knighted when they accompanied the Lord Mayor and Sheriffs to deliver a loyal address to the King. The Company felt proud that one of its own had 'broken the mould' and, for a time, given the Coopers a position of prominence in the City.

THE WORSHIPFUL COMPANY OF COOPERS

The relative prosperity of the Company made possible the replacement of the barge in 1718. Its furnishing and decorating was costly and done to achieve a rich spectacle on the river. The work of the joiners and carvers cost £75; the painter £45; and the herald painter, responsible for the Company's arms carved in high relief, received £45. For its first outing in October 1718 for the Lord Mayor's procession to Westminster, 100 yards of silk ribbon in crimson, green and blue were used as decoration, as well as silk streamers fixed to staves along the sides of the barge. More colour and movement was provided by Company's banners which normally served as decoration in the Hall. These increased in number as each Sheriff and Lord Mayor provided the Company with his personal banner. During these years, the Company was afflicted neither by penury nor puritanism, so hired musicians were on

Below and opposite: panorama depicting the Lord Mayor going to Westminster, 1740. Until the nineteenth century, the Lord Mayor's show was a river procession of barges carrying members of the City livery companies to Westminster where the Lord Mayor took his oath of office. From 1661 until the mid-eighteenth century, the Coopers had their own barge which was decorated with ribbons and banners on ceremonial occasions. Earlier the Company had hired a barge.

122

board to entertain and add to the jollity in the procession. There was a plentiful supply of cakes (biscuits) and wine both for the barge party and the remainder of the Livery who were left to while away the time at a riverside tavern, usually on Three Cranes Wharf. Two hundred pounds of cake were consumed in 1698 when there were 126 Liverymen.

There were other occasions on land when the streamers, ribbons, banners and staves were used, particularly on state occasions when the Company's 'standing' was set up alongside the other livery companies. In 1696, King William's escape from attempted assassination was marked by a thanksgiving at St Paul's. Other thanksgivings followed as Marlborough's victories checked French ambitions in Europe. When George of Hanover was welcomed as King by the City in September 1714, the Coopers' standing was 150 feet long and charged at 12 pence a foot. On this occasion they were provided with music as a diversion while they waited.

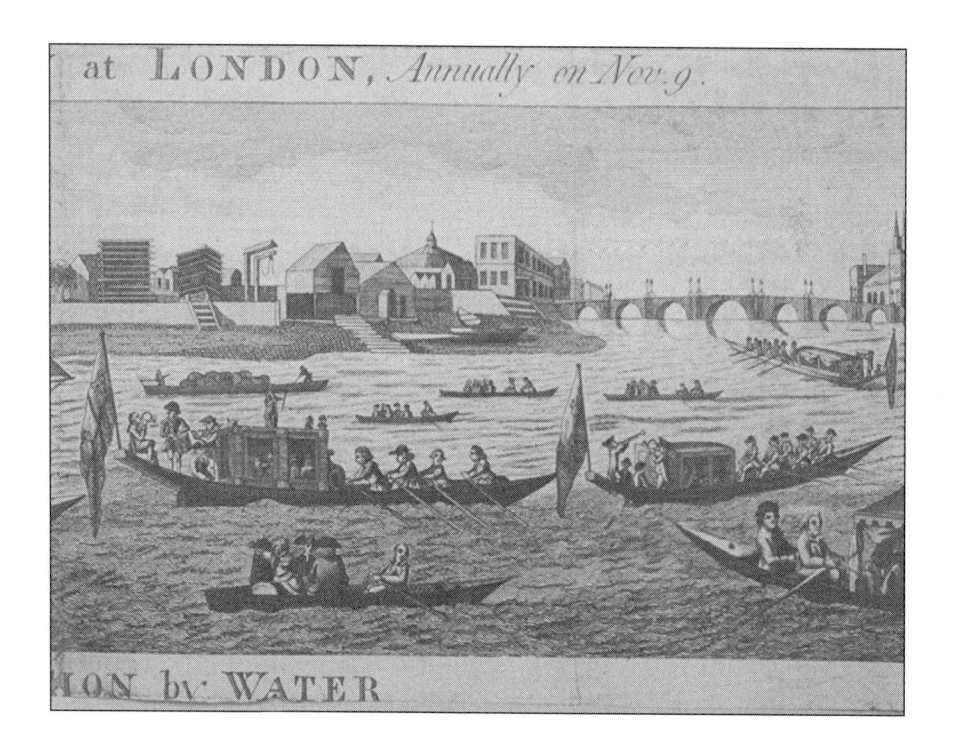

Domestic entertainment tended to become more stylish, in part reflecting greater affluence among those members who became Assistants. The custom of wives attending Livery dinners had grown up during the latter years of the seventeenth century but was ended in 1704. Instead, the wives of the Assistants attended a dinner on the opening day of the St Bartholomew Fair. In 1714, the dinner was transferred instead to Twelfth Night but in 1716, the Bartholomew dinner was revived and the January dinner remained in place, setting a pattern of Court dinners for wives and guests which continued for over a century.

Livery dinners could occasionally create an uproar and on at least one occasion a dispute resulted in the parties going to law. In 1723, there was great difficulty in finding Liverymen prepared to act as Stewards for the Lord Mayor's Day dinner. Nine had been summoned by July but had refused and when, eventually, some were found to serve, they did so with reluctance. They ignored the normal procedure of discussing a bill of fare with the Court and reaching agreement on what they would provide. Instead, they dispensed with the services of the Company's cook, hired their own, omitted a meat course and generally made such scanty provision that there was nearly a riot on the day. Even refinements such as candlesticks were missing and lumps of clay had been used as holders instead.

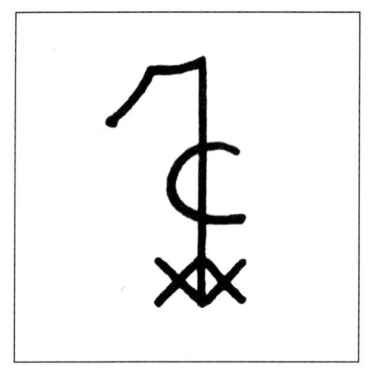

Mark of Benjamin Carter, 1711, later assigned to John Carter, 1723.

The culprits showed no remorse and were referred to the King's Bench after they had committed contempt in the Lord Mayor's Court, answering their charges insolently and with bad language. Subsequently they boasted that they had treated the Coopers' Court as it deserved: that is as a 'pack of Villains and Rogues', who 'only met together to contrive means of spending the Company's money'. Their delaying tactics combined with the natural slowness of justice, kept them out of the King's Bench for two years. The purpose of the proceedings was to disenfranchise them, by stripping them of their membership and freedom of the Company. The row was public and did the Company no good. It decided to drop the case; a reconciliation followed with the errant Stewards apologising, paying a token fine each of £5 and jointly putting £5 into the poor box. For its part, the Company declared it held 'no personal pique or prejudice'.

Although serving as Steward remained unpopular, there followed a couple of decades of better co-operation and often a preliminary dinner for Stewards and the Court to reach agreement on the bill of fare. There was probably no more feasting and drinking in the Company than in earlier times but these domestic matters appear to have more prominence in the eighteenth century. The explanation is that the Company had lost its major responsibility, controlling the craft, and it had not fully realised that its charitable commitments could, perhaps should, become its major new purpose.

CHAPTER EIGHT
Marking Time 1750–1800

> *From two European wars—those of the Austrian succession 1740–48, and the Seven-Years' war 1756–63—Britain, led by William Pitt, Earl of Chatham, used sea power against France to gain control of Canada (Wolfe), and India (Clive). The growth of trade and population stimulated investment in manufactures—iron smelted with coal; steam pumps for mines, and improved transport by roads and canals. John Wesley took evangelism outside the Anglican church. George III, 1760–1820, and his governments, provoked rebellion in the American colonies and lost the war which followed, (1776–83). Revolution in France (1789) was first welcomed, then feared because of its violence. Pitt the Younger formed a European coalition to check French aggression. Income tax imposed.*

NEW TRENDS WHICH emerged in the Company's watershed years at the end of the 1600s, became more dominant after 1750. But the rearguard action to keep some degree of control over the trade was a distraction, a diversion which proved to be a blind-alley. It prevented the Company from putting its energy into the proper care of its enlarged charitable work. There was a failure to give the charities regular attention and it was only when a crisis occurred that the Court was stirred out of complacency and into action. Occasionally, the Company was led by men of talent and vision who tackled long-standing problems; but their efforts were not sustained by others. Strains which developed within the Company between the Court and some of the Livery, in particular those who were working coopers, were not new phenomena. However, greater extremes of wealth and lack of purpose from the leadership exacerbated these tensions. Sometimes, they spluttered to the surface only to subside quickly. Perhaps the tradition of brotherhood, or a strong sense of deference, overcame the Livery's determination. It is just as likely that it lacked leadership.

Some of the issues sound familiar: how to adapt old institutions to rapidly changing circumstances; how to ensure that an elderly and collective leadership is dynamic, forward-thinking and responsive to external pressures; and how to maintain the sense of communal endeavour and fraternity while the gap between the Court and the Livery remained wide.

Once the Company had assumed direct responsibility for the Egham Charity from Henry Herring, it soon faced a problem which began with the need to fill two vacancies in the almshouses. In September 1747, the Clerk was asked to expedite matters and 'wait on the Minister and Officers of the parish of Egham' to discuss nominations. Months passed and the Clerk wrote to say that 'unless they do acquaint the Company what resolutions they are come to with regard to the right of presentation to Mr Strode's charity by next Court day, the Court are [sic] determined to present at that time such persons as they shall think proper'. No answer came. The Court waited five months (not one, as threatened) and then presented two ladies to the vacancies.

The immediate response was a suit in Chancery brought by a wealthy Egham lady, Mrs Helden, claiming for the Egham overseers of the poor the right to present to vacancies in the almshouses from among the poor of the parish. The claim to nominate pensioners was not sustained, but that they should be Egham parishioners was confirmed. Matters settled down quickly and no further disputes about presentation occurred during the time John Paget junior and his successor, William Jones, were schoolmasters. Both were also curates at Egham church and had long-standing family links with the parish. The Clerk continued to collect rents, present accounts for audit to the Company and treat the tenants with understanding. When the elderly tenant of some of the charity's property in Staines was robbed of his rent in 1777, the Court approved a payment to him of £20.

After William Jones became schoolmaster and chaplain in 1766, the Court continued its somewhat relaxed oversight of Egham, unaware that while Jones maintained good relations with the parish authorities, he was not a forceful character and often failed to discipline either boys or almspeople. Matters came to a head when members of the Court made their annual visit in July 1782 and found no boys in the school. They sought out the churchwardens for an explanation and summoned Jones to London to impress upon him his duties and his powers. Within two months, he was told to use his authority. His inadequacy and lack of confidence convinced some of the Assistants that Egham needed a more interventionist approach from the Company. Therefore in November 1783, Michael Tayleure (Master 1775) was made chairman of a committee to investigate the running of the Egham Charity and to provide a prop for Jones.

Within weeks, Tayleure had removed George Newell, an almsman who had misbehaved and misused the charity for years. He had been served with an eviction order two years previously and yet was still in residence. Tayleure gave him a guinea and sent him packing. The need for a resident nurse to help the sick and incapacitated almspeople was recognised and a survey of the accounts showed that the charity was accumulating surpluses from income and could afford to do more. Having taken views from the vicar and leading parishioners, Tayleure recommended increasing the pensions by one shilling a week, increasing the clothing allowance, appointing a nurse and paying two supernumerary pensioners who were non-resident. One of the more imaginative and effective reforms was the introduction of rewards for good attendance at school. Initially, the six boys with the highest attendance marks were each awarded a pair of shoes and socks. Then six more prizes were added; this time of a pair of shoes each.

Tayleure's work was recognised by the Company in 1790 with a specially-struck gold medal. It was agreed that his committee should remain in existence to ensure Jones had the support he needed. These were the years of unusually efficient government in the Egham Charity.

There were many parallels between the Egham Charity and the older establishment at Ratcliffe. The Court had the right to nominate to vacancies in the school and almshouses but there were many occasions when the schoolmasters had to be sharply reminded of their duty. From 1760 to 1763 the Court received no notice of scholars to be admitted and therefore issued a reminder that all admissions were to be first submitted for approval. Thereafter, scholars' names appear for about two years in the Court minutes only to disappear again, until the Court noticed their absence or some problem arose. The Court tended to hold quarterly meetings at Ratcliffe and was therefore more frequently in touch with problems there than at Egham. The schoolmasters in the 1760s and 1770s were quick to pass over to the Court their problems with unruly bedesmen and women. The nurse, Mary Clark, was dismissed in 1763 for misbehaviour in harbouring 'disorderly People in her apartment... and other Misconduct'. Almspeople were dismissed for breaking the rules in 1764, 1767 and 1775.

The schoolhouse and chapel were almost 250 years old and in need of substantial repair. In spring 1786, plans were approved to rebuild rather than repair again. A contract for £970 was agreed with Winckworths, a firm of builders who were allowed to have the old materials for a payment of £120. Progress was rapid and completion in September 1787 was celebrated with a dinner for the Court and the almspeople.

During the rebuilding, a house, next to the school in School House Lane, was destroyed by fire. Five years previously another house in the same lane had also been destroyed. Fortunately for the Company, both were insured. Fire was an ever-present risk in the area, which had become very overcrowded with new buildings obstructing access roads and infilling courtyards and alleys. Many were workshops filled with inflammatory materials, but the biggest threat was the saltpetre works and stores which had long been a source of anxiety to Ratcliffe residents.

A great fire began, on 23 July 1794, which continued the next day. It was started by a pitch kettle being knocked over on a barge which was quickly set alight. The fire spread, fanned by a strong wind and fed by very combustible materials in the river-side warehouses: sugar, timber, saltpetre and the flimsy wooden homes of the poor crowded in narrow lanes among the warehouses. The fire fighters were halted by the lack of water. Exploding timber was hurled into the air so that 'it had all the appearance of raining fire'. Between 600 and 700 houses, that is over half of Ratcliffe, including most of the Charity's buildings were destroyed and 2,700 people, mainly poor and uninsured, were made homeless. The area of destruction covered 55 acres. In the fields beyond Ratcliffe, the government quickly provided tents for the refugees. Many of them had lost everything. A relief fund was started with £1,000 from the government, £700 from Lloyds and 100 guineas from the Company's tenants at Free Trade Wharf, the East India Company. An open-air sermon preached in the fields the following Sunday on 'the inexhaustible Mercies of God in the Preservation of his People' raised a collection of £67 for the relief fund.

The Court met privately on the morrow of the fire 'to afford such relief to the almspeople as [the Court] think necessary'. The first decision was to make a weekly allowance to each pensioner of six shillings and a further three shillings and sevenpence to Nurse Douglas who appealed for help, 'having lost her all'. The schoolmaster and his family found accommodation in School House Lane, where he continued to teach as best he could. Power to act quickly was delegated to the Clerk and a small committee, which met frequently in Ratcliffe during September, to allow the Company's tenants to make their claims. It was reminiscent of the fire court which had sat in London after the 1666 fire.

The Company's new surveyor, Dugleby, was commissioned to survey the whole of the Ratcliffe estate and ensure that walls in danger of collapsing were made safe. Permits were granted to tenants to erect temporary shelters on condition they would remove the shelter and their possessions at one hour's notice. It must have been with some relief that the Hand-in-Hand Insurance Company paid the Company's claim of £3,788 in October. The money was invested promptly in five per cent Government stock. In spite of the bitter blow of having a recently rebuilt school and chapel destroyed, there was relief among the members of the Court that reforms in their handling of the Company's property had included insuring all buildings in 1793.

The ruins of Ratcliffe after the fire of July 1794 which destroyed over half the houses and businesses. Sir Thomas Coxhead, a member of the Court, presented each Assistant with a copy of this engraving.

Rebuilding was fairly brisk. The contractor was Thomas Burrell, a carpenter, and he tendered for £2,255. Dugleby was clerk of works. The foundation stone was laid on 1 September 1795 and the occasion was marked by a dinner which had to be held at the Hall. By December, work was sufficiently advanced for the schoolmaster to move back and the following March the Court went to Ratcliffe to view the near-completed building. Members were so pleased with the rapid progress, that five guineas was voted for the workmen to be given a treat when the roofs were finished.

It took another year to re-equip the almshouses, perhaps because the Court took a keen interest in the smallest details of coal cauldrons, door scrapers, the chapel reading desk, which had to be on castors and the fire irons for each hearth. There was an attempt at small economies such as trying to re-use the old grates and the old copper for heating water. There were also delays caused by the bitter weather during the winter of 1796–97. Extra coals were ordered to heat the Court room, where quarterly meetings were held, and to try and drive the dampness from the walls of the almshouses. Life at Ratcliffe gradually returned to normal during the spring and summer of 1797 and regular Quarterly Court days began again in September.

The Company's management of its property went through an overhaul, first in the years after 1758 and again under the guidance of Dugleby in the 1790s. In 1758, a committee under Alderman Scott was set the task of releasing the properties in Ratcliffe. The estate was divided into eight lots and tenders were invited. Three of these failed to produce an offer and in 1759 were granted to one lessee, Francis Hall, on a rebuilding lease for 61 years. Detailed conditions were attached about removing old buildings which were mostly small and tightly packed in alleys and courts, away from main thoroughfares. New building was to be substantial and of brick, with proper foundations, double thickness for party walls and roadways wide enough for carts and carriages. The scheme was partially successful; in 1772, the Court was once again having to deal with complaints about encroachments from householders into lanes, against the back of the school and in School House Lane, which seems to have still not been wide enough for carriages.

As leases in London became due for renewal, the Court took the opportunity to standardise terms, usually 21 years, which carried full repairing conditions and with covenants governing how much was to be spent and when. In general, rents increased: the Thames Street properties doubled between 1758 and 1779; Fenchurch Street increased from £43 to £63 between 1762 and 1797. Once the French wars broke out in 1793, war taxation began to eat into these modest increases, because it was usually the landlord's responsibility to pay the new taxes on property unless special provision had been made in the lease. The Company continued to try and ensure its property was well-maintained and improved in the fashion of the time, often with new facades, and that, through advertising, it obtained the most favourable tenders. It was perhaps a sign of the times that the old City communities and networks were breaking down and that word of mouth could no longer attract the best tenant at the best price.

The Woodham Mortimer estate in Essex was insured for £500 in 1759. It had been in the hands of Kelham Bulley since 1738 and had caused the Company little anxiety. Visits by members of the Court were infrequent, and a 'very light rein' would best describe the control the Company exercised. A thorough survey of timber was ordered in 1755 and again in 1762, when 80 loads of oak and 15 of ash were advertised for sale. Subsequent surveys in the next century expressed regret at the improvident timber-felling in these years. At the time, the income from sales allowed urgent improvements to be made. Bulley fell behind with his rent and was twice threatened with distraint. The Clerk was sent to issue a distraining order in October 1761 but two years later the Court had obviously relented and Bulley was granted another 21-year lease. Within six months, he was once more in trouble and this time the distraint order was executed. A local farmer took over the lease for five years and then business partners Edward Codd and James Wright took a 23-year lease in 1769 at an annual rent of £120 and with an undertaking to spend £1,200 on the farm.

In spite of the difficulties with Kelham Bulley, the estate was supporting 50 pensioners from 1760 until the 1790s, when the numbers were allowed to fall to 30, by natural wastage! Occasionally, grants were made to liverymen in temporarily distressed circumstances. Lady Grosvenor, the widow of Sir John, who had been compelled to withdraw from the Court in 1742 when his business failed, was granted a £20 pension from 1767 until her death in 1775. The members of the Court, in rotation, nominated candidates for vacancies on the pension list. It was a practice which continued well into the next century and probably helped to maintain personal links when the gulf between senior members of the Company and practising coopers was becoming much wider.

Just as the Company exercised moral discipline over pensioners in their almshouses, so it sought to control out-pensioners in a continuing effort to ensure that only the 'deserving' poor benefited from its charity. One lady pensioner had her grant stopped in 1786 because she had been involved in a quarrel. She was told that payment would be resumed when 'she had asked pardon of the person with whom she quarrelled'. The incident suggests either alertness of the Beadle to gossip or close links between the pensioners and their nominators on the Court.

In spite of failing to maintain and exercise most of its statutory control of the trade, the Company did not abandon all hope. Two attempts to petition Parliament to grant the Company fresh powers failed in 1737 and 1744. Then in 1761, without any warning, the Court began to seek the help of the brewers to enforce the clauses of the 1531 statute. These restricted brewers and alemakers to keeping no more than two coopers to repair casks. There was an exchange of correspondence between the Brewers' Company and the Coopers' and a number of meetings. The outcome was that the Brewers agreed to abide by the old rules.

Following this outbreak of fraternal co-operation, the two companies agreed to make a joint approach to Parliament in the autumn session, 1762. With the support of the City's four MPs, a petition was presented and a Bill drawn up at considerable expense, to amend the 1531 Act and give more strength to the Company's regulatory powers. By March 1763, the Bill had passed all its stages in the Commons but it faced great opposition in the Lords and, possibly on account of the expenses already incurred, together with advice that failure was very likely, the Companies decided to drop the matter. The Brewers contributed £50 towards the costs.

In spite of this disappointment, the spirit of co-operation continued and in 1772 it was decided to resurrect the practice of sealing casks. The scheme was launched with newspaper advertisements and in August, four Sealers were appointed. So much time had elapsed since sealing had last been carried out, that there was much uncertainty about procedures and even a challenge on the accuracy of the standard gauge, kept by the City authorities. The Sealers demanded that the more accurate gauge kept by Winchester be used. The experiment proved an expensive anachronism. The seals yielded an income of £160 after 18 months while the cost had been £300. The Company, which was moving towards one of its periodic financial crises, decided to abandon the scheme by Lady Day 1775. At this point, the Brewers stepped in and offered to 'answer any deficiency' for a trial period. The offer was accepted and accounts for the seal were sent to them the following year.

In spite of this reprieve, the scheme drifted into oblivion. By 1783, there were only two Sealers and in 1786 they were left to run the seal entirely at their own expense, without the annual £50 subsidy they had been receiving from the Company. No more is recorded other than a request from the Livery in 1791 that a committee on sealing be set up. The request produced no action but it marks a resurgence of activity among the Livery to try and protect the trade and seek ways of asserting the Company's control.

There had emerged, sometime after 1773, an organisation of working coopers known as the 'Gentlemen of the Trade'. They had become alarmed at the weakness of the Company's position when faced with obdurate offenders, for example, coopers who had not completed their apprenticeship or had not taken up their freedom.

After the failure of the 1762–63 Parliamentary Bill to strengthen the legal position of the Company in enforcing its powers, many working coopers thought that the Court might be timid in pressing ahead with prosecutions in law, lest the Company's own jurisdiction were challenged. The Gentlemen of the Trade became a self-appointed watchdog organisation, channelling information to the Court about breaches of the old rules in breweries. The period of co-operation with the Brewers' Company seems to have dissolved in the 1780s, probably as a result of greater prosperity in the brewing trade and the creation of larger firms. The new vigour with which offenders were summoned to the Court and fined was due to the activities of the Gentlemen of the Trade. They had some effect, for some coopers summoned for practising the trade while being 'unfree', subsequently applied for the freedom of the Company by redemption so that they could trade legally.

The activities of the Gentlemen of the Trade concerned trade rather than constitutional matters. However there are a few examples of the Livery becoming less complacent with the way in which the Court governed the Company. The official records are tantalisingly reticent; they reflect the attitudes of the Court. In 1734, there was an uproar on Election Day because the Livery did not approve of the nominations for Master and Wardens. So much clamour ensued that the election could not go ahead. The Court then behaved in a foolish, high-handed way and declared they had the authority to proceed to an election. They therefore elected their original nominees and these three were sworn into office.

All this meant that the matter was taken to the Court of the King's Bench and Henry Neale, the Master, was indicted for acting in an office into which he had not been properly elected. The decision went in the Crown's favour, but the Livery had won only a victory of principle. The decision was not made until the last month of Neale's term of office. The Livery did not go any further; for example it did not challenge the legality of the past year's decisions. There was no stomach for a sustained battle, and perhaps no outstanding leader.

Another issue on which members of the Livery became assertive was the state of the finances. During the second half of the eighteenth century, the

Company lurched from crisis to crisis. Part of the problem was using old methods, which were quite unsuited to the Company's new responsibilities of running three charities and managing a portfolio of investments and properties. Some improvements in record-keeping were made in the middle years of the century: standing orders were collected and collated in a single volume: a new Livery list was compiled and the annual accounts accommodated those of Egham after 1759 and had to remain in the Clerk's hands for inspection after the annual audit. The improvements also revealed hitherto unknown deficiencies. In 1758, it was discovered that an Orphan tax, imposed by Lord Mayor's precept in 1696 when each apprentice was bound, had not been paid for several years and a sum of £122 was owed for the binding of almost 1,000 apprentices. There was another lapse between 1774 and 1785. On this occasion £84 was owed for 675 apprentices bound during the period. Was this the only item which slipped and was missed by the Court?

By 1760, a financial crisis was imminent but some speedy measures, which included borrowing from a member of the Court and selling, in stages, £900 worth of government stock, enabled the deficit on the Company's revenue account to be removed. A house in Threadneedle Street, bought with Henry Strode's £500 bequest to the Ratcliffe charity, was sold at this time and the proceeds invested in Government stock. This brought the reserves in investments to £2,200. For a year or two, it seemed that the crisis had been averted. It was, however, only delayed by the device of clearing each year's deficit by the sale of investments. In 1768, these had been reduced to £1,500 and there was £300 owing on the year's accounts.

The problem was next tackled in the traditional fashion by curtailing expenditure on dinners. Venison was omitted from menus and the normal Court Day dinners were cancelled for May, August and November. These measures were not enough. Probably influenced by Michael Tayleure, who was one of the auditors in 1770 and Renter Warden in 1771, a committee of the whole Court was set up to review the Company's finances. Its deliberations led to an obvious conclusion: 'The Committee do find a necessity for abridging the expenses of the Company'. Accordingly it was decided to reduce Court dinners still further so that all were cancelled except Quarter Day dinners. There is little doubt that dinners were a heavy drain on funds and it is to the Court's credit that it judged itself to be the first victim of strict economy. Election Day and Lord Mayor's Day celebrations were not much restricted, because the Court felt that these Livery occasions should continue to be marked with the customary cakes, ale and music.

Expenditure was sufficiently curbed by these economies to solve the problem of annual deficits for three years. However, it was only a temporary solution and expenditure began to rise again until July 1782 when, once more the Company was in deficit. The pattern was repeated: another committee, another period of restraint and after two years a precarious, small credit balance was achieved. In 1785, the first substantial surplus in years was reached, amounting to £570. The Court took a hard decision and voted to rebuild the Ratcliffe School and chapel rather than continue to pour money into repairs. The costs were met by a high risk strategy; borrowing £1,000 at five-per-cent from John Adams (Master 1762) and negotiating a £1,000 annuity with the Company's cook. The latter device was particularly risky at a time when actuarial skills were little known. Adams' loan was expensive when compared to the Company's investments, which yielded only three per cent.

There ensued three years of such confusion and difficulty that in two of them, 1789 and 1791, no audit could be done and in 1790 it was delayed by a month. More economies were agreed in 1791 but these could no longer mask the seriousness of the situation. The Company was living beyond its means and again resorted to the doubtful strategy of selling annuities. It is easy to attach blame for these recurring crises to negligence on the part of the Court. It is true that there was a tendency to let matters ride when all seemed to be going well, but there was an underlying factor which the Court could do little to amend. That was the fact that the Company had quite modest endowments and did not attract many men of substance whose generosity might enhance the income of its charities at Ratcliffe and Egham. For the time being, Egham was self-contained and no cost to the Company, but Ratcliffe's income in these years was insufficient to bear the essential cost of replacing old and decaying buildings. It took only a couple of adverse factors, in addition to this finely balanced situation, to plunge the Company's finances into difficulty.

Whatever the explanation and justification of the Court's predicament in 1791, the latest in a series of financial crises provoked unprecedented action and protest from the Livery. A group met at Paul's Head Tavern, set up a committee to represent the Livery's interests and drew up a plan of campaign to put a programme of reforms into action.

Led by Thomas Richardson, the group presented eight resolutions to the Court. They demonstrate how wide the gulf had become between the Court and the Livery. It was sufficient to prevent any serious communication as part of the normal Company procedure. The group claimed that the Livery knew nothing of the Company's affairs. It felt dispossessed, kept in ignorance and helpless. Liverymen were ignorant of the Company's charters and bye laws. They knew nothing of the Company's finances. They claimed the right to know and asked for access to all books and papers covering the past 14 years dealing with the Company's estates, rents, income and overall financial position. They also asked for a list of all the Livery with addresses. The group's approach was moderate and reasonable. It met with an appropriately civilised approach from the Court, which allowed the presentation, reading and recording of the eight resolutions. This provided the members of the Livery's committee an opportunity to move on to the detailed issues which so concerned them. They asked for a simpler method of keeping the accounts and that measures be taken to liquidate the Company's debt and 'bring Expenditure within the Compass of the Court's Income'.

Next they focused on the Company's 'public festivals', Election Day and Lord Mayor's Day, which were the only occasions on which the Livery participated in the social life of the Company. Superficially, it seems that they were seeking to recommend economies, but after suggesting it would be best if those dinners were held at a tavern, where members would be more disposed to pay some of the cost themselves, the Committee then lost its way. It put forward several resolutions on the smaller details of arrangements, none of which had any bearing on the expenses. Rather they are a reflection of long pent-up irritation such as not being informed of the precise hour of dining and delays in serving wine during the long waiting time before dinner. They also touched on the old problem of the Stewards. Here they were again dealing with constitutional matters. They questioned the Court's competence to compel four Stewards to serve. They recommended changes in the way in which Stewards were appointed and that the Court should have scope to appoint between three and six as seemed appropriate. The final point returned to the essential subject and was well made: '…It would lead to harmony and to advantage of its affairs that auditors be chosen as well out of the body of the livery'. There should be two from the Court and two from the Livery. It was not a new idea. For many years in the 1690s, senior liverymen were invited to serve as auditors. However, given that old minute books were seldom consulted, it was a tradition which had long been lost.

The Court's reaction was gracious. Compliments flew between it and the Livery committee and agreement was reached that the two sets of resolutions submitted from the Livery would be officially minuted. The Court readily agreed to there being two Livery representatives at the 1793 audit. The Livery nominations for auditors were confirmed at Common Hall on Election Day, but only one, David Griffin, appeared on Audit Day. In two subsequent years,

Livery auditors were appointed but none was present in 1796 and thereafter it seems the practice ceased. It may have helped reduce the sense of urgency that the Court succeeded in reducing expenditure, improving some of the rents and balancing the Company's current account. These modest achievements took away pressure from the Court and removed the target for the Livery protest. One innovation survived and may have been sufficient to satisfy the leaders of the Livery: at Election Day, the final statement of the accounts was read out to the assembled liverymen. Another small victory for this brief foray into pressure group politics, or representative government, was the introduction of three separate accounts: one for the cash received at the Hall by the Upper Warden, one for the Ratcliffe Charity and the Renter Warden and one for the Egham Charity, which at this point was being administered by its own committee.

It is tempting to see the protest of the Livery as a sign of the times when many rivulets of liberal political philosophy fed the mighty torrent of revolution, first and chiefly in France but then spread by war to many parts of Europe. In London, there were powerful social tensions on which sound political ideas could feed. Changes in trade, manufacturing and the consequent organisation of business along lines more familiar to the twentieth century than the seventeenth, provided ready audiences and readers eager for new ideas about social and political organisations. Until legislation in 1799 made a crime of workers combining into clubs, societies and unions to press for better wages and conditions, London was the centre of spirited debate among the intellectual leaders of workers in 'new' trades, that is ones which had never been subject to regulation by livery companies. Influential leaders such as Francis Place, the Charing Cross tailor and Thomas Hardy who created a network of Corresponding Societies, may have emboldened the actions of the Coopers' liverymen.

Although the attempt to give the Livery a voice soon vanished from the records, it was not without precedent. In 1774, the Livery had tested its constitutional power by nominating and electing as Under Warden, one of its members, David Trinder. His election meant that there were more than the permitted number on the Court. The result was overturned and ignored by the Court, which went on to defend its action successfully in the King's Bench. Trinder had responded to being black-balled by taking out a writ of *mandamus* against the Company. These events may be quite unconnected to the 1793 Livery protest. There is no means of knowing whether there were other intervening attempts by the Livery to assert itself, to demand to be better informed about the Company's affairs or to seek representation on the Court. The value of the 1793 events is that they were recorded in the official minutes. They may well have been the culmination of long-standing concern at the way the Company appeared to lurch from one financial crisis to another.

During the years of stringency, the Company had cause for celebration: one of its liverymen became Sheriff in 1766. James Esdaile had been apprenticed in 1730 but he never claimed a mark and did not practice as a cooper. He was the third generation of a protestant family which had left France after the Revocation of the Edict of Nantes in 1685 to seek a more tolerant society in London. The family business, making military equipment, flourished during a period of several European wars, and was particularly prosperous under his guidance. In 1766, the Company offered him the use of its barge in the Lord Mayor's procession and afterwards the use of the Hall. This was probably the last occasion the barge was used. Its condition was the subject of serious discussion in 1763, when the proposal to replace it was shelved on account of the deficit. Esdaile was further honoured by the Company when a vacancy occurred on the Court during his year of office, and he was elected as an Assistant.

At the end of his shrievalty, Esdaile continued his political career in the City by being elected Alderman for Cripplegate Ward. Ten years later it was his turn to be chosen Lord Mayor. He seems to have been a popular choice: 'no man is more amiable or more universally respected', was the verdict of the 'City Biographer' in 1800.

The Company celebrated the day heartily and took a leading part in the processions. Few in the Company would have had a clear memory of the last occasion that a Cooper became Lord Mayor in 1742. It was unfortunate that the aftermath of the celebrations produced a rather sour atmosphere. Several resolutions were passed of which the chief was that for the future, the expenses of attending the Lord Mayor should not be borne by the Company; and that liverymen were not to be elected out of turn on account of honours gained in the City. The latter was a reference to Esdaile's promotion to the Court out of turn in 1767. It seems a particularly churlish reaction to a member who showed great ability, ambition and experience in the affairs of the City.

The incident gave prominence to a dilemma: how to reinvigorate the Court whose members served for life, without upsetting the tradition of promoting to the Court by seniority. The case for bringing a few younger men on to the Court, when the opportunity arose, was strengthened in 1762 and 1763. The Master elect in 1762 was paralysed and too ill to serve in office. Nonetheless he was duly elected, but died before he could take his oath. The following year, the elderly Upper Warden died in office and the Clerk had to deputise until the end of his term. The Company deserved and needed more dynamic leadership. The challenge to improve matters and provide a link between the Court and the Livery was thrown down to Coopers of the next generation.

CHAPTER NINE

PART ONE: Schools, Schoolmasters and Reformers
1800–1870

> War against Napoleon until his defeat at Waterloo, 1815. Nelson and Wellington were the national heroes. Post-war depression and popular protests against factory work, machines replacing crafts; repressive laws. Working men supported chartism which demanded the reform of Parliament and universal suffrage, Queen Victoria succeeded her randy uncles in 1837 and, with Prince Albert set new middle class standards of propriety. In the 1840s, railways transformed the landscape, Manchester set the pace of urban boom and civic pride and Sir Robert Peel broke the Conservative party but achieved a policy of free trade. The 1851 Great Exhibition demonstrated the return of prosperity which trickled slowly to some of the urban masses. They benefited from better drains, cheap food and cotton clothes. Householders were given the vote.

THE COMPANY STRUGGLED to survive during the early part of the nineteenth century. It had lost its purpose and still had not understood or grasped a new mission. With some honourable exceptions, its leaders continued to take the practice of *laisser-faire* to extremes. It neither managed nor supervised its charities. Future events showed that the charities at Egham and Woodham Mortimer were still being neglected. The Tayleure Committee, which had rescued Egham from chaos, was inexplicably wound up. The neat little incentive of half-yearly prizes for attendance was stopped. It seemed a churlish economy. Nevertheless, timid Mr Jones, the schoolmaster and chaplain, made no protest. The charity was run quietly under his benign and tentative rule until his death in 1807. This period proved to be the calm before the storm.

The immediate problem, which exercised the Court, was how it could improve its income. It had been badly affected by the destruction of the newly-built Ratcliffe charity in the fire of 1794. Rebuilding was prolonged and its chapel finally came in to use in 1802. After a fiasco of selling annuities and failing to make a profit, the Company found an unexpected, but lucrative income, by letting the Hall to the Commissioners of the national lottery for their twice yearly draw. At first the arrangements were *ad hoc* but £400 a time was a useful windfall and the Court was in favour of continuing the connection. The Clerk and Beadle were quite well rewarded with £80 and £20 respectively 'for the inconvenience'. Both lived at the Hall. The Court was not averse to enjoying the celebrity which the lottery's antics brought the Hall. It gave the clerk, John Edison, *carte blanche* to negotiate a contract. By 1809, the arrangement became an annual one for a fee of 600 guineas. It lasted until 1824 and probably saved the Company from bankruptcy.

There were other gains. Necessary repairs to the Hall became affordable and the Commissioners demanded some modernisation. In 1816, they asked that gas be installed. It seems not to have been extended beyond the Court room because the Beadle continued to receive his annual allowance of 12 pounds of candles. The downside of the arrangement was the disruption of the offices caused by the lottery equipment, having to plan repairs around the lottery times and needing to move the date of the monthly Court meeting.

The lottery continued on an *ad hoc* basis until 1826, but both sides were ready to end the deal. The lottery was less popular, its purses less lucrative and the Company less financially dependent on its letting income. There were draws for a lottery promoted by the City of Glasgow held at the Hall in 1834 and 1835.

Rents were the Company's life blood, but they were hit hard by the economic consequences of the prolonged struggle against Napoleon. Taxation, particularly on property, became a heavy burden. Inflation of prices was another consequence but the Company, saddled with rents at old rates for property let on long leases, could do little but wait until it could catch up with the rise in property values. Insurance valuations reflect this situation. Company property in Miles Lane doubled in value from £500 to £1,000; in Little Tower Street one house was valued at £600 in 1802, £800 in 1816 and £1,600 in 1827. As leases expired, the Company was able to raise the rents, but meanwhile it depended on the lottery and £1,000 lent by the Clerk.

The last splutter of trade regulation occurred during the war years, when, for example, the brewers, Thrale and Company, were challenged for making casks against the Coopers' ordinances. However, the Company's efforts were not sustained nor did it prosecute after 1809. There was also little chance of enforcing strictly the rules about apprenticeship. Evidence was hard to find and probably would not have stood up in court. Increasingly the Company was challenged by practising coopers who had neither been formally apprenticed nor taken the freedom of the Company. When summoned to the Hall to answer for breaking the ordinances, they came accompanied by their solicitors. The Court issued a warning letter to brewhouses in Limehouse, Walworth and Hackney, but there was nothing further to be done. Breweries were becoming large-scale industrial

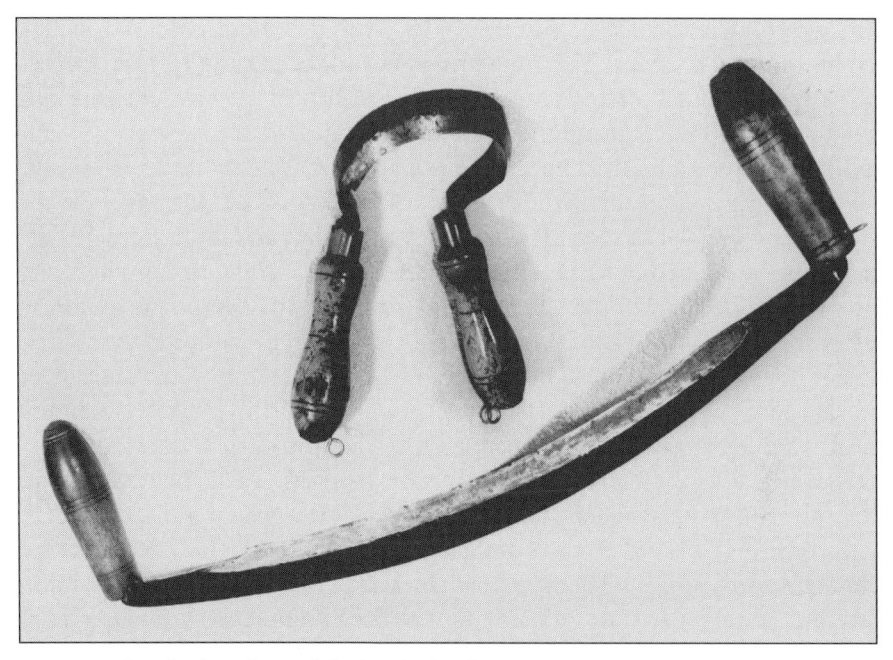

Heading knife and round shave. The heading knife is used for cutting the edges (the basle) round the head of the cask.

operations, the result of amalgamations of successful family firms. They had little to fear from the warnings of a livery company which had no statutory backing for its claims.

The Company turned increasingly to the care of its charities and their endowments, which were its responsibility to manage well. It was not, however, well-prepared. The state of its records illustrates the point. In 1805, a committee was set up to examine its old papers and see what could be destroyed. The committee decided to destroy nothing but ordered that the papers be placed in boxes and labelled. It proved inefficient as a means to making the papers accessible and useable. No catalogue was made and when a lease, relating to property in Birchen Lane, was needed in 1816 during a legal dispute, it could not be found. Some repairs to 'old books' were carried out in 1813 and then nothing more was done until 1823–24 when the Company's administration broke down completely. An indication of the confusion was an order, in January 1824, for the Beadle to sort and label the papers, separating the Company's properties from those of Ratcliffe and Egham and placing the relevant indentures, leases and other title deeds in three tin boxes — secure from mice — with schedules attached.

The immediate cause of the crisis in 1823 was the fragile hold of the Clerk on his duties. That year no accounts could be produced and there was, consequently, no annual audit. As usual, senior members of the Company had been appointed to carry out the audit but having 'used great industry [were] sorry to find the labour had not been more successful'.

The full extent of the problem was revealed once a Committee on the Accounts set to work in September 1823. Among its early discoveries was the fact that the Company had been so indebted twenty years earlier that it had borrowed £1,000 from the Clerk and in return allowed him control of the whole rent collection from its properties, 'to the great prejudice of funds'. The Committee members spent long hours trying and failing to make sense of the account books. They selected the Woodham Mortimer estate, as a relatively simple enterprise with a mere hundred-year history in the Company's possession, to try and trace back the income from rents and the payments to the Company's pensioners from 1726 to 1823. They found the Clerk too ill and confused to assist. He had probably had a stroke. They were unable for some time to discover what property belonged to each bequest. But at length, after many days 'perusing and attentively examining many ancient books of accounts', they produced a statement on Woodham Mortimer.

Some glimpse of the chaos can be gained from the recommendations made by the Committee. The accounts of the Company, the Ratcliffe and the Egham charities were to be kept separately. All bills must be in writing and must be presented to the Court for approval before payment. There must be up-to-date lists of all freemen and all liverymen. Entries in the Wardens' accounts must be precise and clear. Arrears in rent must be listed and followed up by legal action if need be. A new table of fees for entry of apprentice, freeman and liveryman was approved. And to show that reform was no joking matter, the quarterly Court dinners were suspended.

It was obvious that the Clerk, John Edison, had to be replaced for he was 'incapable of performing his complicated duties'. But it was an unpleasant task from which the Court shied away. Depriving Edison of his post also meant removing him from his home and taking away his security. The proposed solution was to appoint a joint Clerk, promoting to this post Edison's assistant, James Smith. The matter was solved by a deterioration in Edison's condition and his resignation, written and delivered by his wife in April 1824.

These events were responsible for the revival of the Livery's concern with their interests and rights in the Company's affairs. The movement for reform in the 1790s had disappeared without trace. Even as early as 1796, the representation of liverymen on the audit group had lapsed and no objection was raised. Perhaps alarm at the stern legislation against the first trades unions and any 'combinations' of workmen had dampened enthusiasm for reform. But the research involving the Company finances may have depended on the skills of a young liveryman and archivist, James Firth, who worked in the Town Clerk's office at Guildhall and had the opportunity to study the Company's Charters.

The Clerk's resignation coincided with the nomination of the Master and Wardens. The Livery submitted its own nominee, Abraham Algar for Under Warden and, on Election Day 1824, easily outvoted the Court. It seemed an unprecedented action to choose as Warden a man not already an Assistant and member of the Court. Firth, however, knew of at least one precedent since 1662 when the Charter had limited the Court to 17 members. He was sufficiently confident of the legal and historic facts to allow himself to be nominated in 1825 as Under Warden. Algar was elected Upper Warden.

The new Clerk was instructed to seek Counsel's opinion on the matter. The problem was how Wardens from the Livery could be accommodated on the Court and the number of Assistants kept to 17, without there being two 'reserved' vacancies on the Court. Eventually the opinion was delivered. There was no objection in law to the Livery's right to choose one of their number as Warden. However, there was no right for the Warden to remain as a member of the Court once his term of office ended. He would simply return to the Livery.

While the legal decision was awaited, confrontation was skilfully avoided. First, Robert Carter was elected Master in 1825. He was a traditionalist, a member of a long-standing 'Cooper' family, but he supported the Livery's claims. Second, a head-on clash was avoided by the simple device of re-electing the Master and Wardens of 1825 in 1826 and 1827. Contested elections were thus avoided. It gave the Company a cooling-off period while the lawyers' views were being considered and it also gave an opportunity for a remarkable trio, Carter, Algar and Firth to set about a mighty overhaul of the administration and finances of the Company.

Between them, the three had expertise in property surveying and management, in the law and in historical precedent. These skills they added to reforming zeal and strong characters. They cut through much of the muddle and confusion by applying simple, common-sense methods. Livery elections had become a major issue since Algar's election in 1824. After the next elections in 1825, a new Livery list was ordered. Notices were placed in the *Morning Advertiser* asking liverymen who were out of touch with the

Company to come forward and establish their credentials and addresses. When plans were ready for repairs at the Ratcliffe Charity, public tenders were invited in three metropolitan newspapers. The trio sought efficiency and value for money. The long-delayed Banfield bequest of £1,000 for the poor at Ratcliffe was prised from the grip of the lawyers with interest of £200 which it had accumulated. An enquiry was held into the chaplain's duties at Ratcliffe and it was felt he could do more.

When, in 1828, fully contested elections were held again, the Company's thanks to Carter, Algar and Firth were unusually fulsome and honest. The motion passed to the reformers at Common Hall referred to their 'indefatigable exertions in the financial department' and to their assistance to the Court 'by their researches into ancient Records which have brought many important matters to light … and discovered gross errors, the exposure of which is creditable to themselves … and the removal of which bids far to be highly beneficial to the finances of the Company'.

These fine words did not prevent the elections from being contentious and, in the end, probably illegal. A new force in the Company was the Society of the Livery created in 1827 to uphold the rights of the Livery in the matter of electing Wardens. It may have been the Society's involvement in the 1828 elections which resulted in two candidates from the Livery standing for election to the office of Under Warden. There was no contest or opposition from the Court about James Firth stepping up from Under Warden to Upper Warden. But a poll, instead of the usual show of hands, was demanded. Instead of its being held immediately, involving only those present at Common Hall, as the 1661 Charter prescribed, the poll was taken over three days and 83 votes were cast. The Court did not surrender its claim to nominate the Wardens and though it usually accepted the nomination of the Under Warden as the next Upper Warden, it continued to nominate its own candidate as Under Warden until 1883, when 'next business' was moved at the point when the Court's nomination would normally be made. Only in 1886 did the Court accept it would be 'inexpedient' to make its own nomination.

During the intervening years, the Livery chose their Wardens and these Wardens brought another point of view as well as a more youthful attitude to the Court's deliberations. On completing two years as Under and Upper Warden in succession, the Wardens returned to the Livery, perhaps better able to understand and interpret the Court's decisions to the rest of the Company. The Society of the Livery, meanwhile, provided a constitutional watchdog on the Court. It was not afraid to express its viewpoint occasionally by memoranda to the Court, while it also became a social club for those liverymen who wished to participate. As a body, it is unusual to have begun as a revolutionary organisation and to continue as a social one.

Of the three liverymen who were pushed into the forefront of the Livery's campaign in 1823, Abraham Algar had the briefest influence on the Company. Having served his two years as Warden he returned, in 1826, to the Livery until his turn came by seniority for election to the Court as an Assistant in September 1834. He refused, however, to pay the fine required in the Company's 1741 bye laws for an Assistant, declared the Court was not legally entitled to claim a fine and he then took out a suit in the King's Bench. His election to the Court was declared void and no more was recorded in the Company's papers of Mr Algar. In 1857, his wife, Mary, applied for a Company pension, presumably because she was widowed. The other two champions of the Livery, Robert Carter and James Firth, continued to serve the Company with great panache and distinction. Their knowledge and wisdom can be detected in the complex affairs of the Egham and Ratcliffe charities over the years from 1825 to Carter's death in 1844.

Robert Carter was a powerful figure. He had enormous energy and not much patience. He disliked inefficiency in all its forms. As an architect and surveyor he found, or was given, plenty of scope to bring change and order to the Company's property, charities and procedures. His proposal, that notice should be given of motions for the Court's consideration, improved its dealing with business matters. He was the instigator of simple, but practical, reforms dealing with finance, and later he persuaded the Court to draw up a calendar of business, listing annually recurring items. At his suggestion, vacancies at the Ratcliffe almshouses were advertised. Court minutes were checked for accuracy and to see that actions agreed had been taken.

He became deeply involved with reforms at Woodham Mortimer, surveying the whole estate, marking the boundaries with iron posts, settling a dispute with the parish church and compiling a list of repairs estimated at £1,200. A little later he dealt with settling the payment for commuting the tithe due to the parish.

The Court entrusted him with several property matters, in particular securing tenders for repairs. By 1839, he was acting for the Company's surveyor in completing rebuilding works at Egham. He handled a difficult case where the leaseholder had disappeared, having failed to fulfil his covenants on a group of the Company's houses in Hatfield Street. These small cottages were left in such ruinous condition that they had to be cleared. Carter even secured a reduction in the land tax for this property. But it was at Ratcliffe that he showed his determination to end years of neglect and inertia. He believed that the schoolmaster should be removed. To Carter, he appeared incompetent and weak, and an obstacle to the development of the school. Carter did not succeed as he would have wished but he set in motion the process and inspired the collective will of the Court to effect the changes in 1848, just four years after his death.

Some years before these events at Ratcliffe, the Egham Charity dominated the Court's agenda. The administration of the charity, of which the Company was the trustee, had already created such sensitivity among the parish authorities as to lead twice to cases being brought in the Court of Chancery against the Company. The first had been in 1708–09 and had ensured that the charity had been properly endowed, the founder's will observed to the letter and sufficient funds were available to support the school and almshouses. Such concern arose from the heavy burden of the poor rates on the parishioners of Egham. Henry Strode's charity was a very valuable subsidy from which the parish wanted to derive maximum benefit.

The catalyst for the third chancery case brought against the Company was the appointment, in 1807, of a new schoolmaster, Thomas Jeans, a Wykehamist and former fellow of New College, Oxford. He was already 58 years old and in need of a post where he could secure his income by taking private pupils, who would lodge in his house, while the teaching of the charity boys could be delegated to an usher. The Egham parish officers were clear about the kind of schoolmaster they wanted: 'respected in moral character and qualified to instruct children in the inferior branches of education … but … he should not be a person too much raised above the situation of a Master of such a charity by his affluence and rank in life'. Jeans, however, was a clergyman of 'considerable church preferment', a Surrey magistrate who took into his house as private pupils 'young gentlemen of rank and fortune'. His character was well delineated in Parson Woodforde's diary. During the 1780s, Jeans had held two Norfolk livings and was a neighbour and often a guest at Woodforde's table. But Woodforde soon wearied of the inconsiderate demands made by Jeans—to take his services while he went to London—and had little regard for the airs and graces of fashionable London society, which Mr and Mrs Jeans adopted.

The suitability of the Company's appointment was only one part of the case brought by the 'Relators' (plaintiffs). The removal of the poor children to a nearby cottage and the conversion of the schoolhouse to a private dwelling was another complaint. Perhaps most telling of all was their argument that the Egham Charity's income was much less than expected, given the size of its endowment. There were personal animosities, as well, which

Plate 1: Dame Avice Knyvett, *c.* 1540 (*see p. 250 for full caption*)

© *The Worshipful Company of Coopers*

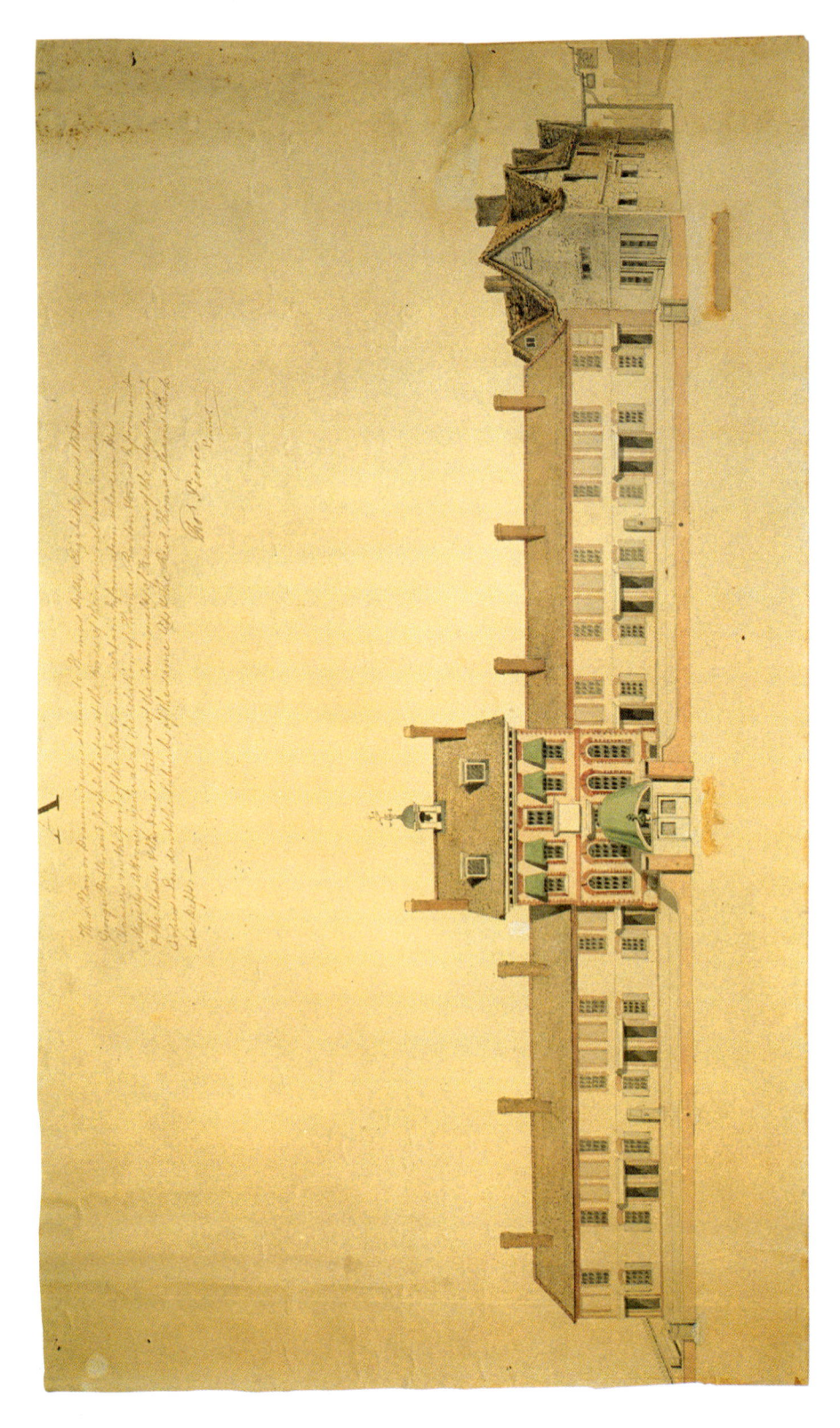

Plate 2: The Egham Charity (*see p. 250 for full caption*)

Copyright of Surrey History Service

Plate 3: Woodham Mortimer Hall (*see p. 250 for full caption*)

© *C. E. Doe*

Plate 4: Memorial to William Alexander (*see p. 250 for full caption*)

© *C. E. Doe*

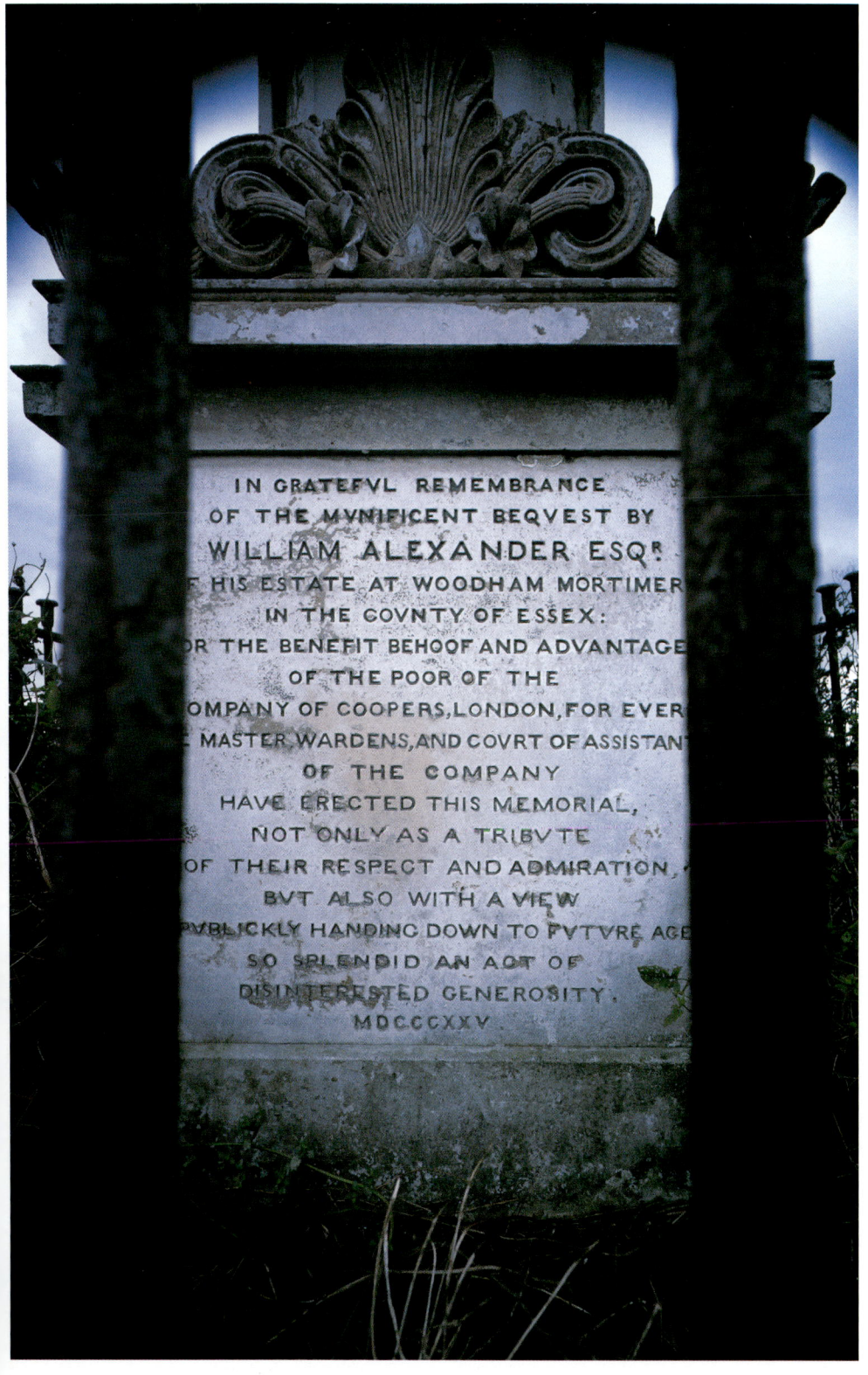

Plate 5: Memorial to William Alexander: the inscription (*see p. 250 for full caption*)

© *C. E. Doe*

Plate 6: Plan of The Egham Charity's Lands at Staines (*see p. 250 for full caption*)
Copyright of Surrey History Service

Plate 7: Drawing the Lottery at Cooper's Hall in 1803 (*see p. 250 for full caption*)

© Guildhall Library, Corporation of London

Plate 8: Sir David Salomons (*see p. 250 for full caption*)

© Guildhall Library, Corporation of London

Plate 9: Henry Capel (*see p. 250 for full caption*)

© *Worshipful Company of Coopers*

Plate 10: Chapel in the Ratcliffe Charity (*see p. 251 for full caption*)

© *Guildhall Library, Corporation of London*

Plate 11: Dining Room in the Company's third Hall (*see p. 251 for full caption*)
© *Guildhall Library, Corporation of London*

Plate 12: Sir Henry Murray Fox (*see p. 251 for full caption*)

© *Worshipful Company of Coopers*

Plate 13: Dining Room at 13 Devonshire Square (*see p. 251 for full caption*)

© *Worshipful Company of Coopers*

Plate 14: Coopers' Court, Maplin Street, Bow (*see p. 251 for full caption*)

© *Bailey • Garner*

Plate 15: Jonathan Manby, the last brewery apprentice of the twentieth century (*see p. 251 for full caption*)
© *Theakston's Brewery, Masham*

Plate 16: Cooper Lew Jones at work (*see p. 251 for full caption*)

© *St Austell Brewery Co. Ltd*

added spice to the proceedings. Several of the Relators were local tradesmen, owed money for alterations ordered by Jeans but not authorised by the Company. One, Carey Turner, who seems to have been the leader of the Egham group, had been expelled in 1790 from Strode's school on the orders of the Tayleure committee, because as a son of a prosperous tradesman, he did not qualify as a poor scholar.

The Lord Chancellor made an interim judgement in 1812. He ordered that the children be taught in the schoolhouse but he recognised its inconvenience and lack of privacy for the schoolmaster's family. Under his orders, the Court carried out some improvements. The charity's accounts were also to be investigated and, when the report was published in 1817, it confirmed the Egham Relators' allegation that income had accumulated and was lying unused in the Company's accounts. The report also revealed that the Plaistow estate, the main source of income, had been let at too low a rent in 1800. It confirmed, once again, that the Relators were right in claiming that the charity could support more almspeople and double the number of pupils.

The Lord Chancellor's order was received in 1818. The Company had to raise the Plaistow rent, by a new lease, from £260 to £430 per annum. It also had to pay the charity the difference between the two rents from 1801 to the present and it had to pass over £1,114 to the charity, being the accumulated surplus. The most important requirement was a new scheme of management to expand the school and increase the number of pensioners.

In spite of the embarrassment which Dr Jeans caused the Company, it was he who had the foresight to purchase land which would make possible building a new schoolhouse, chapel and almshouses to the rear of the existing building. Jeans went further. Having examined the original bequest he realised it was in favour of the poor children of Egham. He asked the Court of Chancery to declare 'that the Education of Female Children was within the terms of the Testator's bounty'. The point was well made but it was ignored.

The Lord Chancellor approved the other part of Jean's scheme. He ordered the Company to purchase the necessary land from Jeans. The Relators involved themselves fully with these developments and mellowed sufficiently to put forward, for Chancery's approval, a scheme jointly agreed with the Company.

While these developments took place, the Company had appointed a special Egham committee to supervise the new building and to implement the new charity scheme. The committee showed diligence in visiting many almshouses in and around London to gather ideas of the latest practice. To some extent it must have felt under pressure to act responsibly. It had to answer to the Lord Chancellor and comply with the requirements of the Charities Act, 1812, which set up a commission to enquire into the behaviour of the trustees of charities. The tenders for the new building were supervised by the Lord Chancellor. The lowest, from Richard Dean, was just over £3,000 and was the one accepted.

In September 1828, a foundation ceremony of some grandeur took place at Egham, in the presence of the Company's special committee, consisting of the Master, Wardens and Robert Carter, the Relators, representing the interests of the Parish of Egham and the almspeople and boys. After processions, speeches, the burying of a selection of contemporary coins, there was a blessing, the National Anthem, three cheers, wine, a silver sixpence for each boy and a new half crown for each almsperson. In a gesture of reconciliation, the Coopers' party entertained the Relators to dinner at the King's Head.

Building continued during the winter but mistakes and deficiencies in the work were so numerous that the whole scheme was well behind schedule in April 1829. Only the foundations of new almshouses had been laid, the schoolhouse had no floors or water closets and even the Coat of Arms was wrong. Carter tried to sack the clerk of works without due notice and merely succeeded in antagonising the Relators.

Clearing and landscaping the grounds took another 18 months. So great was the mess that for once Egham residents came to the Company's aid. The schoolmaster's accommodation was so ill-planned that Jeans refused to move in. Rain seeped under the front door; there was no window in the entrance hall, so a candle had to be lit when anyone called; the stoves failed, the pump broke, the chimney smoked and the cesspool serving the new water closet created such a stink that half the house was unusable. It is small wonder that Jeans became ill in February 1833 and the Court had to agree to his wife and daughter taking charge.

The full scheme was not completed until 1839, four years after Jeans' death, at the age of eighty-five. Six of the old almshouses remained to house half the pensioners until the second new range could be built. Under Jeans' successor, George Hopkins, son of the limner and painter to George III, the school expanded to take 100 scholars. In 1839, the charity had run out of funds and was made a loan of £1,300, at first from the Ratcliffe Charity, but later this was replaced by a Company loan of £1,400-worth of stock. It was slowly repaid in the following decade.

The Ratcliffe Charity provided challenges of property maintenance, legal entanglements and awkward personalities to match those at Egham. The

Company followed the completion of rebuilding after the 1794 fire with expanding its income from speculative development. In 1804, a 66-year lease was granted to a builder from the West End to build small tenements on vacant land in School House Lane, the western perimeter of the charity. In all, 21 small houses formed Dunstan's Place and from these the charity benefited from ground rents of £3 or £4 pounds each. The yield enabled the pensions to be increased from £5 to £8 a year for the women and from £9 to £12 for the men.

For the first time in centuries, the exact sources of the charity's income were researched, first by the new Charity Commission in 1819 and then by James Firth in 1826. He established that the Fenchurch Street property should be assigned to Ratcliffe and not to the Company. The result was to show an income of over £1,000, but expenditure only a little over £500 a year. Two extra pensioners were provided for and there was a modest increase in pupils.

This increase proved to be only a brief revival in the school's fortunes. The schoolmaster appointed in 1820, Edward Burrow, was already middle-aged and temperamentally unable to match the zeal for improvement shown by the reformers on the Court and in the Livery. Matters were made worse by Burrow's lack of authority, particularly over the almspeople, and by the Court's tendency either to let matters ride or to intervene on issues which were properly in the schoolmaster's domain. The result was that what little authority Burrow might have asserted was undermined by interference from Basinghall Street. The almspeople were skilful at circumventing the rules about no lodgers or dependants using their houses. Several took advantage of Burrow's weakness and his foolishness in being frequently absent from his post without leave. He thus put himself in the wrong with the Court which might otherwise have helped him assert himself over the unruly elements in the almshouses. He survived a vote of no confidence and consequent dismissal in 1831 only on the Master's casting vote.

His problems, which were not all of his own making, are well illustrated by his encounters with the Archer family. Exceptionally, because almsman Archer was over eighty and disabled, his wife was permitted to 'live in'. Custom and practice since the sixteenth century ruled against couples in the almshouses. Mrs Archer did the cleaning in the school and chapel and frequently provoked incidents to humiliate and annoy Burrow. She would block his way in doorways, abuse him verbally, doing so once in the hearing of his dying daughter and causing great distress. Her offensive behaviour made his life a misery. He was, at length, provoked into a lengthy written complaint to the Court, which felt compelled to investigate. The Archers had the right to respond and almspeople were called as witnesses. The latter confirmed Burrow's statement that he had 'long been a total stranger to every domestic comfort'. They also made it clear that the Archer daughters ran a brothel from their parents' almshouse.

The Court backed away from an open scandal, gave the Archers the benefit of age and infirmity and merely cautioned them. Next time they would be dismissed. Poor Burrow! He must have felt let down and desperate at having to continue living and working in the same building. He had to endure the Archers until the almsman's death 15 months later in November 1835.

Burrow lost heart and his health declined. The grounds, school and chapel were ill-kept and their untidy, dirty appearance annoyed visiting members of the Court. There was a complaint in 1839 about 'dissolute boys at Ratcliffe' entering the courtyard and vandalising the garden. A few weeks later Robert Carter happened to catch a pupil running over the garden. Carter dismissed him from the school immediately. He did, however have the grace to tell the schoolmaster that he might reinstate the boy if the parents appealed against the dismissal.

Thereafter, Burrow was harassed, particularly by Carter. He was summoned to attend the Court for a number of small errors such as not dating orders for books. Then he was ordered to attend Thursday and Sunday prayers and see that the almspeople did so too. The following month he had to produce full details of the numbers in class and admitted, the names of monitors, the names and ages of the boys and the time allocated to each subject. It smacked of a mini-inspection and was probably provoked by stirrings in Stepney where some parishioners were dissatisfied with the elementary level of instruction.

In 1839, the Court was petitioned by some local residents in Ratcliffe and more widely in Stepney. They complained that the education provided was 'only adapted for children of poor working people'. In 1840, there were 18 children in the school. Carter believed the time had come to remove Burrow as the main obstacle to increasing numbers and returning to the founder's intention. By this time, James Firth had begun systematic research into the early documents of the Company and discovered that the school was intended to have a master 'skylfull and taught in gramer, letters and in the science of gramer' to teach and instruct the boys in those skills. The boys were expected to have skills in reading and writing their own language before being admitted. The grammar they would be taught was, of course, Latin.

By 1841, Carter indicated it was his intention to have Burrow removed. Burrow responded with a lengthy vindication, but when asked if this amounted to a resignation he quickly replied that it was not: he could not possibly resign without a pension. Carter pressed his case when the annual re-election of the schoolmaster took place but only succeeded (on several occasions) in having Burrow's election deferred. Although Carter died in 1844, the Court was convinced it had to proceed with reform and respond to more complaints from Stepney. A special committee was set up to find a solution and the Reverend John Smith of the Mercers' School was called in to advise. Burrow refused to change. At 67 years of age he was too old a dog to learn new tricks. He was asked to retire. He gave the impression he would do so but at the right price. He wanted a pension equivalent to his salary. Given that he received £74, only half of what was then the normal headmaster's salary, he was not being too unreasonable. The whole matter was left in abeyance for a further two years, pending the outcome of a nine-year legal battle between the Company and the East India Company.

The dispute concerned a lease granted in 1770 to the East India Company of the saltpetre wharf at Ratcliffe Cross. It was probably the most consistently valuable of the charity's property. The terms of the lease were surprisingly generous, comprising the remaining term of the existing lease granted in 1758 for 61 years, and a further 200-year lease, for which an entry fine of 200 guineas was paid. In 1837, the East India Company wanted to dispose of the lease as profitably as it could, but the Coopers' withheld permission. In response, the East India Company sued for losses incurred. Although the Coopers' made available their papers, the East India Company lawyers failed to gather evidence or to present a case. So dilatory were they, that the Coopers' threatened twice to have the case dismissed.

Instead, in 1840, an ejection order was issued against the East India Company and the first hearings were held in January 1842. The Coopers proceeded cautiously and at first did not seek to recover rents which had been withheld since the legal contest began in 1837. However in 1844, they had assurance that seeking the rents which were owed would not compromise their main cause.

There was an added complication when three of the Company's Assistants used James Firth's historical research to bring a private prosecution against the East India Company. Their argument was that in 1774, without the Coopers' Company's permission, the East India Company had granted a sub-lease of part of the wharf to one David Trinder. By this action, the three 'Relators' argued that the lease had long been forfeited.

The scene was set for arguments of the length and complexity of Jarndyce v. Jarndyce, in *Bleak House*, but wise counsels prevailed, arguing that the need for income for the Ratcliffe Charity was paramount. After another two years of wrangling, a figure acceptable to both sides was agreed. The East India Company surrendered its lease for £5,500. It was more than the Ratcliffe Charity could pay as a lump sum but a further agreement allowed the immediate payment of £2,500 and repayment of the remainder by instalments at five per cent interest. The wharf itself was the security offered and accepted by the East India Company. To complete the settlement, the 'Relators' dropped their case.

It was a timely solution, limiting the Company's legal costs, allowing a new lease of the wharf to go ahead with the Thornley Coal Company at a much improved rent of £700 and it cleared the way for bringing to fruition plans for a new kind of school at Ratcliffe. After Robert Carter's death in 1844, the lead was taken by James Firth. His researches had clarified the extent of the charity's property and his calculations of its likely income made the school's future look secure.

There remained the problem of Burrow, the schoolmaster. Where Carter had harassed and bullied, Firth worked more subtlely and swiftly to exploit Burrow's increasing inability to perform his duties. The schoolmaster wrote pathetically in March 1848 of his poor health which put 'utterly out of his power' attendance to his duties. The Court agreed to his retirement in May 1848 on a pension equivalent to his salary. He was 69 years old, a sick and weary man who had never been the right person for the post.

The speed with which the Ratcliffe school was reshaped was largely due to the zeal and confidence of Firth who, as Master in 1847, was in the ideal position to push through reforms. He was clear in his own mind about the objective of creating a grammar school but he had the patience and skill to carry with him the few waverers on the Court. As soon as he had secured a decision about one stage in the process, he was ready to move to the next, having quietly put in hand the necessary preparations. The first step was to make a temporary appointment as schoolmaster, Mr Hart, who ran a private school in Stepney Causeway. With the help of an assistant, the school was ready to re-open in July 1848. Within a few weeks, Firth had secured agreement on salary, time-table, hours, terms of admission and curriculum. It was astonishing speed for the Court, used to more leisurely consideration of such momentous matters.

The school remained true to its founder's intention, free for tuition and writing materials but parents were asked for 20 shillings a year towards prizes and were offered textbooks at reduced prices. The latter were 'to be confined to works of acknowledged utility' according to Firth's instructions. The

SCHOOLS, SCHOOLMASTERS AND REFORMERS 1800–1870

The Ratcliffe Charity, 1857; an engraving by Thomas Hosmer Shepherd (1793–1864) showing the building as restored after the 1794 fire. The school was rapidly growing in numbers as a result of a new headmaster and a technical curriculum, introduced by James Firth in 1848–49

curriculum consisted of the three basic skills of reading, writing and arithmetic to which English grammar, geography, book-keeping and composition were added. It proved its popularity with parents. It met their need for a practical and vocational education which would fit boys for careers in new industries and as clerks in the expanding docks and in City offices.

Within a few weeks of opening, the school was so popular that the Court felt confident of its success and made Hart's appointment permanent. He had rent-free accommodation, and £180 per annum from which he was expected to pay his assistant. For a few years, he continued to run his own 'Finishing Academy, Commercial and Naval'. Firth was ready with a suitable appointment as soon as the Court approved the addition of Latin and French to the curriculum. His grasp of the development needs of the school was recognised as crucial to its early success and led the Court to take the unusual step of re-electing him to serve a second, consecutive term as Master with the same Wardens. He used his second term of office to set up a scheme for monitoring and examining the school and making its finances secure.

Formal inspection was provided twice yearly by the Rector of Stepney, a useful way of linking the school and its community together. The Company's involvement was improved by a rota of visitors from the members of the Court and by holding Quarter Day Courts at Ratcliffe. These meetings provided the opportunity for occasionally inspecting books and conducting viva voce tests. Prize-giving was instituted twice yearly in the chapel which was always full to overflowing with parents. For many years, the tradition of providing the boys with a bun and a glass of marsala was maintained and probably helped to make prize-giving memorable. By 1850, so many boys wanted to enter the school that the waiting list was temporarily restricted to 100 names.

Firth's solution to the school's indebtedness was to persuade the Court to make a loan to the charity, so that the debt to the East India Company could be paid off. The deal made sense, for the debt was costing five per cent interest, while the Company's investment, used to repay the debt, yielded three-and-a-half per cent at most. The establishment of two Gibson scholarships (commemorating the founder) for further study meant that the most academically gifted pupils could do more than just dream of Oxford spires and Cambridge courts. The Company had last helped members of its community to enjoy a university education with occasional bursaries to Oxford and Cambridge in the seventeenth century. The Gibson scholarships signified a renewal of one part of the Company's mission, but in an appropriate, modern context.

When Firth retired from office as Master in 1849 there were many plaudits for his character and achievements. He was praised for his 'discretion, judgement and ability' in 'remodelling and re-constituting the Grammar School at Ratcliffe; and more generally for his urbanity, kindness and constant attendance to business'. In 1851, to mark 25 years of service from his election as Under Warden in 1826, the Court voted that his portrait should be commissioned to hang in the Hall. (It was, alas, one of the casualties of the blitz in 1940.)

Firth's own scholastic achievements survived. Among his discoveries was the 'Vellum Book' which contain the Quarterage records from 1439 to 1524. In the same old chest, in the Beadle's apartments, were other treasures: the earliest Minute book of the Company dating from 1553, the Warden's accounts for the early years of the sixteenth century and the quarterage books up to 1622. Firth produced a manuscript catalogue of the Company's books and papers, listing the deeds relating to all its properties and those of Ratcliffe, Egham and Woodham Mortimer and including extracts from the wills which contained bequests to the Company or its charities. From all these sources he produced the first history of the Company, *Historical Memoranda*. It was very much a volume of its time, treating history as a science in which the facts, once they were all known and assembled, would speak for themselves. Firth presented a copy to each member of the Court and continued for some years to encourage the study of history at the Ratcliffe School by means of donating books to the embryonic school library. These included David Hume's *History of England* and Smollett and Hewson's *History and Description of London*.

Government intrusion into the affairs of City institutions and their trusts gathered momentum in the second half of the nineteenth century. In 1860, the Charity Commissioners carried out an investigation of the Ratcliffe Charity's rental and made a comparison with its income in 1836. The conclusion was that the charity was well placed to increase the scope of its work. The commissioners suggested that the charity should help the parish of Stepney by setting up a grammar school more centrally situated than the charity school at Ratcliffe, which was near the river in the far southwest of the parish. In practice, the Ratcliffe school was already developing its curriculum in the direction of becoming a fully-fledged grammar school but it was increasingly seen as being situated at a distance from its main catchment areas, Stepney, Bow and West Ham, and the rough character of the neighbourhood presented a threat to the safety of young boys.

In 1864, the school was investigated by Commissioners for Endowed Schools enquiring into the efficiency and potential of trust schools such as the Ratcliffe school. There was little doubt of demand locally for an extension of provision; the school's waiting list numbered over 300 applications. The outcome of the investigation was a recommendation in line with the view of the 1860 Charity Commission statement. The Court was not averse to expansion and, in November 1864, ordered a survey of the site to see how the school might be enlarged. It was agreed that 100 more places could be provided if a new building could be squeezed into the northern part of the site. This depended on gaining possession of two adjoining properties in Dunstan Place, which were leased by the Company to a leaseholder who could not at first be traced.

The decision to build was taken in January 1868. It took a comparatively short time to produce drawings and go out to tender. There was a year's delay because it was found that leaseholder was in New Zealand. The total cost was a little short of £3,000. At the laying of the foundation stone on 16 September 1869, a hymn, especially written for the occasion, was sung. The new upper school for 200 boys opened on 24 May 1870. The old buildings continued to be used by the lower school.

By this time yet more legislation had been passed to regulate endowed schools, in spite of a vigorous and united campaign to restrict the intervention of central government in what were seen, particularly in the City, as private trusts for the public good. The new Act required the submission to the Endowed Schools Commission of a scheme of management indicating the scope, size and admission arrangements for the school. German was new to the curriculum but, in spite of the best efforts of Cyrus Legg (Master 1872 and 1873) to promote music by the offer of instruments for a school band, the majority of his colleagues declared that music fostered conviviality and 'attracted those least disposed to study'. Music was deemed both unnecessary as a school subject and not contemplated by the founder, Nicholas Gibson.

In spite of this heavy-handed attitude, the boys were allowed treats. Buns and oranges were distributed to them at the new building's opening; most of the senior boys were allowed to visit the 1873 International Exhibition at the expense of the Company and a select few, probably the senior class, were occasionally invited to the gallery overlooking the room where the annual Livery dinner took place. One of the examples of the close personal links which a few members of the Court developed with the school is illustrated by the annual birthday greetings which the boys offered each March at the Quarterly Court, held at Ratcliffe, to Henry Capel. This custom continued from 1870 for the rest of his long life. He died aged 93 in 1887. Among his many manuscripts was a history of Ratcliffe.

Having successfully launched a new stage in the Ratcliffe school's long existence, the Court took the view, contrary to strong urging and advice from the Endowed Schools Commission, that it would be imprudent to consider creating a parallel school for girls. There were sound reasons to argue for financial prudence. The public reason against such a venture was that the 'locality is one where it would be undesirable to assemble girls'. Like the girls themselves and their increasingly determined champions, Henry Sidgwick, Canon F. D. Maurice, Barbara Bodichon and Emily Davies, the issue of secondary and higher education for girls would not go away.

The healthy condition of the Ratcliffe Charity's rental income, which continued to improve during the decade of the 1870s, made it difficult to put off indefinitely the consideration of making provision for girls. The effective use of educational charity funds had been a major objective of the the Endowed Schools Act and the Act had specifically sought to promote some transfer of funds to set up girls' secondary schools. In September 1877, the Education Committee of the Court produced a report on the feasibility of the Ratcliffe Charity being capable of making provision for girls. It was agreed that an annual surplus on the charity's account of £115, together with a small charge of £6, for each of 60 girls, would produce an adequate sum to sustain a small school.

Market research was not initially encouraging. In response to a press advertisement in February 1878, there were only 24 enquiries for 60 places. The site was of critical importance. It must be in a respectable area. Several places were investigated by the surveyor and Education Committee members and resulted in taking on the lease of 141 Mile End Road, already run as a school. The Company paid £200 for the goodwill and the fittings. From 12 applicants, Miss Sarah Chell, from the North London Collegiate School, one of the pioneering schools for girls, was chosen as the headmistress. She held a first class Cambridge teaching certificate and, though a difficult personality, she proved a first class leader, uncompromising in setting high standards for herself, her staff and the girls. A decade later in a letter to the Court she set out her views on the management of schools: 'teachers [are] ... taught how to teach, while the idle and incompetent ones are ruthlessly weeded out. Such management as this, drastic as it may appear, is the real secret of the unprecedented success of the girls' school'. When the school opened on 1 July 1878, there were 43 girls in two classes and one assistant mistress, Miss Evans. The curriculum was light, virtually featherweight on mathematics and science. Only arithmetic appeared alongside English grammar and literature, reading, writing, French, German, needlework and the rudiments of music. But the aim was to prepare girls for the Oxford and Cambridge local examinations which would open up to them further study, training for a career in teaching and the opportunity to compete by examination for a range of clerical grades in the Civil Service. It was a serious education and it already responded to the needs and aspirations of the middle classes in the East End of London. Celebrations at the end of the school's first year drew in the wives of members of the Court to view samples of the girls' needlework. During the school's second year, successes in the Cambridge locals and College of Preceptors' examinations resulted in a day's holiday. The school was full to overflowing with 80 girls crammed into accommodation which was hardly enough for the 60 planned places.

In 1880, the search for better accommodation resulted in a lease being taken on a handsome mid-century house at 86 Bow Road which had a double-sized site giving it a good yard with stables and a coach house. There were two conservatories and 'superior residential accommodation' for the resident headmistress. Initially, small alterations were made to allow for 150 girls but by 1884, the school's success made necessary the construction of extra classrooms on the site of the stables. The Court debated the expansion of the curriculum with some passion. In the end there was a narrow victory, after several amendments, for adding algebra and Latin, allowing an advanced class and increasing the numbers to 180. As a generous tribute to the school, the Court also provided the costs of a reunion of old girls and mistresses. Seven hundred attended.

Some of the increase in numbers was the result of widening admission to the school to girls from outside the parish of Stepney. Much of the increase, however, came from other schools in the area which could not compete. Nearby, the Coborn Girls' School, which had been re-founded in 1880, decided to close in the face of Coopers' Girls' competitive edge. It recommended its remaining girls go to the Coopers' school in May 1886. The Court faced a dilemma: once more the school had outgrown its premises.

Chapter nine

Part two: Surviving Change 1800–1870

THE COMPANY HAD other responsibilities demanding its attention apart from the complexities of the Egham Charity and the Ratcliffe School. One of these was William Alexander's bequest at Woodham Mortimer in Essex. This comprised an estate of just over 300 acres of arable and woodland. The income was used to provide upwards of 30 pensions, so it was a constant obligation on the Court to administer the property soundly and prudently.

The Woodham Mortimer estate came under scrutiny in 1825 when the Company's financial collapse forced the Court to take careful stock of all its possessions and responsibilities. As part of the investigations, Woodham Mortimer had been selected as a simple, but substantial item for research. James Firth undertook the task and revealed, for the first time in many generations, the exact holdings, the history of the rent charges, fines, timber surveys and sales, and repairs to the manor house and outbuildings.

The Committee on the Accounts, which produced the final report on the Woodham Mortimer estate, was trenchant in its comments on past failings. It was not the first time criticism had been recorded. In 1805, the Company's surveyor, John Dugleby, had commented on the neglect and waste of timber in 1755, when £256-worth was removed and 13 hedges grubbed out. The 1825 report added that there was no piece of woodland on the detached portion of the estate at Little Baddow which was in as good order as when the current lease was granted. Although the house itself was in good repair, in all an estimated £1,200 needed to be spent on repairs, but 'there is no timber on the farm for that purpose'. The list of short-comings in management went on to indicate that the property was under-insured, and the rent was too low. The lease, held since 1769 in the Codd family, had been granted in 1804 to Edward Codd's son for a fine of £400 and a rent of £212 and was to run for 30 years. By 1815, Codd was in arrears with his rent and two years later declared insolvent. For a few months in 1817, Codd's Chelmsford bankers ran the farm until the lease was assigned to William Hart and William Ferris. It was argued by the 1825 Committee that the fine was illegal, the rent too generous for such a well-situated farm and that there had been private agreements, presumably between Codd and the Court, which were quite inappropriate.

The report produced prompt action. A group of members from the Court travelled to Maldon where they stayed overnight and walked over to the farm to give notice of their visit of inspection on the next day. The outcome was approval for all necessary repairs, agreement with the tenant, William Hart, that any timber used must be replaced with new planting and, their most permanent decision, to commemorate the benefactor, William Alexander. Even at so late a date it was thought appropriate to record 'so splendid a Donation inducing in the minds of others equally well-disposed, similar acts of benevolence and generosity'. The form of the commemoration, a stone obelisk set on a platform bearing an inscription which names the donor, trustees and purpose of the bequest, was set up in 1826 opposite Woodham Mortimer Hall and set back a little from the main Chelmsford to Maldon turnpike. It provided a stately focus for a double avenue of elms and continued to be kept in repair and the inscription occasionally re-cut until 1943 when the estate was sold. To complete the new works, 23 iron posts, embossed with the Company's coat of arms, were ordered to define the boundaries of the estate. (A similar set of posts had been placed on the lands of the Egham Charity in Staines and Egham in 1817 after enclosure.)

After putting to rights many years of neglect, the Court made more frequent visits of inspection to Woodham Mortimer. Robert Carter was also a valuable link and used his knowledge of surveying to alert fellow Assistants to incipient problems. In 1835, he acted for the Company to settle the amount owed by the estate for tithe when it became possible to negotiate commutation of tithe for a rent charge. The advent of James Boyer as Clerk to the Company in 1843 established another link with Woodham Mortimer. He gave an organ to the new parish church which adjoined the Hall.

The practice of visiting the various parts of the Company's estates once every three years had been adopted in 1825 as part of the reform movement. Each summer, led by Carter, Algar and Firth, a deputation from the Court would visit, in turn, the Plaistow and Woolwich properties (which had been Henry Strode's endowment); then the London properties, and finally Woodham Mortimer. The land at Staines and Egham was inspected at the same time as the annual visit of the Master and Wardens to the school and almshouses, as ordered by the Chancery decree of 1828. This system went some way to avoid the long periods of drift, neglect and mismanagement which had characterised the eighteenth century.

It did not prevent all instances of maladministration. In 1847, there was another report on Woodham Mortimer very critical of the Court. It appeared that Hart's rent had not been increased as the 1825 report had suggested and that there had been certain impropriety in the way repairs and new building had been carried out. The estate was in debt because of the low rent and heavy repair bills which amounted to just short of £1,000. Improvement followed. The renewal of the lease was by public tender in 1851: it remained in the same family but was raised to £350. In 1855, the Company agreed to take advantage of a government scheme to subsidise the laying of land drains. In all, over 20,000 sections of drainage pipe were laid. Within two years, the Company felt able to increase the number of pensioners it paid from the estate by 10, making in all 50 who received £5 a year. In 1860, the amount was increased to £6 and the number, which had fallen, was kept at 34 pensioners, a restoration of the number supported from 1800 until the 1820s.

These pensions were referred to as the London pensions to distinguish them from pensions supported by either the Ratcliffe or the Egham charities. Since 1746, it had been the custom for each member of the Court in turn to select the successful candidate for a vacancy from a list of nominations. Qualifying rules also remained substantially the same, that the applicants must be of good character, usually over 70 years of age, have no other pension and in the definition used at Egham 'neither [be] or ever [have] been a common Beggar or maintained in a workhouse or received parochial relief'. This amounted to a definition of 'deserving poor'.

The qualifications for admittance to an almshouse were more restrictive than for the London pensioners. As part of the tidying up at Egham while the final verdict from the Chancellor was awaited, application forms were printed which defined eligibility, in terms which were the same as for out-pensioners, with the addition that candidates must be single and have no estate, salary, pension or certain income whatsoever. At Egham, the age limit was 60 and evidence was sought; either a baptismal certificate or an affidavit with witnesses. In addition, the Rector had to certify the candidate as a 'person of sober life and conversation…in every respect a proper and deserving object to partake of the late Henry Strode's charity'.

It was usual to avoid granting an almshouse to the really elderly in case they quickly became ill, unable to care for themselves and thus become a drain on the charity's funds. In 1844, Almsman Evans at Egham became insane. The Court ordered that he was to be removed if his friends or the parish could not nurse him. An 80-year-old applicant was granted an out-pension in 1852, instead of an almshouse. When the daughter of a Ratcliffe almsman, who had fallen ill, neglected him, she was ordered by the Court to pay one shilling a week to cover the cost of his nursing or he would be removed. In 1864, an awkward situation developed when a deranged almsman had to be removed from Egham to the Windsor workhouse and Mr Beattie, the schoolmaster, continued to pay the man's six shillings a week pension. It was against the rules of the charity: the Court ruled Mr Beattie's action wrong but relented when told that otherwise the man would have been discharged.

There are many such sad and harrowing examples of the distress and anguish which overcame the elderly poor. There was little room for sentiment where the pressure of need on very limited resources was great. The number of applicants (between 15 and 21) for each vacancy points to the fact that the world beyond the almshouse or charity pension was much harsher than within. Nor was destitution confined to people in the lower economic strata of society. Insecurity was a fact of life for most when the unexpected death of the main breadwinner could plunge a prosperous, middle class family into penury. In business, the risks were great, particularly during the frenzy of speculative investment in the 1840s and 1850s on railway building both at home and abroad. James Firth suffered serious losses after his retirement in 1855 as the principal clerk in the Town Clerk's Office at Guildhall. His embarrassment was such that he sought to resign from the Court but he was persuaded to remain and unconditionally granted £100 to ameliorate his situation. Another master from an earlier date who fell on hard times was Gregory Pember. In 1803, he resigned from the Court in order to apply for the vacant post of Beadle. It had the added advantage of accommodation. On his death in 1808, his widow, Elizabeth, became a £10 pensioner of the Company.

Although the rules seem harsh by later standards, there were occasional treats at Christmas and on special days. The Ratcliffe pensioners each received an extra five shillings when the Prince of Wales married Princess Alexandra of Denmark in 1863. When the Company poor box was generously full, there was a supplement, usually half-a-crown, added to each London pension. Sherry and port were used, sometimes too liberally, as medicine at Ratcliffe, supplied by Henry Capel (Warden 1840, Master 1868). A major advance at Ratcliffe came in 1865, when it was decided that couples could be admitted to the almshouses. There was no express exclusion by the founders and three instances were found in 1555. The historical precedent was sufficient to head off objections.

In 1858, the Company augmented its own pensions from a fund set up in 1844. The initiative to extend the Company's almshouses or increase its number of out-pensioners came from Robert Carter, recently made an Assistant and son of the Robert Carter who had steered the Company so tactfully through its constitutional crisis in the mid 1820s. The younger man was as vigorous and determined as his father and wanted to take advantage of the Company's greater financial security once it was certain of victory over the East India Company in the dispute about the lease of the wharf at Ratcliffe. In December 1844, £100 was invested, and added to in subsequent years until 1857, when an Annuities Committee was set up to review all the Company's pensions. Its members were the Master, Wardens and Robert Carter. From the accumulated fund, six new pensions of £10 a year were created, the fund was to be topped-up annually with £100 of which £60 was to pay the pensions and £40 was for investment. There was also a somewhat distant project for providing four more almshouses, but it remained in abeyance and was then forgotten as the need for almshouses diminished in the latter part of the century.

The Annuities Committee made administrative improvements. The system of nomination by each member of the Court in turn was ended and instead, vacancies for pensions and almshouses were advertised in Stepney. A system of 'promotion' was also introduced: existing pensioners could apply for one of the Company's higher pensions and have preference over new applicants. Six new annuities of £20 a year were set up in 1858 for liverymen. By 1870, the pension list comprised 30 pensions at £10 for freemen and their widows; a further 12, also at £10, for liverymen and widows and six at £20. The improvements reflected the buoyant state of the Company's finances.

A commitment to maintaining and improving pensions gave urgency to the proper management of the Company's property. The reforms in finance and administration which accompanied the Livery's successful constitutional challenge in the 1820s, contributed greatly to the Company's ability to manage its affairs more effectively than in the recent past. It became the custom to bring all bills to the monthly Court meeting for approval. A refinement from 1831 was the checking of these accounts by the Master and Wardens before the meeting. In 1837, three accounts were opened at the Bank of England for the Company and for the Ratcliffe and Egham charities. The books were audited in January and June and a closer eye was kept on the Ratcliffe accounts by holding quarterly Courts at Ratcliffe. Egham, too, came into line under Dr Jeans' successor, the Reverend George Adolphus Hopkins. He submitted detailed monthly statements.

The resignation of the Clerk, James Smith, in 1840, gave another opportunity to overhaul the organisation of the Company. Instead of making a straight replacement of the Clerk, the post was divided into two and a solicitor-clerk was appointed as well as a clerk-administrator and accountant.

It was a recognition of the expansion of business, of the need to be pro-active and of the importance of the Company's property. The solicitor-clerk was Alexander Weir, who remained until 1870. The other Clerk was a liveryman, James Boyer, who remained in office until his death in 1863 and was succeeded by his son, John. In all, five Boyers served the Company and gave continuity until 1927 either as Clerk, assistant clerk or solicitor.

James Boyer's appointment in 1840 was accompanied by more research into the archives, led by James Firth, to produce a definitive rental, listing the title deeds of properties and allocating their income correctly, in some instances, for the first time in centuries, to the charity which they endowed. The discovery was made that the Fenchurch Street property was part of the Ratcliffe Charity's endowment and that the Cloker bequest in Miles Lane had not been correctly apportioned between the Company and Ratcliffe. This matter became the subject of a Court of Chancery case. Judgment given, in 1844, allocated the income to Ratcliffe and the Company in the proportion of eight elevenths and three elevenths respectively.

There were plenty of opportunities for the Company to expand its property holdings in the years after 1800. London's size and wealth grew spectacularly as the century advanced. The successive spates of new building which produced the grandeur of Nash's Regent's Park scheme, the widening of streets in the City, new bridges and new offices all provided opportunities for speculation. The building of the new London Bridge destroyed not only St Michael's, Crooked Lane, which had been the venue for centuries of the annual reading of Henry Cloker's will, but it also cleared away one of the Company's Miles Lane houses. With the compensation, of almost £2,000, new freeholds were purchased at Ratcliffe and long leases taken on cottages on the Dover Road in Southwark and in Little Tower Street.

The advent of railways, new roads, and other industrial construction, enhanced the value of the Egham Charity's property. There were ten proposed railways which in 1846, might go through the charity's lands at Staines and Plaistow. Almost £1,000 was eventually paid for four acres next to the new railway bridge over the Thames at Staines and £800 was paid as compensation at Plaistow by the Gravesend Railway Company. Plaistow also provided a windfall from the gravel digging in 1860–61 when nine acres of land was exploited to construct a main sewer which crossed the Charity's land. The price agreed was £250 an acre, part of which was granted to the leaseholder. The consequences for the Egham Charity were a dramatic change in fortune from being in debt to the Company after the rebuilding in 1828 and 1839, to having a modest annual surplus and £1,200 invested in Government stock.

These developments encouraged the Company to look to the future when both the Plaistow and Staines land might become more valuable as building land. The coming of railways had stimulated the growth of Staines while the creation of the Becton gas works had caused new roads to be built across the Plaistow estate by the Gas and Lighting Company. In 1875, the Company bought 30 acres of land next to the Egham property at Plaistow but also giving frontages on to the new roads. It was let on short-notice terms. At Staines, the Company bought road frontages along the Ashford-Staines toll road and along the Staines-Laleham highway with a view to future building.

In spite of the astonishing growth of London during these years, property ownership was a hazardous form of investment. Accident and fashion could play an important role in determining what were good and bad properties to hold. The Company could not act quickly, as a business speculator was able, to off-load property which was likely to decline in value, nor was it wealthy enough to have surplus cash to buy investments in anticipation of a rising trend. Much of its property was old and with years of neglectful management, much had decayed in spite of covenants on leases stipulating lessee responsibility for repairs and dilapidations at the end of a lease.

One of the more extreme examples of neglect was an estate of small houses in Hatfield Street and adjoining courts near Goswell Road. The property was already judged as 'ruinous' in 1828 and, in spite of the Company's new vigour and regular inspections, it proved impossible for the Court to regain control over the lessee and his numerous tenants to carry out repairs. In their turn, the tenants disappeared and could not be found. When the lease expired in 1833, the Clerk managed to track down the lessee's son and obtained formal surrender of the lease but no compensation for dilapidations. There ensued a nine-year struggle to lease or sell the property, but it was an unattractive area and the Court was at first disinclined to concede a lower sale price than £2,000. Unfortunately, Hatfield Street was within one of the notorious London liberties, that of Golden Lane, outside the jurisdiction of any ward. It had, therefore, become a safe haven for criminals of all kinds, thieves, pimps, extortioners, and racketeers. The longer the Court delayed a decision, the more the property suffered depredations. Anything movable or detachable was stolen, particularly the lead. The sewers became blocked, and rubbish accumulated. So bad did the area become that the parishioners of St Luke's petitioned the Court to take the first offer it received and relieve them of a local nuisance. There was some prospect of a sale for factory development and at length, perhaps a little shamed by the pleading of St Luke's representations, an offer of £1,500 was accepted for the freehold. It was an amount which had been rejected a few years earlier.

There were other potential 'Hatfield Streets' in the Company's portfolio of properties but none was allowed to get so out of hand. The older properties at Ratcliffe were liable to overcrowding and subletting so that, by the 1840s, the tenements off Broad Street (Ratcliffe Highway) built in the 1790s as Dunstan Place and Burlington Mews contained 'a low class of tenant'. According to a survey in 1842, the inadequacy of sewage disposal and drainage caused 'soil to run into the yards'. In spite of being served with notices of offences under the sanitary laws, the Court dithered and delayed a decision about rebuilding for forty years. Some minimal improvements kept the Company just within the law. In 1856, it responded to a damning report of the Commissioners for Sewers and removed the old wooden privies in the forecourt of Burlington Mews. At a cost of £150, two new privies and a communal washhouse with a copper for heating water were provided. Otherwise, essential repairs were all that was needed to keep these wretched houses standing and fully occupied. When the lease was put out to tender in 1877, the Company received 35 offers. There were still profits to be made from desperate people seeking cheap accommodation.

It was fortunate that much of the Company's Ratcliffe property was alongside the river, with wharfage and warehousing which were in great demand as trade of all kinds, river, coastal and global grew rapidly. Equally fortunate were the reliable lessees who replaced the East India Company and had the capital to strengthen the wharves to take steamships and their heavier cargoes. With increased values attached to Ratcliffe's City properties in Fenchurch Street, Miles Lane and Upper Thames Street, the charity paid off its debt to the East India Company and by 1854, had an annual surplus of almost £900. It was therefore able to admit an extra 50 boys to the school in 1859, bringing the number up to 200.

Two riverside properties, which might have expected to flourish and profit from the mid-century burst of commercial and industrial activity along the Thames, were public houses, one on Stone Stairs, Ratcliffe (the New England Lighthouse), and the Bell Watergate Inn at Woolwich. Both suffered badly because the trades on which they depended declined in the face of competition from new industry. The seaborne trade in coal, which had provided them in the past with dusty, thirsty coal hauliers as customers, was transferred to rail transport by the 1860s. Railways also killed off the trade of watermen who favoured the Bell Watergate. The New England lost its licence in 1872; the Bell had a new tenant who survived by smartening up his business and providing a 'luncheon' window, an 1860s version of a take-away.

Property in the City itself proved to be more profitable and less troublesome than the outlying parts of the Company's estates. Where there was also a reliable lessee who was able to offer investment in the property which increased its value, the Company also benefited from increased rents. The Little Tower Street premises were described in 1815 as being 'most eligibly situated in the immediate vicinity of the new Custom-house and Commercial sale-rooms, and an easy distance only from the docks'. One of these properties was leased by Henry Capel in 1828 for his wholesale wine business and was kept in first class order. In 1847, Capel negotiated an extension to his lease so that he could invest over £1,000 in improvements. He sub-let to a wholesale grocer and soon re-couped his outlay while the Company's rent doubled.

Investment in government stocks became an increasingly important part of the Company's wealth. Purchases began in 1804 as a result of the income produced from the lottery rents and £5,500 had accumulated by 1830. Banfield's £1000 bequest to the Ratcliffe Charity, received only after many delays in 1826, was held in government funds rather than being laid out in property as was normal in past times. These investments gave the Company greater flexibility in managing its affairs. When, for example, the Egham Charity's money ran out before the 1839 rebuilding was completed, first the Ratcliffe Charity and later the Company, transferred stock on loan to Egham until compensation from the South Western Railway Company restored the Charity's balance. Similarly, the Ratcliffe charity was helped with a loan of stock to enable it to repay the loan which secured the surrender of the East India Company's lease of the saltpetre wharf at Ratcliffe.

After 1818, however, there was a new factor supervising, restricting and restraining the activities of charities. This was the Charity Commission which, by the Charities Act, required a return from charities indicating the nature, value and income of their property. It was generally unwelcome and seen as intrusive government interference, detrimental to liberty and to the special privileges of City institutions such as livery companies. The influence of the Commission was felt in the Egham Chancery case and in the subsequent diligence with which the Court conducted the annual inspection of the Charity and its lands. It was a great contrast to the outcome of the Chancery cases brought against the Company in respect of the Egham Charity in 1707 and 1747. In both instances, the Court's requirements were soon forgotten and then ignored.

The vigour of City opposition to further parliamentary encroachments on their freedom to administer trusts was demonstrated between May 1845 and June 1846. The rest of the country was absorbed by the violence of the debate over the repeal of the Corn Laws in the wake of the Irish Famine. In the City, the political temperature ran high over another charities Bill. Three livery companies briefed Counsel while the Coopers relied on their solicitor-clerk, Weir, to find means to bring in amendments in the House of Lords. There was great indignation when the Lords refused admittance to the Companies' representatives at the Committee stage and refused to take any evidence at the bar of the House. Further outrage was felt by ancient City institutions that the Universities of Oxford and Cambridge were exempted from the jurisdiction of the new Bill.

A committee of the Court, composed of its most respected members, was given the task of drawing up a petition to Parliament and of lobbying the City's MPs. James Firth was responsible for putting the Company's case. He argued that the Coopers in common with over 70 other livery companies, had been entrusted with gifts and bequests by members in times past because of the strong sense of brotherhood within the Company. This fraternal bond provided the surety that the donors' intentions would continue to be honoured. No outside interference was needed.

The combined efforts of the companies impressed the Prime Minister, Sir Robert Peel, and he allowed debate. In so doing, the Bill ran out of time and suffered further delay after the Easter recess, in 1846. When the vote was taken in June, the Bill was lost by a single vote. Parliament was by this time engulfed in the final stages of the Corn Laws' repeal and the defeat of the government followed swiftly.

Whatever the merits of the livery companies' case, there is no doubt that the earlier legislation which established the Charity Commission had been a spur to better management of property and funds held in trust. The Coopers' Company followed advice to synchronise the timing of sub-leases with that of the main lease. Neglect of this principle in the early years of the nineteenth century had produced a chaotic situation especially at Ratcliffe, where properties were increasingly sub-divided as they moved down market. Other advice from the Charity Commission was to advertise leases and invite tenders in order to improve the price. Several times in the past there had been too cosy a relationship between lessees and members of the Court. This was particularly so when leases were granted to members of the Company. The East India Company lease and subsequent sub-lease at Ratcliffe in 1770–74 remained a solemn warning against such entanglements.

The Charity Commission also supervised the sale of properties, the investment of the proceeds of sale and compensation payments. None of the windfalls from railway building or road widening could be used for revenue spending. It had to be invested in property or secure funds to increase revenue from its interest. Periodic returns had to be made to the Commission, a requirement which ensured more systematic record keeping and probably alerted the Court to the potential of some properties and the liability of others.

The Commission's permission had to be sought before the contract for gravel-digging on the Egham Charity's land at Plaistow could be completed. The Company had to ensure that any income was invested for the benefit of Egham. In 1860, a return was made comparing the rent on each property in 1836 with that of the current year. Accounts also had to be submitted on request. In 1857, the previous four years' accounts were required and led to the Commission querying the heavy loans being made to the Ratcliffe and Egham charities by the Company. The reply that it was to pay for extensive repairs seems to have been satisfactory.

An investigation of the Company's records revealed to the Commission the existence of four small loan charities set up by members between 1586 and 1635. They totalled £60 and were designed to help young coopers set up in business by lending money to purchase equipment. The Company argued that they were subsumed in its own charitable gifts. These tiny charities passed from the Company's control in 1893, when £50 worth of Consols were given to the City Parochial Foundation.

The Court was always cautious in responding to external appeals for charitable help. It argued that it had its own responsibilities and indeed, it could claim a considerable expansion of its charitable work by means of more and better out-pensions. However, the many appeals by which the philanthropic middle classes sought to ameliorate the worst impact of industrial change were not entirely unheeded by the Court. Responding to a patriotic cause created no difficulty. In 1804, it gave £10 to the Ward of Bassishaw, where the Hall was situated, for the Ward Volunteers against the threat of a French invasion. At the onset of the Crimean War, 50 years later, it contributed 20 guineas to help the wounded and dependents of those killed 'in the East'. Other exceptional gifts were towards the relief of distress in Lancashire, first, in 1826, when hand-loom weavers were being made destitute by the use of power looms; and again, in 1862, when the cotton industry was deprived of raw cotton by the blockade of the Confederacy ports in the American civil war. Appeals to contribute to the Duke of York's column and a statue of the Duke of Wellington were rejected. Instead, the Court gave £20 to the poor of Stepney.

The social diary of the Company assumed a regular pattern by the 1830s. The main dinner continued to be held on Lord Mayor's Day, 9 November, and a small committee of the Court made the arrangements. The old custom of electing Stewards to oversee and provide the cost of the dinner had long been a source of friction. With the growth in the size of the Livery it became impracticable, so the custom developed that the Company would subsidise the dinner. Early in the century they were modest affairs costing nine shillings a head (for example in 1807 and 1811) and were kept going by Assistants taking turns to act as Stewards. There was no dinner in 1823 and in 1828 for lack of Stewards. One liveryman who refused to pay his share of the expense as a Steward was taken to court by the Company and won his case with costs. The costs alone would easily have paid for the dinner. This incident brought the old custom to an end. Thereafter, the system of paying a fine instead of serving as Steward was used as the means of keeping open the pathway for a liveryman to be elected, in due turn, to the Court. Refusal to pay the Steward's fine usually closed off any advancement to the Court.

For many years, the November Livery dinner was held at either the London or Albion Tavern. The numbers remained steady at 160 but with places laid for a few more. The room was decked with the Company's banners, its own coat of arms, the City of London arms, the sword and mace and the Union flag. The banners increased as members gained distinction in the City serving as Sheriff and Lord Mayor.

The meal began at 5pm, a couple of hours later than the dinner-time of the 1790s but the introduction of gas lighting made the later time possible. Entertainment assumed a new importance with the engagement of singers and piano, which replaced the woodwind and brass ensembles of the previous century. A few light ballads must have been a welcome interlude in the long, heavy dinner and before a toast list which seldom had fewer than 15 items.

The general behaviour of the diners seems to have improved in line with a refinement in manners among society at large. Only one unpleasant incident was recorded when, in 1838, a liveryman the worse for drink attempted to throw two decanters out of the window. The police were called but the Court imposed only a temporary ban on the man's attendance at Livery functions.

The Livery dinner on Election Day had had a chequered history and had often been the first victim of financial stringency. No dinner was held between 1816 and 1824. It was revived by Abraham Algar and James Firth in

1825 and by 1830 it had become a cold collation for those who had attended the Common Hall election. For three shillings a head, the Albion Tavern in Aldersgate Street provided veal, a round of beef, ham, bread, cheese and porter. Regular Election Day dinners were not revived until 1868.

Court dinners, following the monthly Court meeting, fluctuated according to the Company's financial health and the preferences of those who dominated the Court at any one time. In the early years of the century they were provided from the pockets of the Master and Wardens. In 1814, the full cost, including cleaning up the next day at the Hall, was calculated and produced a fit of economy. Guests were to be limited to two, butchers' meat reduced in quantity to 25 pounds and the soup course was removed to achieve a saving of 20 shillings. But such attempts at frugality never lasted. The typical Court dinner in the 1830s cost 15 or 16 shillings a head and included port, sherry, bucellas (a sweet wine from Lisbon), two rounds of champagne, followed by tea, coffee and brandy. Small wonder that Robert Carter's proposal to serve no refreshments on Court days met with a decisive defeat.

A feature was introduced to the social calendar in the 1840s. This was the summer dinner for the Court and its guests, who included ladies. It became the custom to go out of the City either down the Thames to the Ship, the Trafalgar or Crown and Sceptre at Greenwich or to Blackwall which was still a pleasant rural setting. Richmond came into favour in the 1850s when the docks, railways and gas works had despoiled the lower reaches of the river. When the Crystal Palace was removed to Sydenham from Hyde Park, it too came into favour for a pleasant summer evening dinner. Until the 1870s, these dinners included the schoolmasters from Ratcliffe and Egham and several of the Company's principal leaseholders.

There were other occasional celebrations when City institutions gave a national lead in celebrating a major event. In 1802, the livery companies took part in a general thanksgiving for the Peace of Amiens which proved but a temporary pause in the European war against Napoleon. The Company was indirectly involved in premature peace celebrations in 1814 after Napoleon had been consigned to exile in Elba. In July that year, the Prince Regent hosted a great banquet at Guildhall in honour of the leaders of England's two main allies, the King of Prussia and the Emperor of Russia. Because the Coopers' Hall was next door to Guildhall, the Company's kitchens and plate were used.

There seems to have been muted enthusiasm for royal occasions. The Court rebuked Dr Jeans for spending £7 on illuminations at the Egham Charity to mark the Prince Regent's coronation. It may have been more a reaction to the troublesome schoolmaster than an expression of anti-royalism. When the

18-year-old Queen Victoria visited Guildhall to mark her accession in 1837, the Court refused an invitation to pay for a traditional standing along the royal route. There was quite a different reaction in 1863 when the beautiful Princess Alexandra of Denmark was given a rapturous reception in the City at the time of her marriage to the Prince of Wales. The Company held a special meeting of the Livery to approve addresses of loyalty to the Queen, the Prince, the Princess and her parents. They were written on vellum by Mr Torre, calligrapher and master at the Ratcliffe School. Both the Company's schools were granted a holiday for the royal wedding day.

For almost 60 years, the Company had played no significant role in the political affairs of the City. Then, in 1835, a newly admitted liveryman, William Thornborrow, asked the Court if it would also admit David Salomons, the Sheriff elect. The pair were members of the Jewish community in the City and two of a group who were seeking office in City government. The group had been encouraged in its efforts to remove discriminatory laws barring Jews from holding civic office by advice given by Lord Denman to the City Corporation in 1831. Lord Denman argued that Jews could be admitted to office by using an oath which would be binding on conscience though not specifically Christian in form. Salomons was the leader of this movement. A successful underwriter, he had founded the London and Westminster bank in 1832 and felt sufficiently secure professionally to spearhead an assault on the remaining old discriminatory practices.

The Company welcomed Salomons, who expressed his pleasure in correspondence with the Master at the warmth and friendship he had been shown. He was duly admitted as Sheriff and honoured by the Company with a special dinner at the Albion Tavern following the swearing-in ceremony. On the following day, Coopers accompanied him in the Lord Mayor's procession: the first time they had done so since Sir Peter Esdaile was Lord Mayor in 1777.

The next year, 1838, found Coopers again prominent in the celebrations of Lord Mayor's day. Thomas Johnson, a liveryman since 1814 and Alderman for Portsoken Ward was sworn in as Sheriff. He, too, was feted with a dinner along the same lines as Salomons' dinner. But on this occasion the Company had had more forewarning and hired a barge so that the Coopers could make a good show in the Lord Mayor's river procession to Westminster. Coloured ribbons and satin bows costing £10 were purchased to decorate the barge.

When Johnson became Lord Mayor in 1840, £70 was voted for the extra costs of Lord Mayor's Day. The experience of the Innholders' Company the previous year was used to determine what should be the proper contribution of the Coopers' Company to the procession. Coaches were hired at 25 shillings each for the land procession from the Hall to the Tower where the Lord Mayor embarked for the river procession to and from Westminster, disembarking on his return at Blackfriars. On this occasion the Company shared a barge with the Tallow Chandlers using the ribbons and bows it had purchased two years earlier and adding its banners and those of its members who had been Lord Mayor or Sheriff. For the land procession, the coachmen and horses had ribbons and cockades. A dinner at the London Tavern completed the celebrations.

An interval of 15 years followed before David Salomons attained the Mayorality. During this time, his attempts to gain office as an Alderman, as the necessary preliminary to becoming Lord Mayor, were frustrated by the requirements of the oath. He was elected for Aldgate Ward in 1835 and for Portsoken Ward in 1844 but could not take up his office. It was only after Parliamentary legislation opened public office to Jews in 1846, that he was elected and took his place as Alderman for Cordwainer Ward. His personal success was celebrated by the Company with a dinner at which he was given the full credit for leading the campaign to remove a shameful barrier. His appreciation of the Company's sentiments was genuine. He wrote the following day of his feelings: 'Few can hope, much less expect to receive so great a compliment...I will endeavour in the new career opened to me to merit [the Coopers'] good opinion...to prove myself in all respects a good, useful citizen'. The lack of rancour he displayed at being so talented, yet so long frustrated, is remarkable.

Salomons' turn to be Lord Mayor came in 1855. He was the first Jewish chief magistrate of the City. The same order of procession was made as for Thomas Johnson but there was an additional silk banner designed to include the Union and French flags, a reference to the alliance in the Crimean War. Lord Mayor's Day began with breakfast at the Mansion House. The Court and the Company's officers took their place in the procession sporting extra ribbons and favours and accompanied by a military band. The day was wet, but all except the poor Beadle up on his box, were protected inside their coaches. For the first time, the Company printed special programmes of the order of the procession and the day's events. The Court granted both schools a holiday. The Ratcliffe pupils were soon able to greet the Lord Mayor when he attended the Christmas Quarterly Court at the school and presented the half-yearly prizes in the chapel.

Two other members of the Company gained high civic office during these mid-Victorian years. They were David Stone a 'professional City man' and

THE WORSHIPFUL COMPANY OF COOPERS

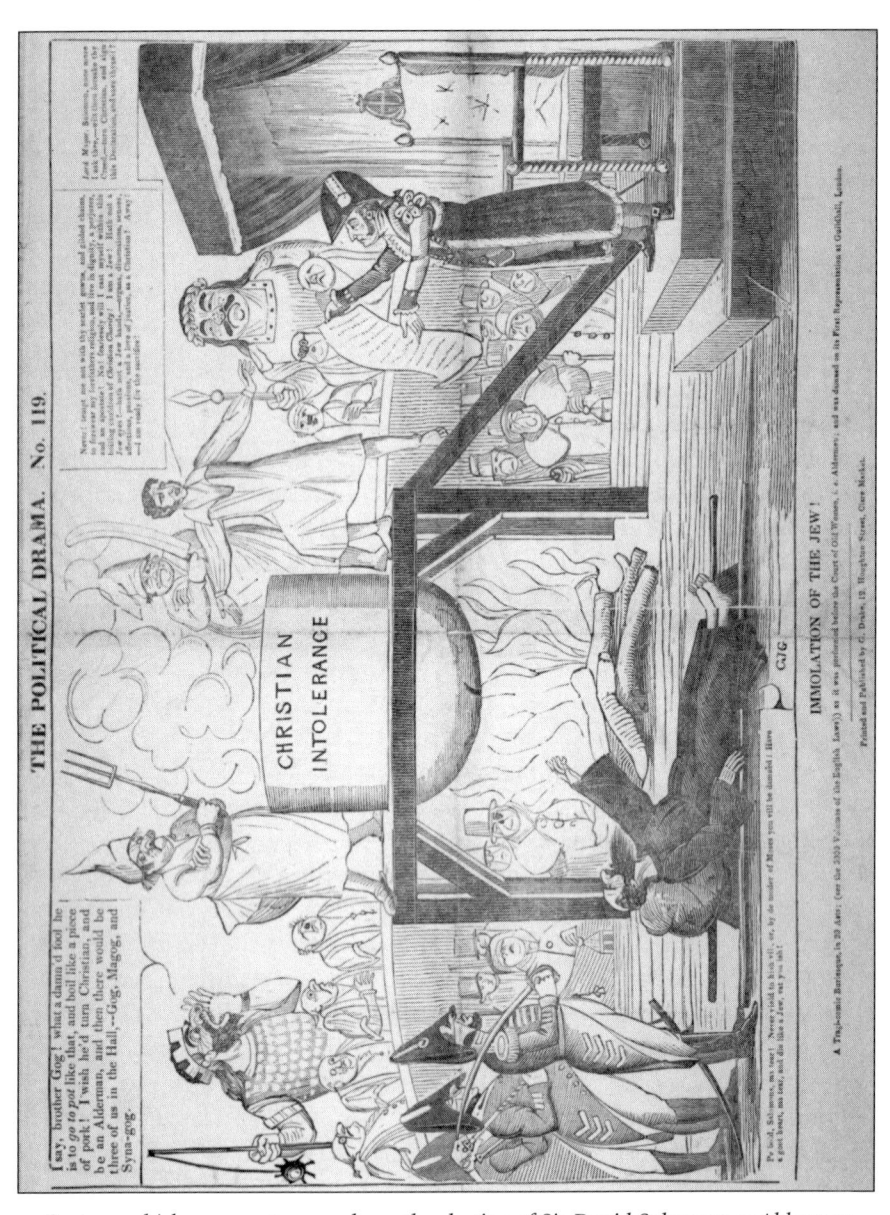

Cartoon which comments savagely on the election of Sir David Salomons as Alderman and his subsequent debarring from taking office because, as a Jew, he was deemed unable to take the oath. In 1835, he had served as Sheriff, being allowed to take the oath under a judgement of Lord Denman. This was subsequently reversed on appeal and it was only in 1855 when a special Act of Parliament was passed that this particular piece of discrimination was removed. (Catholics had been admitted to public office since 1829.)

Edgar Breffit who aspired to City office as a result of business successes. Both used their membership of the Company as a vehicle for attaining civic office and expected to be advanced out of turn from the Livery to the Court. Stone was, for many years, a member of the Metropolitan Board of Works, Treasurer of the Honourable Artillery Company, and of St Thomas' Hospital and the last Principal of Clifford's Inn. He was a member of three other livery companies and became Master of each. He was admitted to the Coopers' Company in 1868, the year when he became Sheriff. His choice of the Coopers' was probably influenced by the fact that he was Alderman for Bassishaw Ward where the Hall was situated.

Stone's admission to the Livery may have provoked debate in the Court about the principle of precedence in elections to the Court. It was not a new issue. In 1778, a resolution was passed that no liveryman should be promoted out of turn simply because he had been elected an Alderman or Sheriff. Robert Carter, the younger, returned to the matter with a more absolute proposal: that no-one should be elected to the Court out of turn. It was opposed with some passion by Warden Bristow, who argued that strict precedence would prevent the Court promoting men of talent, energy and influence before they reached their dotage. Given that there was no age of retirement from the Court, its membership tended to be elderly. Bristow proved a particularly able Warden, energetic and with the intelligence to recognise that the governance of the Company needed a few more robust and vigorous members like himself. His argument won the day and was aptly illustrated when the Masters elected in 1869 and 1870 died in office, and the next Court vacancy following this debate went to John Hazard, an 87-year-old who was also blind and living with his son in Cambridge. He declined his place.

In 1871, Stone was asked for his banner to add to the Company's collection of shrieval and mayoral banners belonging to its distinguished members. He responded that he was merely a liveryman of the Company; that it was true, he had presented his banner to the other Companies to which he belonged as a member of their Courts; and that perhaps he might expect to be made a member of the Coopers' Court as he was their Ward's Alderman. His hint was taken and in February 1872 he was elected out of turn, to the Court. He subsequently presented the Company with his banner. His turn as Master came in 1874 and coincided with his election as Lord Mayor a few months later.

For Stone's procession the Company hired the band of the Victoria Rifles, provided the Beadle with a new gown and the Ward with money to purchase suitable decorations for Basinghall Street which was to be the first stretch of

The old school at Ratcliffe shortly before it was pulled down in 1898.

the processional route. As on previous occasions, the Company's schools were granted a holiday. At Ratcliffe, each boy also received a shilling, wine and cake. It is from Stone's mayorality that the convention of holding the Livery dinner shortly after Lord Mayor's Day came about, thus allowing the new Lord Mayor to be the Company's guest of honour.

Edgar Breffit's election as Sheriff followed quite quickly. He had been the leaseholder of Free Trade Wharf (fomerly the saltpetre wharf and then East India Wharf) at Ratcliffe for 20 years. Since 1865, he had been a Common Councillor for Dowgate Ward and he sought admittance to the Coopers' Company probably because of his long business links. He expressed the wish to restore to the ceremony of swearing-in the Sheriffs, some of the pomp and display of former times. When he became Sheriff in 1875, the Company obliged him with a good display of banners, coaches and a band to accompany him to Guildhall. On Lord Mayor's Day, the Company again joined the procession to Westminster, this time escorting both the new Sheriff and the ex-Lord Mayor, Alderman Stone.

Like Alderman Stone, Breffit was elected to the Court out of turn, a mere three years after his admission to the Company. The murmurs of dissent which had accompanied Stone's early promotion were far less muted and produced a formal protest to the Court from the Society of the Livery, pointing out that there were 83 liverymen senior to Breffit. There were some misgivings on the Court itself, perhaps due to anxiety about Breffit's business dealings. Breffit's civic career advanced, in 1877, when he became Alderman for the Ward of Cheap. His success was greeted with the customary dinner which included the City MPs (one of whom, Roger Eykyn, was a Cooper), the Sheriffs and Masters of several other Companies. Unfortunately, Breffit did not live long enough to become Lord Mayor. He died in 1882, two years after serving as Master of the Coopers' Company.

The Company's most valuable property in London was its Hall. Although major repairs were carried out in 1800, 1806 and 1813 when a strong room was built, it proved a difficult building to adapt to the comforts of modern sanitary appointments, hot water and effective heating. A newly-patented hot water apparatus to heat the Court room proved very temperamental. The supplier attended on the Court when the members had reached a point of desperation at the cold discomfort of meetings, and suggested a new arrangement of pipes with a furnace in the cellar instead of relying on pipes leading from the fireplace in the Court room. He was told to take it all away. Major repairs in 1834, which included the kitchen, a new waiting room and a new ceiling in the Court room cost over £800. Within two years there was more disturbance as a new sewer was constructed in Basinghall Street and the Company wrangled with the Commissioner for Sewers for adequate compensation

The possibility of the sale of the Hall first arose in 1840. There was an opportunity to negotiate with the Corporation of London which wanted space on the Guildhall site to provide offices for the Metropolitan Police. The Court agreed that if it were not restricted by law from disposing of its assets, £6,000 would build 'a respectable hall with suitable offices'. The Company's Surveyor, George Smith, suggested £15,000 would be a good price for the site but it proved much too optimistic and the talks fizzled out. There were other brief and tentative approaches from the Corporation in subsequent years, James Firth being used as intermediary by the Sheriff's office in 1843, but discussions made no progress. The Company settled in to continual repairs and to increasing the creature comforts of the Hall. The gift of family portraits by Mrs Waldo Astley provided an opportunity for repairing, regilding and rehanging other portraits. A new reception room was created and the cellar was kept well stocked. From 1822 there was a stock book in which wine was ordered and new stocks entered. The taste of the day was for port, brandy and sherry in preference to table wine. Later in the century champagne became popular but 'claret [was] so little consumed that it may be disregarded'.

There were changes at Guildhall in 1860 when the Town Clerk's house next to the Company's Hall was pulled down to make room for offices. The Company had to protect its right to light and thoughts again turned to selling the Hall. There had recently been pressure from the Livery at Common Hall for more use to be made of the building by letting it for occasional functions. In 1860, it was used for quarterly wool auctions and for a parliamentary election in 1865. There was certainly a body of opinion in the Company which thought a more modern, stream-lined Hall, with one or two floors of offices for rent would be a sensible solution.

Talks with the Corporation of London about selling the site or a part of it began in 1864 and continued at intervals for almost four years. The delays were caused in part by the innate slowness of decision-making of each organisation and in part by the Company's inability to stick to a decision once it had been made. There were four options: to agree terms with the Corporation and sell the site and seek another building plot within the City for a new hall; to sell part of the site to the Corporation and use the proceeds for a more compact hall on part of the Basinghall Street site; to retain the whole site, and develop its potential for offices as well as a new hall; to renovate the existing building and include office accommodation to rent.

The last of these options was ruled out when the surveyor discovered that the foundations were of timber planking. The first option was tried at the outset but only one reply was received in response to an advertisement for a suitable building plot. Many members were relieved that there was a good reason to allow heart to rule head and keep the Company's Hall on its original site. When no agreement could be reached on the value of part of the site, the Company decided to 'go it alone' and began demolition and clearing the rear of the site in September in 1865. Then came delays because of disagreement over compensation for the widening of Basinghall Street to take a new sewer.

At length, after hesitation and flirting with alternative plans, the old Hall came down during the summer, 1867. In September, the Court and Clerk moved to offices in Gresham's Buildings at the southern end of Basinghall Street and agreement was reached with the Corporation to sell part of the site for £21,000.

Tenders for the new building came in at £4,600 and the foundation stone of the Company's third Hall was laid on 7 January 1868 followed by dinner for the Court, former Wardens, the chaplains and schoolmasters at Ratcliffe and Egham and the MPs for the City of London. To mark the event a silver medal was struck for members of the Court. After the hitches and delays, the Court was euphoric and ordered the additional expenditure of £288 to build substantial vaults to the new Hall.

Presiding as Master and Renter Warden over these changes was Henry Capel, the former wine merchant, who had been such a model lessee of the Company's premises in Little Tower Street. Capel was indefatigable in recording contemporary occasions in the Company's life and in the City. His account of the laying of the foundation stone includes the speeches of all three Wardens and the Master. The latter spoke at length as he recounted incidents in the history of the Company. The Renter Warden (Capel himself), adapted lines of Longfellow to suit the occasion:

> Let us do our work as well
> Both the unseen and the seen
> Make our Hall where gods may dwell
> Beautiful entire and clean…

CHAPTER TEN
Men of Property 1870–1900

> *Disraeli and Gladstone dominated Parliament and by their reforms created the machinery of the modern state — national elementary education; elected borough and county councils; civil service, army, judiciary overhauled and open to talent and an extension of the franchise. The Irish Question became the main political issue and split the Liberal party. The economy faltered in the 1880s, challenged by Germany and America; exports fell, imports remained high and the balance was made up from earnings on foreign investments. The British navy patrolled the oceans, the Empire grew and two royal jubilees concealed the growing conflicts within society at home and with imperial and industrial rivals abroad.*

WITH CRAFT LINKS LOST, the Company was left with its charities. Their management and improvement of income from rents and investments became the Company's main concern. Any notion that membership of the Court was a sinecure, providing good company and even better dinners, is wide of the mark. Those liverymen, who, at length, reached the seniority of the Court found themselves faced with making decisions on leases, covenants, sales and purchases of property which could have long lasting effects on the charities. They had to be acquainted with and respond to a torrent of legislative controls, governing trusts, schools, local government, lighting, roads, sewers, tithe commutation, income tax, railways and reservoirs.

In addition, they had to be managers in a surprisingly hands-on manner. There was an expectation in the Company's schools that the Court would have a view on everything from the curriculum and the behaviour of pupils to text books and staff relationships. The headteachers deferred to the Court on even small administrative matters and seem to have exercised their managerial skills only in the classroom. In 1896, the headmaster at the Egham School was told to discontinue mapping and elocution and replace them with more useful subjects. The epitome of direct management was the running of the Woodham Mortimer estate by a committee of the Court from September 1893 to April 1896.

The practice of a regular 'viewing' of the Company's property by the Master, Wardens and some of the Court had been resumed in 1836. A cycle developed of visits spread over three years so that each group of estates was viewed in turn and a report on their condition and requirements was drawn up by the surveyor. There were tricky decisions to be taken, particularly in the case of London where the market was volatile, swinging from a shortage of offices and warehouses in the 1870s to a glut in the 1890s. Whether to sell or rebuild and develop at the end of a lease was a matter of fine judgement. The Miles Lane property increased in value until the 1870s; then, against all predictions, it fell until in the late 1880s, its rental value was only half that of 1870. A similar fate befell two properties in Fenchurch Street to the extent that abatements in rent were granted in 1890 and 1891.

The expansion of urban railways and the London underground system had a sharp impact on property required for lines, stations and goods yards. The rebuilding of several properties in Blackman Street, Southwark was seriously delayed in the 1880s by the construction of goods sidings nearby. In Little Tower Street, properties threatened by the Metropolitan railway with compulsory purchase, actually increased in value by over 25 per cent as a result of the area being 'improved' and benefiting from better communications.

From the 1870s, the surveyor, G. B. Williams, developed a plan to diversify the Company's property portfolio to take advantage of the buoyant market. As surplus balances on the accounts accumulated, he sought out areas tipped to improve in value. Purchases in Leadenhall Street, near the new East and West India Dock Company's warehouse and near also to Tower Bridge, which was about to open, were considered a good investment. In 1891, 13 Crutched Friars and three houses nearby in John Street were purchased in this same area, which was attracting more trading activity. The search for good ground rents in Kensington went less well. In 1886 and again, in 1888, prices were too high; too many other trusts were seeking the same few properties.

The Company's other properties were held in trust for the Egham and Ratcliffe charities. The Ratcliffe properties suffered badly from the decline of the area and from the decay of buildings, some of which had been speculative ventures in the 1790s. Adequate drainage and sewage disposal in the area was slow in being provided. Landlords, including the Company, were not prepared to spend money on new drains for property which really needed to be demolished at the end of the lease. Dunstan Place illustrated the problem. Three small cottages had decayed beyond repair, to the extent that 36 notices under the Nuisances Act 1852 had been issued by the Limehouse Board of Works. The lessee had also failed to carry out dilapidations at the end of the lease. The Company took possession in 1873 and at first attempted a repairing lease with Mr St Leger, whose agents did a few repairs badly. When St Leger died, his widow had to surrender the lease. The Company took a more radical course; to lease to a developer who would rebuild. The offer was sufficiently attractive to produce 35 tenders. Progress was slow because the successful firm lacked capital but by 1879 the scheme was complete. The 40 new cottages, were let on 21-year leases and yielded £460 rent a year. Such schemes were risky and potentially disastrous, but this particular success may have encouraged the Company to embark on a much larger venture on the Egham Charity's land at Plaistow.

The Ratcliffe Charity's main source of income was the former East India Company Wharf, known by the 1870s, as Free Trade Wharf. The lease was held by Edgar Breffit, owner of the Aire and Calder Bottle Company and many tenants also operated from the wharf. All were at a disadvantage in not being able to attract the larger vessels, which carried the Mediterranean trade, because the Board of Customs judged the wharf unsuitable for the larger tonnage coming into London. It needed either influential patrons to persuade the authorities that it was worthy of a First Class Sufferance certificate or it needed improvements. Between 1868 and 1873, 14 applications for a certificate were refused. Then Breffit, by this time a liveryman of the Company, and the Master, approached Sir Thomas Fremantle, Chairman of the Board of Customs. The outcome was not recorded but it was probably unsuccessful. Breffit persuaded the Company to allow him to make improvements, which involved extending the jetty and extending and enlarging the warehouses. The latter scheme meant three houses on Broad Street (the modern Ratcliffe Highway) were demolished. The neighbouring wharf at Stone Stairs was also improved and strengthened to allow the use of heavy lifting machinery. The Company was content for these changes to go through, providing the costs were borne by Breffit. In the longer term the value of the rental would increase.

However, although all was not well with Breffit's affairs, a majority on the Court was keen to cultivate a man who had ambitions for high office in the City. In addition, there was the temptation of a more general improvement scheme in Ratcliffe to enhance the Company's income. The Charity Commissioners advised against renewing Breffit's lease in 1873. They probably had a less clouded view than the Company.

Breffit failed to keep to the timetable for rebuilding which was part of the new leasing agreement. In 1875, he had not begun what should have been completed in that year. He was granted an extension and made some progress but, when the Company's triennial view took place in 1879, much needed to be done and parts of the Company's estate in his lease were in a poor state of repair. Breffit had a serious financial problem. After his death in 1882, his business collapsed, his son had to find other employment and his wife was virtually destitute. She twice appealed to the Company for assistance and in 1890 was granted an almshouse. There was no requirement placed on her to reside there. She drew her pension and remained in the family home in Yorkshire. Breffit's affairs were in such confusion that it took years to deal with his creditors. In 1896, his daughter wrote that she had still received nothing from her father's will. Edgar Breffit's later career well illustrates the opportunities as well as the high risks which were open to the ambitious businessman. The task of the Company was to find a middle way between high risk and excessive caution.

The Tees Union Shipping Company took over the leases of both the Free Trade Wharf and the Stone Stairs Wharf, together with most of the Company's Broad Street property. Breffit had made the wharves fit to take heavier goods than the cattle which had been the main cargo in the 1850s but the Shipping Company had its sights on using steam ships. It took four years to re-negotiate its lease to achieve a 70-year term at double the old rent. In return, it undertook to construct new warehouses valued at £5,000 and to combine the two wharves in a major rebuild. The improved income was welcome; it came just as the Ratcliffe School was preparing to leave Ratcliffe for a new site in Bow.

The Egham Charity's lands provide a contrast in many ways. Whereas Ratcliffe was already an overcrowded and decayed area, both Plaistow and Staines were areas poised for development. Riper was Plaistow, already under cultivation for market gardening to supply the voracious needs of London. The lessee, who followed the Ireland family, was granted a new lease at a rent of £525 in 1877. The Company purchased 30 acres of land to ensure that the Egham land was not boxed-in by other speculative developers, and to have access to main roads. In its recent dealings with the Becton Gas Lighting Company, the Court had first-hand experience of the higher value of frontages on main roads. In 1888, the Company bought Sion Villa which gave access to Becton Road. It was let at £1,500 for building.

The initial impetus to begin building came in 1879 from Robert Carter (the younger) and resulted in 12 cottages being built in Prince Regent Lane by a small-scale builder named Merralls. It proved a nerve-racking and reckless experience. Merralls was provided with capital in instalments by the Company, agreeing to repay at six per cent when the cottages were sold. He soon ran into trouble when the early onset of winter weather stopped work in November. He wrote to the Court, 'Jack Frost has stopped my building … a little help now will save me from sinking'; and a little later; 'frost has destroyed 1,000 of my blocks'. The Company lent him £1,500, which he was then unable to repay. Tenants had to be induced to take the cottages by a rent reduction to six shillings a week. When the Court saw the cottages, it was shocked to see they were built of concrete. It immediately decided no more would be built. The Company's profit was very small and then further squeezed by reducing the interest charged to Merralls on his loan. It was important to save him from bankruptcy while he owed so much to the Company.

The episode was a warning which the Company only partly heeded. It made a different deal with J. Clever, another speculative builder. Clever was granted up to five acres at £40 an acre on which he was to bear all costs of roads and sewers. The houses were to have a value of £175 and he was to take a mortgage, not with the Company, but with a building society. Clever proved unreliable and failed to begin building by the agreed time. His contract had to be re-drawn to give him longer. The houses, in Hastings Terrace, were incomplete when the building society, the National Standard Land, went into liquidation in March 1888. The Company had to assume possession of 30 houses.

Problems multiplied on the Plaistow estate. Clever had to be evicted in 1892 because of mounting arrears of debt. A third developer had to be evicted in 1895. The market garden business somehow kept going, but the tenant, Mills, was affected by floods in 1888, and had to contend with gypsies encroaching and the threat of two projected railways to Woolwich. He was granted £100 abatement in 1890 and thereafter a ten per cent reduction on his rent for the general disturbance.

Until 1896, the Egham Charity had seen no gain from these activities but its reserves of stock were committed to meet the expensive costs of providing roads and sewers. At this point, the Court asked the surveyor to draw up a more systematic plan for the medium and longer-term future, taking note of the pitfalls already experienced. The report was careful, tactful and a little too optimistic. It analysed the difficulties associated with the Court's leisurely procedures. Decisions could easily take two or three months because they depended on the Court awaiting a committee recommendation and often referring a matter back to committee. The approval of the Charity Commission for capital spending also was required. Its practices were even slower than the Company's. What was needed was a mechanism for a quick decision and more responsibility to be devolved onto the surveyor.

The 1896 report suggested dividing the estate into three sections, each nominated for development in sequence over a period of seven years. The plots on each section would be given outline specifications by the surveyor and approved by the Court in advance of any bids the surveyor might make.

In this way, the surveyor would be at liberty to act quickly within broadly agreed guidelines and the Charity Commission would be the only delaying factor. The report also recommended that road construction, the biggest expense, should be provided by borrowing at four per cent for the term of the lease. During the development period, the report suggested keeping rentals low for market gardening. The estimates of net income, assuming rents of four to seven shillings per foot of road frontages were £822 per annum by 1902, and by 1917, £1,764 for the Company and £3,222 for the Egham Charity.

At Staines, the Company followed the same policy of securing frontages on main roads as a preliminary to development as it had in Plaistow. In 1873, it purchased land at Laleham, south west of the town and it exchanged land with the Staines Lodge estate to the east, near the Ashford road, so that a new road could be constructed to connect the estate to the main road, now the A30. However, the Court was in no hurry to carry out new building.

The main leaseholder at Staines until 1884 had been ill for some years and, when a triennial view was made in 1876, members of the Court were surprised to find the farm run by Denyer's 17-year-old son. The next lessee, Stolley, was burdened with high initial costs to get the land back into good heart and also faced falling agricultural prices as the depression of the 1880s deepened. Stolley appealed for a lower rent and received annual abatements on an *ad hoc* basis ranging from 10 to 15 per cent.

The Company faced the full impact of the agricultural crisis on the Woodham Mortimer estate in Essex. From 1817 to 1863, it was fortunate in its tenants, William and Robert Hart, father and son. However, when a family trust took over the lease on Robert's death, farming standards declined. Further concern was caused by the drainage laid in the 1850s but, by 1870, showing every sign of having been installed faultily. The Company sought expert advice from a Chelmsford land agent. He said new drains were essential. The cost was estimated at £1,800, but the tenant rejected the proposal that he should make a contribution. With only two years of the lease to run, it was not the best time to make such a large investment.

Only with difficulty was a new lessee found in 1875 but he had to withdraw because he had overstretched himself financially and from the outset was in arrears with rent. Just in time for a Michaelmas transfer, a new tenant, an experienced local farmer named Bartlett, was found. He took over a neglected farm with poor land, untidy hedges, despoiled timber and decaying farm outbuildings. He agreed to pull down and rebuild the stables for 12 horses but declined to share the cost of the drains.

There was little choice for the Company other than redraining the land at its own cost. Work began in 1878 with the ordering of several thousand two and three inch diameter sections of pipe, and continued for another four years. Meanwhile, farming plunged into the worst and longest depression of the century. It was heralded and then accompanied by bad weather; cool, wet summers, late and spoiled harvests and severe winters, often beginning early with frost and snow in November. Prices for grain had already begun to fall by 1870 and then gathered momentum. Wheat, the main crop in Essex, fell in price by almost one third between 1883 and 1895, oats by a quarter and barley by a little less than a quarter. Following this disaster, came a fall in meat, livestock and dairy prices, exacerbated by general drought in 1892 and 1893. At last some of the prophecies of doom, which the debates over Free Trade in the 1840s had produced, were coming true. Without protective tariffs, the British market was wide open to the food exports of North and South America, Australia, New Zealand as well as Russia, South Eastern Europe and Denmark. Their products could undercut home produce because steamships were so numerous and fast that freight costs fell dramatically.

The impact was felt on all the Company's landed estates but with particular intensity at Woodham Mortimer where grain production was the main activity. Bartlett asked for a ten per cent concession on his rent in the autumn of 1879. He spoke of a 'perennial depression throughout the country' and said that it was 'impossible to make the farm meet its expenses'. The Court refused and continued for two more years to appear indifferent to his pleas. He asked and was granted an allowance of £13 for 100 tons of chalk; and in 1880 was granted a deferment of rent from midsummer to harvest; otherwise there was no real understanding of his plight or of the crisis gathering over the whole agricultural sector of the national economy. While the Court complacently recorded 'Mr Bartlett is doing justice to the property', their tenant was complaining that the Company was the toughest of his landlords.

Eventually, Cyrus Legg persuaded his fellow Assistants of the gravity of the situation and the prudence of granting an abatement to a good tenant, who, at the very least, was keeping the farm land in good heart. There were reductions of 15 per cent, and 10 per cent on the rent for 1881 and 1882, respectively and then came a correspondence between landlord and tenant so full of misunderstandings that Bartlett assumed the Company was about to terminate the lease. The Court's limited appreciation of farming in the current difficulties was becoming all too obvious. Bartlett explained that for five years, since taking up his lease, he had been compelled to pay the whole rent charge from capital. The Court went down to Essex to view the property in July 1883 and was very satisfied with what it saw. The draining was well done and almost complete, the buildings in good order and the land well cultivated. Indeed, it felt congratulations were due to the Company for having the farm 'properly and skilfully cultivated by so responsible a tenant as Mr Bartlett in these times of agricultural depression and difficulty'. Eventually a rent reduction from £560 to £550 was agreed. Bartlett was able to write a nice letter and refer to his 'understanding landlords'.

The lease was due to end in 1893 and Bartlett decided on retirement. The Court offered the lease to his son, Arthur, on a yearly basis with taxes and insurance paid at £300, but he was a dairy farmer and Woodham Mortimer had only a small amount of pasture. By spring 1893, time was short and only one offer was received by the Company's land agents in Chelmsford. There was a glut of farms to let after a disastrous year and the only possible market consisted of Scottish dairy farmers seeking good pasture to fatten cattle for the London market. After the one possible tenant backed out of the agreement, the Court took its agent's advice and made an offer to Arthur Bartlett, to take on the role of steward for two pounds a week until the Company could find a tenant. A committee consisting of Leonard Shuter, George Elkington and Henry Boyer was constituted as the management team and ran the farm for the next two and a half years, visiting monthly and making all the decisions on crops, sales, purchases, changes from cereals to pasture and the hire of labour. Arthur Bartlett provided professional advice. After the first winter, the three reported to the Court about the delay in ploughing; none had been possible by February because the ground was either wet or frosty. They had to borrow capital from the Company to rebuild the cart shed, destroyed by fire and to purchase stock. During 1894, not a single offer was made for the farm. It was not until the following autumn that Stevens, a Maldon farmer, offered £210 annual rent for an eight-year lease. It was less than two fifths of the old rent, but the Court accepted with relief, realising it 'would be ruinous to allow it to go uncultivated even for a season'.

In April 1896, the Court counted the cost. Over the two-and-a-half years of direct management, the Company had laid out £5,282 on Woodham Mortimer, achieved an income of £3,321 and made a loss of £1,961. It had been compelled to sell stocks at the worst time of the market and had survived 'the two most disastrous years that farmers ever knew'. Nevertheless it had been a brave undertaking, which had averted a much worse disaster. The working relationship between the management committee and Arthur Bartlett was apparently harmonious. It was certainly crucial to the success of the enterprise and was recognised by the gift of one dozen bottles of champagne and half dozens of whisky and brandy sent to Bartlett by the Company in January 1895.

During the 1870s, the Company's finances had become more secure. Rental income rose during the decade from around £1,700 per annum to almost £7,000. In addition, there was a useful portfolio of investments, in part the result of the sale of some of the Basinghall Street site to the City Corporation when the Hall was rebuilt in 1868. From 1885 to 1891, these investments almost trebled in value. Thereafter, times became harder. Interest rates fell to two-and-a-half per cent and the troubles at Woodham Mortimer left the Company, in effect, subsidising its losses. To compound matters, the Company had embarked on developing the land it had purchased at Plaistow. It had lent £1,500 to the builder, Merralls, who was unlikely to be able to repay his debts. It invested in roads, sewers, drainage and repeated repairs to this infrastructure at Plaistow with little return from ground rents. Its rental income, hitherto so buoyant, was less so as it felt obliged to agree to lower rents on some of its London properties which were run-down and unattractive as leases.

In 1896, the Court discovered with some degree of shock that it had a small deficit on its revenue account; 'An unsatisfactory state', according to one Assistant. An investigation of the past ten years showed that the deterioration began in 1888. The Court declared that, had it known, it would have curtailed the cost of its entertainment. The unpalatable revelation led to a resolution to proceed with economy. There were to be no Ladies' dinners and only four Court dinners a year. This last decision was confirmed again 1904.

The finances of the charities largely reflect the mixed fortunes of the Company. Woodham Mortimer became totally indebted to the Company, unable to support any pensioners; the Egham Charity's income declined until its overdrawn account prompted the Charity Commission to advise the school's closure in July 1900, while the Ratcliffe Charity went from strength to strength as its properties gained in value and improved rents flowed into the Company. Ratcliffe's strength meant that the Company's pensioners did not suffer in spite of Woodham Mortimer making losses.

The problem with the Egham Charity's endowments was that they needed long-term investments in the infrastructure of roads, before they were likely to match the Ratcliffe results. Items such as roads, sewers, fencing and fees for surveyors and solicitors needed greater resources of capital than the Egham Charity possessed. Its investments were modest, amounting to almost £3,000 but a decade of largely unsuccessful attempts to develop part of Plaistow reduced the charity to dependence on its income from rents, which at just under £500 was less than a fifth of the Ratcliffe Charity's income. The difference can be explained by the rise in rents from urban property and the fall of rents from agriculture.

The school at Egham served its community well, but in a limited way, during the 30 years that John Beattie was schoolmaster and chaplain. His dominance was such that it was generally known as Beattie's School for many years, even after his death. He managed to stem a decline in numbers by persuading the Court to allow him to admit new applicants straightaway rather than wait for the Court's approval. Many had drifted away during the waiting period. Eventually he had a waiting list and was seen as a competitive nuisance by the local Board schools. Beattie's improved admission policy was preferred by parents to waiting for the result of tests on which government grants to the Board schools were based. During the 1870s, visits from members of the Court became more frequent, usually coinciding with the annual inspection by an independent examiner. Two members of the Court who took a particular interest in Egham were Alfred Chantler, who also represented the Company in the Council of the City and Guilds Institute, and Cyrus Legg.

Locally, the school's reputation was good and it could point to some notable successes. Two ex-monitors gained studentships at Coopers' Hill College near Egham, the training college for engineers for the Empire. One boy matriculated, another took holy orders, went to British Columbia as a missionary and became an expert in the languages of the North West Pacific coast. These were the exceptions. It was not unusual for a third of the top class to leave before midsummer. The attraction was work on local farms for wages of 12 to 16 shillings a week. Beattie also had to contend with uncooperative and unappreciative parents. Not only did they remove boys from school to take on casual work at hay and harvest time, but also they would not see that their sons did homework.

New pressures on the school came from the parish authorities and a number of liverymen whose spokesman was Warden Bristow. Independently, he and Dr John Monsell, the vicar of Egham, raised the issue of changing the school from an elementary one to a grammar school to satisfy the aspirations of a growing number of middle class families in Egham. In response to Monsell's proposal, the Court set up a committee to examine the case and report back. The Committee came to a swift conclusion, that the charity's funds were insufficient for such a change. Furthermore, at the time (1869) it was difficult to extract rents for Plaistow, Egham's main source of income.

However, support for the idea came from Beattie and Edward Budgen, one of the churchwardens. The vicar resumed the argument in January 1870 and suggested that the parish school should undertake 'the education of the poor boys hitherto taught in the [company's] school' and that the Company should have *ex officio* trusteeship of the parish school. Among members of the Court who favoured the idea was Henry Capel, who argued for free places in both the parish and the Coopers' school, while the remainder should be charged fees. 'The poor', he said 'are likely to value what they pay for'. The argument was defeated on the grounds that it would be against the spirit of Strodes' will and none should be 'deprived of the blessing of education through their inability to pay for it'.

Another attempt to influence the Company to change its mind was made in 1881 when the parishioners of Egham sent a petition to the Court. The Clerk, James Boyer, was asked to do some research to find out likely demand for a 'middle-class school'. In his report, Boyer noted the rapid growth of Egham from 5,880 inhabitants in 1871 to 8,680 in 1881. Rateable property showed almost half the population lived in houses assessed in the middle and upper bands. In addition there was extensive building in Englefield Green, already popular with members of the Court at Windsor. The evidence convinced the Company that a further investigation ought to be made into the case for a middle class school in Egham.

From 1882 to 1886, plans were developed for building a small grammar school costing between £600 and £850 either on land behind the Crown Inn or, as eventually settled, on the site of three of the old 1706 almshouses. The building was to be 44 feet by 22, set back from Egham High Street, and with a masters' room and a cloakroom. The annual fee was to be £6. At this point the whole scheme was shelved.

The reason for the postponement was the plan to remove the Ratcliffe school from its ancient site by the river to one more central and convenient for most of its pupils. Few came from Ratcliffe; the majority came from Stepney, Bow and West Ham. Ratcliffe had become an area of slum tenements, a drifting maritime population, as well as being an area somewhat threatening to young pupils. One site in the Mile End Road, found in September 1886, proved to be too small, but its consideration prompted the delay at Egham. It took another six years of argument with the Charity Commissioners and local organisations, which declared an interest in the school, before a solution was reached.

There were two main options. The one, which was for some time favoured by a majority on the Court, was to move to West Ham. The other, favoured by the Charity Commissioners, was to amalgamate with the two schools in Bow run by the Prisca Coborn education foundation. The arguments for West Ham were that over half the boys travelled from there to attend the Coopers' school. There was considerable moral pressure from the parish of West Ham, the local MPs, the High Sheriff and the Bishop of Stepney, to persuade the Company to move its school into a rapidly growing borough, already with 15,000 inhabitants but with no school beyond the level of the National (Board) School.

The Company was, at the same time, approached by one of the governors of the Coborn foundation in October 1887, to suggest a meeting to consider amalgamation. The decision had already been taken in 1886 to close the girls' school and many of its pupils transferred to the Coopers' Girls' School. At this point, the Charity Commissioners entered the negotiations, at first expressing surprise at the very existence of the Coopers' Girls' School. It was an example of how overwhelmed the Commission had become with reform of charitable trusts and the work it had generated. It admitted that it had not once examined the annual accounts submitted by the Girls' school since 1879. It also regretted that the Coopers' had chosen for its school, a site so close to the Coborn Girls' School. Altogether this was not an auspicious beginning.

However during 1888, the Commissioners stepped up their pressure on the Court to consider seriously their favoured solution; an amalgamation of the Gibson (Coopers') and Coborn foundations. Understandably, the Court hesitated. It did not want to lose control of the Ratcliffe assets nor take on the liability of the £900 debt of the Coborn foundation. On the plus side, there were the Coborn Boys' School buildings in Tredegar Square which would make a better physical environment than the Ratcliffe site. Eventually the Court was persuaded of the advantages but two sticking points remained to delay the outcome. First was the proportion of Company governors on the board which would take responsibility for the new schools. The board had to be representative of the community and local government as well as including Coborn foundation representatives. In the end the Company had to concede and give up its aim of securing a majority of governors. The other point was naming the two schools. A compromise was reached in 1891, with the Ratcliffe boys joining the Coborn boys in the Tredegar Square buildings under the name of the Coopers' School. The Coopers' Girls' School, which had swallowed up the Coborn girls' was renamed the Coborn School. At Common Hall in 1891 these arrangements were accepted and it was agreed there should be no more opposition. Two members of the Livery were allocated places as governors and the new educational charity came into being as the Stepney and Bow Foundation. Its first meeting was in February 1892 at Coopers' Hall when the Company's Assistant Clerk, Henry Pelham Boyer, was appointed Clerk to the Foundation.

For the time being, the holding of Quarterly Courts at Ratcliffe continued. It must have been a strange, quiet place after the removal of the school with the only sound of children coming distantly at playtime from the new Board school in Broad Street. The almshouses had reached a twilight zone where arrangements were temporary. Nurse Davies died of cancer; her husband, who was caretaker, received his pension (£10 per annum) at the age of 79 and the new chaplain,

Coopers' School from Tredegar Square, Bow. This was the building to which the School moved from Ratcliffe in 1891, amalgamating with the Coborn Boys' School whose trustees owned the building.

appointed in 1895, was temporary. The Charity Commissioners advised the Company to provide out-pensions to replace the almshouses. It was a solution being considered at the same period in Egham. Certainly it made more sense to concentrate resources on pensions rather than on the upkeep of ageing property and the salaries of caretaker, nurse and chaplain. Generally, there was still family support in the community for the elderly. If evidence were needed, there were several recent examples of families taking in chronically sick almspeople.

Delay in reaching a conclusion on the future of the almshouses was caused by a dispute with the Charity Commissioners on whether it was wiser to sell the Ratcliffe freehold or lease it for a commercial purpose. Meanwhile the Company tried to reduce the waiting list of 25 people seeking a pension or an almshouse by adding £300 to its budget for pensions. Before agreement was at length reached in 1898, there was some acrimony from local organisations which wanted a benefit to the community rather than a purely commercial transaction. The Ratcliffe vestry was annoyed because it wanted to acquire the site to build baths as a commemoration of the Queen's

Detail of the Coopers' School at Bow.

diamond jubilee in 1897. The conclusion was a lease for 80 years at a rent of £150 to Poulter and Co, a distribution firm, who built a new block north of the School and added stables.

The almspeople were given notice to quit by Lady Day (25 March) 1898 and allowed to take with them the bed, chest of drawers and wash stand provided in each house by the Company. They continued to receive their pensions with enhancement. There was little sentiment or concern to preserve any tangible remains of a charitable enterprise which had lasted 362 years on the same site. It was left to C. P. Ashbee, chairman of the newly established Survey of London, to secure the memorial tablets from the chapel and almshouses for the London County Council Museum.

After 1826, craft matters ceased to appear on Court agenda. A minute for June in that year notes the examination of papers which gave guidance and quoted precedents for coopers working outside the Company, never having taken their freedom. It was a matter beyond recall. The next time the craft of coopering was discussed was during the setting up of the structures for technical education by the City Corporation. The result was the City and Guilds Institute. Henry Capel was appointed the Company's representative at an initial meeting called by the Lord Mayor in 1872 and became a founder member of the committee which established the new technical institute. In 1878, at the launch, six of the Great Companies each promised 2,000 guineas, the Coopers promised 100 guineas, then tried to withdraw and finally paid their subscription, when told they would otherwise lose their representation. Until 1902, the company continued its support through its subscription and its representatives, Leonard Shuter and Alfred Chantler. Thereafter, it halved its contribution to 50 guineas a year but gave 100 guineas a year to encourage technical education in its schools in Stepney.

The City and Guilds initiative prompted others. In 1887, Alexander Chalmers, the Upper Warden, suggested schemes for reviving interest in the craft of coopering. His ideas included an exhibition, prizes for examples of outstanding work and a registration scheme. This last idea was being adopted by the Turners and the Plumbers, while the Merchant Taylors and Leathersellers encouraged more systematic vocational courses run under the aegis of the City and Guilds.

Chalmers succeeded in launching an exhibition of coopering in 1888 at the People's Palace in Poplar. It was opened by the Lord Mayor and featured 24 cooperages as well as attracting 600 entries for eight prizes sponsored by coopering firms. During its ten days, between 11 and 21 July, it attracted 15,000 visitors while over 100 journeymen and 24 apprentices took part. Although it produced a small deficit (£82), it created new links between the Company and London cooperages and gave encouragement to those members of the Livery, who had at some time in the past, made casks. A trade committee within the Company was set up, including in its membership H.W. and J. E. Putley, Alderman James Newton, Herbert Russell, Percy Gilling and Leonard Shuter. From this group eventually sprang a registration scheme.

The Company's corporate life, meanwhile, needed no special effort to encourage the well-established pleasures of regular Court dinners, two Livery dinners on Election Day and Lord Mayor's Day and the occasional grand dinner, usually in February, to which the Lord Mayor was invited. This replaced the summer dinner, so popular in the middle years of the nineteenth century when there were still rural charms at Blackwall, Woolwich and Greenwich. Instead, the Company preferred the baroque grandeur of the Hotel Metropole, near Trafalgar Square or de Keysers on the Victoria Embankment. The formality of the dinners, the ponderous menu and the long toast list were felt to be too grand for cosy entertainment by singers round the piano and, instead in the 1890s, the Bijou Orchestra was engaged to play during the meal. From 1903, it became customary to allow members of the Court to invite guests, including, for the first time, ladies. These were the years when traditions such as passing the loving cup became established.

CHAPTER ELEVEN
Holding Fast 1900–1952

> *Liberal governments until 1916 faced the challenge of Irish nationalism, Trades Union and Labour agitation and the Suffragettes with a spate of social and welfare reforms. War against Germany caused huge and unnecessary casualties and a desire for a more democratic and socially just world. The 20-year peace from 1919 was a great disappointment, marked by world-wide depression, high unemployment and complacent politicians. The rival claims of Socialists and Fascists to have the answer to all these ills marked the drift to a second European War in 1939 which became a World War in 1941. War bankrupted Britain, undermined the Empire, destroyed the old social certainties and caused dependence on America. War-time rationing and punitive taxation contributed to the growth of a more equal, though still deferential, society, a foundation on which Labour governments, 1945–51, created the welfare state.*

AS THE CENTURY TURNED, the Company's responsibilities contracted. Since 1898 there had been no almspeople at Ratcliffe and since 1892 the school had been in Tredegar Square, Stepney. More significantly, it was managed on behalf of the London School Board for education by a governing body which represented the local community as well as the Company. The educational part of the former Ratcliffe Charity was administered by a new trust, the Stepney and Bow Foundation, while the Company continued to manage the remainder of the charity's property and paid the pensioners, some new, some former almspeople.

There were parallel changes in the Egham Charity. The proposals, during the 1880s, to create a small grammar school within the grounds of the existing school had been left in limbo, in 1886, by the urgency of dealing with the Ratcliffe Charity. The opportunity at Egham was lost and, though there were many schemes and meetings about reorganisation during the 1890s, it was clear that there was not enough money for Egham to follow Ratcliffe. It would become a grammar school, primarily dependent on income from its endowments but with some small support from Surrey and Middlesex County Councils. For some time, hope triumphed over reality: a draft scheme to convert the school into a grammar school was agreed by the County Councils, the Company, the parish of Egham and the Charity Commissioners in 1899. It would have established the Strode's Foundation but, at length, the Court felt it could not be launched with the charity still in debt to the Company. In May 1900, the decision was taken to close the school for the time being and the teachers were given three months notice.

It was a sad and sudden end. From Mr Beattie's retirement in 1893, young Mr Cooper had taken a strong lead as headmaster in raising aspirations and standards. The curriculum expanded to include French and music. Mr Cooper's sister was the unpaid music teacher and even provided the piano. All the signs were that sensible preparations for becoming a grammar school were in hand. However, the buildings were very dilapidated, roofs leaked and sanitary arrangements were so bad as to make the Company liable for prosecution. The Company's surveyor indicated that because of the deterioration, rebuilding was becoming the only option. Given the existing state of the charity's finances and the high risks involved in speculative development on the charity's estates in Plaistow and Staines, closure of the school was the only sensible option in 1900.

The Egham Charity continued to suffer from the worst aspects of speculative development, mainly in Plaistow, and the continued depression in agricultural prices. In Plaistow, development, which had begun in 1880, continued to be costly and fitful. Rents had to be reduced on the remaining island of market gardening to compensate for the builders' encampment all around. It was beginning to be clear to some, that the bulk of the charity's land was not well situated to take advantage of the existing, albeit, skeletal infrastructure of roads and sewers. To exploit its potential would require the kind of investment which neither the Company nor the charity could afford. Even then, good returns would be likely only in the long term.

The surveyor's report of 1896, which projected planned development, with costs and probable income, for the coming 20 to 25 years, contained warnings beneath its superficial optimism. It warned of the disadvantages of the slow, cumbersome workings of the Court itself and of the unattractiveness to speculators of leasehold land by comparison with freehold. The new surveyor, appointed in 1898, was George Elkington. He had boundless energy and great enthusiasm for the Plaistow project but he soon discovered that the day-to-day problems were too numerous for any one person to manage at a distance. A local agent with considerable freedom to act was needed. Without such a presence, and in spite of Elkington's energy and skill, there was constant vandalism; fences were pulled down, 'For Sale' boards destroyed, there was trespass, dumping by other speculators and West Ham Council workmen, gypsy encampments, Sanger's circus, performing without permission and constant complaints from the Company's tenants about the conditions of innumerable badly organised building sites around them.

Constructing the necessary roads proved expensive and dragged the Egham Charity into debt on its current account as well as depleting its investments. A large part of the problem was that the charity land was not immediately accessible from the two main roads across the area, Barking Road to the north west and Becton Road running east-west to the south of the estate. Much more construction was necessary to connect these two roads before any builder would be interested in taking building leases. Once built, the road surfaces quickly broke up with the movement of the builders' heavy vehicles.

Elkington's annual report to the Court, in 1901, gives a snapshot of recurring frustrations. 'Denmark Street is worse than ever. There is very lawless conduct chiefly by boys or louts ... The Police seem inert or powerless.' Nevertheless, he was still optimistic. The West Ham authorities were about to widen two of the (roughly) north-south lanes connecting Barking and Becton Roads and there were plans to extend a tramway along the length of one of them, New Barn Street. Against the inclination of the Court, Elkington persuaded its members of the advantages of reserving three good corner sites for public houses. The local magistrates were disinclined to grant more licences, so an alternative strategy was pursued, seeking help from the brewers, Charringtons.

The achievements of 1902 and 1903 amounted to £227 in lettings from ground rents, but Elkington estimated that to put the existing roads in order would cost £220, while repairs on the very first development, Prince Regent's Villas, 1880, would cost £388 'to put these wretched houses into condition'. Some progress was made in the following three years but it was slow and financially hazardous since the builders themselves had little capital and depended on letting a few completed houses to pay their creditors for supplies for the next few. By 1906, the whole area was falling silent as depression settled on the property market. The builders were in difficulties and there were no more enquires for new lettings. The surveyor's report noted only £36 had been acquired in new ground rents for the year ending April 1907. Only one builder was still at work and he needed help.

The Court wisely said no to more expenditure on developing the area. It faced a bill of over £1,300 for road works and was already concerned at the overload of work in the Clerk's office. On further investigating the Clerk's work, a Committee of the Court revealed for the first time the full extent of the Plaistow venture and its potential for bringing financial disaster on the Company. The Committee was convinced that it was 'quite beyond the powers of any single individual adequately to manage the Company and

Charity affairs unless those outlying and troublesome properties at Plaistow and Woolwich are got rid of'. The Committee discovered that the Clerk was supposed to look after and collect the rents of over 200 houses. It concluded: 'It is essential that we should put our house in order and this, in the opinion of the Committee, cannot be done until the Court returns to the City and gilt-edged securities and gives up building speculation'.

As a follow-up to this internal investigation, the Court, reluctantly, invited W. S. Ogle, accountant to the Coopers' School Governors, to appraise the Company's administration and finances. Ogle's report, in July 1908, produced a five-year analysis of the Plaistow operation up to the end of 1907. It showed a deficit of £600. In his evidence, the Clerk argued for selling the estate. Of the 108 acres owned by the Egham Charity, less than 5 had been developed. In the previous 10 years, only 37 houses had been built and none in the last 4 years. The bulk of the Charity's land lay on the eastern side of Prince Regent Lane and compared very unfavourably with the western portion, where the Company had bought 18 acres and had developed roads. By contrast, the eastern part needed roads and sewers at an estimated cost of £15,000. The Clerk concluded it would take 44 years before there would be any return on the development. When the West Ham Council made an offer to buy the land, the Court applied promptly to the Charity Commissioners for leave to sell. The deal was eventually completed in May 1910: 50 acres of the Plaistow estate was sold for £8,339 and the proceeds invested in 3 per cent London County Council stock.

During the months when the sale of the Egham property was being negotiated, the surveyor did his best to limit damage from vandals on the rest of the Plaistow estate. One of the more reliable builders was appointed custodian at five shillings a week, land was let out for allotments and football pitches, fences repaired again and the surveyor himself undertook the collection of rents. He made another attempt to re-start the building process by putting to the Court a proposal for letting single plots but met with a refusal to consider any such private treaties.

Rescue for the Company came in the form of a surprising approach by the Ilford MP, Sir John Bethell, who made an offer for between 40 and 50 acres of land for playing fields. He indicated he had backers interested in buying land in areas which were developing rapidly, so that open space for recreation could be secured. Some of the costs would be defrayed by developing frontages along main roads. A price was agreed, after almost a year of negotiations, on the basis of £7,000 for the uncovered land and £7,838 for the built area, allowing for ground rents leased for 25 years. In November

1912, the Company had freed itself from Plaistow and following its Finance Committee's report, five years earlier, it invested the proceeds prudently in gilts. George Elkington's fee was £262, although the great reduction in his responsibilities for the Company caused his salary to drop a third. He was doubtless very relieved to be free of the nuisances of Plaistow.

The property at Woolwich was another embarrassment. It had been purchased with the £500 Strode left to enhance the pensions paid by the Ratcliffe Charity. In the 1730s, it was referred to as the Woolwich estate and included several cottages as well as the Bell Watergate public house. There is no record of any substantial rebuilding at Woolwich. By the middle of the nineteenth century, the area was depressed as a result of railways taking away much of the Watermen's trade from the river. In turn, the Bell suffered a serious loss of custom and received some abatement of its rent. Thereafter its fortunes fluctuated with those of the neighbouring dockyard and it seems to have become increasingly disreputable. In July 1907, the landlord was convicted and fined for keeping a house of ill-repute from which prostitutes were allowed to work. Its licence was refused a few months later. At auction it failed to reach the reserve price of £500 but Elkington managed to find a private buyer. After two centuries, the Company had recouped its investment. The Beadle was probably the most satisfied person involved: he had been obliged to visit Woolwich fortnightly to collect the rents.

Another area where building development was expected was the Staines land owned by the Egham Charity. The problems were similar to those at Plaistow: the threat of development reduced the value of the land for farming, made the Company reluctant to spend money on repairs, particularly to the cottages scattered on the land at Laleham, and leasehold land was less attractive to developers than freehold. Apart from sites along the Kingston Road, the charity land was next to low-quality buildings which depressed the value. The construction of the Staines reservoir held up development on the Ashford Road where the Company had prudently purchased land to acquire good frontages. The navvies working on the reservoir gave the area a poor reputation and harassed the Company's tenant farmer. An abatement of 15 per cent on his rent was more than matched by compensation of £1,142 for land compulsorily purchased for the reservoir in 1900.

In spite of this windfall, there was only small interest from builders. The first serious offer fell through in 1904; then the Company hesitated because it believed a scheme to separate the almshouses at Egham from the educational part of the Charity was imminent and it was felt unwise to embark on a major commitment until the Charity Commissioners' approval had been gained. In 1909, an opportunity was lost because the adjacent Staines Lodge estate, with which agreement on boundaries and co-operation over roads had been made in 1880, failed to honour part of the agreement. The Company was left to sell more Egham Charity stock to pay for making up roads without any sign of a contract with a builder.

Meanwhile, reaching a decision about the future of the school and almshouses at Egham proved a tortuous business. Once more the parish authorities, by this time represented by the Egham Urban District Council, were deeply suspicious of the Company and critical of its delays.

When the school closed suddenly in 1900, the Egham School Board was faced with the problem of accommodating most of the Strode's pupils. There was such overcrowding at the Station Road school that the Company was persuaded to re-open Strode's buildings and lend them to the School Board for a term from January 1901. It took four more terms before the old school was vacated.

The arguments about the future organisation, governance and nature of the new Strode's school raged between the Court, the Charity Commissioners, whose approval of any new scheme was essential, and the representatives of Egham. Since the establishment of district councils in 1894, the spokesmen tended to be urban district councillors rather than churchwardens. The Egham view was that most places at the new school should be free, in the spirit of Henry Strode's will. The Charity Commissioners argued that if more than one third of the school's income were devoted to providing scholarships, middle class parents, who could afford fees, would be deterred. There would be no social mix and the school might well remain an elementary one.

The Commissioners' views prevailed; a scheme was published in 1903 and the first Governors' meeting took place at Coopers' Hall in July. It was intended that the Governors should meet twice yearly. The death of the chairman, Barnes Williams, the former surveyor to the Company, and the realisation by all closely involved that the prospect of a Company school was diminishing as rapidly as the charity's funds were being spent at Plaistow, removed the urgency of replacing the school. The Egham Charity seemed to be in limbo. In 1905, the Charity Commissioners began to show impatience at delays in agreeing a new scheme to place the almshouses under a separate trust. The Company pleaded that its difficulties at Plaistow were compromising the financial settlement. It also failed to nominate a successor to Barnes Williams.

Meanwhile at Egham, the buildings were given only the minimum of repairs, which ceased altogether in 1907. By 1909, only three of the twelve almshouses were occupied. The grounds were neglected, the lawn uncut. One small improvement was the removal of the old cottages, two groups of three, which bordered Egham High Street and were the last survivors of the original 1706 almshouses. Nevertheless, the patience of local people and other interested parties was growing thin. Letters from the vice-chairman of the Governors, William Paice, who was also a district councillor, went unanswered. There were several requests that the Company cut the grass and allow band concerts on the school lawn twice a week during the summer months. The district council wanted to see the accounts. The Middlesex County Council, which intended to award scholarships to the proposed grammar school, asked when the governors had last met.

Delays and indecisiveness were understandable once the Court had learned the bitter truth about the losses sustained in Plaistow. Ogle's report in 1908 established that the Egham Charity had already lost £600 and was liable for more payments for roads on the estate. The experiences of Plaistow made the Court more sceptical about any early increase in income from the Staines estate. West Ham offered to purchase the Egham Charity estate in Plaistow; but until then there was little the Court could do other than sit tight and hope for an improvement. The apparent discourtesy in not answering letters was explained by the breakdown suffered by the Company's Clerk in 1909 and the subsequent discovery of a large backlog of work. By August 1909, permission to use the lawn had been given, and the district council had agreed to keep it and the paths in good order for the rest of the summer.

The Court found it less easy to respond to the query about governors' meetings. Since the death of the chairman in September 1905, there had been none. Mr Paice made plain his anger at 'the short-sighted policy on the part of the Trustees [the Company]. The people of Egham are ready and willing to work with the Trustees for the benefit of the Charity, but if the Trustees continue to treat them in this manner you may depend upon it, it will lead to ructions again.' By the end of 1909, the governors agreed to the separation of the school from the almshouses and the provision of a new building by Surrey and Middlesex County Councils. Once the purchase money for part of the Plaistow estate had been received, in May 1910, a conference of the interested parties at Coopers' Hall agreed schemes for the grammar school and a separate pensions charity. The latter was named the Egham Eleemosynary Pensions Charity and was endowed with £12,000 of stock to yield an income of £300 annually. Two of the three remaining almsmen died in 1911 and the third was removed with a pension of five shillings a week plus coals and clothing.

It took another two years before a scheme of governance was agreed for the new school. Since the charity's funds could not sustain the costs, the new school would pass from the Company's trusteeship and become a county grammar school, with a few scholarships reserved to Egham boys. The remaining assets of the charity (£1,000) passed to the official trustees and the cash (£700) to the governors. All the deeds and papers relating to the charity's endowments were passed to the new Clerk to the governors and it seemed that the links between the Company and Henry Strode's charity had, at last, been severed. An important tailpiece to this saga, was the sale of the remainder of the Plaistow estate to the Port of London Authority, completed in August 1914. The proceeds of the sale were £10,000, sufficient to build the new school, leaving the Surrey County Council responsible only for the maintenance of the teaching staff.

The rest of the Company's property caused comparatively little trouble. Although the Essex estate at Woodham Mortimer was in debt to the Company, there was a reliable farmer as leaseholder and sound advice to hand from the Chelmsford's land agents. At the insistence of Sir David L. Salomons, nephew and heir of Sir David, the debt was steadily reduced from 1903 by investing all net balances in a separate account from which the interest paid off the debt. By 1914, the debt had been reduced from almost £2,000 to £1,400. A recovery in agricultural prices meant that, when a new seven-year lease was agreed in 1910, the rent could be raised from £210 to £300. The Company felt able to share with the tenant the cost of a very necessary improvement, a bathroom.

The main properties at Ratcliffe were the Free Trade Wharf, still held on a long lease by the Tyne and Tees Shipping Company, the old school site, occupied by Poulter Brothers and the newly rebuilt Dunstan Place, known after the builder as Cosh's Buildings. The tenants were reliable and, until 1912, no major changes were needed. Discussions in 1912, about the shipping company's plans for changes to meet the decline in demand for riverside warehouses, while wharfage and landing facilities remained valuable, led the Company to consider selling the freehold. Its value was put between £35,000 and £40,000 but the majority view was that its rents would yield more than would the sale price invested.

The properties in Blackman Street (which had been renamed Borough High Street) were all eventually the subject of a compulsory purchase by the Post Office. They were the subject of an out-of-Court settlement of £14,592, which continued to be held in the Court of Chancery and was invested on behalf of the Company. The Court was advised not to apply to the High Court for its transfer. This puzzling decision was explained only in 1947. The Court was anxious to reinvest the principal in new, more profitable stocks and so it investigated the opinion given in 1912. This argued that the Company's charter did not permit it to sell its property. Fortunately the opinion was overturned.

In London, the surveyor kept a vigilant eye on the Company's property threatened by new developments. Each year he provided a full report on the condition, value and necessary repairs to all the property. Just occasionally he showed frustration at his advice being ignored. In his forties, he must have seemed a 'young' man in a hurry to the old men who governed the Company's affairs.

The Court was increasingly dominated by old men. By the turn of the century there was insistence on following strict seniority to fill vacancies on the Court. In turn this meant passing over distinguished liverymen who had experience in public affairs as well as vigour to offer the Company. One such was Sir David Lionel Salomons. When, eventually, he was elected to the Court, the younger Salomons proved a wise counsellor and guided the Company very astutely in the affairs of the Egham Charity as well as more generally advising on investments. Another liveryman who was passed over, was Alderman Newton whose 'out of turn' nomination was more warmly debated than usual. Newton was defeated by one vote in 1897 and again in 1898. The Society of the Livery joined the controversy and issued a 'Memorial' criticising the attempts to elect him out of turn. The Society's action drew a response from the Alderman regretting being a source of ill-feeling among the Livery and promising he would reject any further invitation to join the Court.

Newton was elected Lord Mayor in 1899. His election was well supported by the Livery at Common Hall in September and the celebrations accompanying his inauguration in November followed the pattern of Alderman Stone's in 1874. The band of the Lincolnshire Regiment was engaged, the Hall and Basinghall Street were decorated and pride of place was given to the Company's banners. There was even extra seating erected outside the Hall to view the start of the procession in which the Company, of course, played a leading role. The day's events began with a breakfast at the Hall. The accounts book recorded numerous expenses including new poles for the banners, a scarf for the Beadle, and refreshments for the band. It seems that on his big day, the new Lord Mayor was given a worthy reception by his Cooper brethren but there remains a lingering suspicion that he had previously been treated with less than the courtesy he deserved. He never became a member of the Court.

Between 1903 and 1905, eight of the 18 Assistants died. These deaths mark the passing of a group which had embarked on the Plaistow development. They are commemorated in the street names, where early development occurred between Becton and Barking roads. Several of them had devoted much time and effort to the complexities of moving the school from Ratcliffe to Stepney, amalgamating with the Coborn Charity and establishing a new governing board, which had extensive responsibilities. Some, although quite elderly, had worked hard to conduct the detailed management of Woodham Mortimer when it had proved impossible, for several years, to find a tenant. All showed in their different ways a deep devotion to the Company and a desire to enhance it by their work and gifts. The father of the Court was John Bressey, who died, aged 91, in 1905, having been an Assistant since 1871. He was the third generation of his family to serve on the Court and his two sons, John Thomas and Edward, became Assistants in their turn.

It is perhaps not entirely coincidental that the changes in membership on the Court were followed by an investigation in 1907 into the Company's management and finances. In part, this was precipitated by the Clerk's distress at the amount of work he had to undertake, but it probably also indicates that there were some new brooms at work. The Clerk, Henry Pelham Boyer, was a member of another Company dynasty. His grandfather, James, became Clerk in 1843, his father followed in 1863 and he himself acted as Assistant Clerk from 1888 until his father's death in 1902 in his eightieth year. He had inherited his father's systems, which came under severe strain as the Company's business activities became more complex. He had asked for assistance in 1905 but after some discussion about employing a clerk-book-keeper at £100 a year, no further action was taken to ease his burden of work.

The Committee of the Court, which was principally concerned with finance, reported that 'the system is confused, antiquated and unbusinesslike'. The report continued: '[it is] open to grave objections and it is practically impossible to master the intricacy of the accounts without assistance from Mr Boyer'. With the Clerk already showing signs of overwork and stress, this was not good news for the Court. The situation in the Clerk's office, together with the Company's entanglement at Plaistow, gave added urgency to a reform programme.

Such a programme was put in place by W. S. Ogle. His investigations had revealed that there was no register of pensioners and as a result six Egham pensioners appeared in the books although they had died. Confusion over collecting and recording the rents meant that 12 houses were missing from the list. Ogle introduced the age of bureaucracy. There were warrants for paying pensioners, printed receipts and counterfoils, schedules to regulate annual reporting and two new bank accounts to separate the Company and its property from the Egham and Ratcliffe pension charities. Ogle continued his link with the Company as its auditor.

The Clerk's health did not return after a three-month absence and he died in February 1911. His cousin, Edward Lawrence Boyer, the Company's clerk-solicitor, took over during Henry Pelham's illness and then succeeded him. He had to wind up his legal business but he was compensated by a rise in salary from £500 to £600 and the appointment of a type-writing clerk. With Ogle's assistance he brought more modern methods and more transparent systems to the Company's business.

All these investigations involved a search of the offices and the cellars and brought to light records and historic relics which had probably not seen the light of day since the Hall had been rebuilt in 1869. By good fortune, the Master at the time, 1909, was John Jackson, who had a keen amateur interest in history. He made an inventory of the records and ensured they were rebound and placed in an improved strong room. Among other treasures rescued from the cellars was the 1591 pall chest. The Court was galvanised into beginning the restoration of the Company's pictures, which had last been cleaned in 1870. Sir David L. Salomons gave £100 to speed up and complete the process. Jackson was encouraged to continue his research and produced a pamphlet history of the Company.

The Company's own revived interest in its past was matched by interest in the City and its institutions among many newly-formed history societies in and around London. Several were welcomed by Jackson on Saturday afternoon visits to the Hall. It is very likely that the creation of a new Benevolent Fund sprang from his historical revival. Newton Dunn, Master in 1914 and 1915, discovered that a fund to augment the number of the Company's pensioners had been set up in 1844 and been added to each year until 1858. It proved impossible to trace it through the accounts but it was re-established (by Newton Dunn's efforts) as the Old Coopers' Livery Fund with an initial investment of £500. It was immediately augmented by Newton Dunn's gift of £250, £100 from William Burn, Master in 1916, £100 from Sir David L. Salomons and a further £100 of war bonds owned by his son, who was killed in the Dardanelles in 1915.

The outbreak of war against Germany and Austria-Hungary came as a shock and surprise to most people. The Court did not normally meet in

Topping plane and inside shave. The topping plane is used to smooth the ends of the staves; the inside shave smooths the inside of beer casks.

August, but in 1914 it reacted swiftly with donations to emergency appeals: the Prince of Wales' fund, Belgian Relief and the Red Cross. By 1915 there was alarm at the prospect of air raids, particularly at Woodham Mortimer, which was so near the east coast. Precautions included constructing a fire escape over the Hall roof to Guildhall and taking out special premiums on insurance for Woodham Mortimer until the government put its own scheme in place. The first bombs fell near the Hall in October 1915. The major treasures, plate and pictures, were placed in the cellars, the paintings, enclosed in felt, were turned to the wall and blue, Holland blinds were fitted at the windows. The air raids increased in number in 1917 and caused slight damage at Ratcliffe and to the Company's property in Crutched Friars.

There was a strong desire 'to do something' towards the war effort and it found expression at Common Hall in 1916. It was perhaps provoked by the stalemate in the war and by the introduction of general conscription. The Livery voted to send a letter of encouragement and a gift of 300 cigarettes to each member of the Company and each old boy of the school on active service. Letters of thanks with accounts of experiences flowed back to the

Hall over the following months. In August 1917, the Company inaugurated its Roll of Honour.

Apart from the devastating casualties and the grief at the loss of young lives, the war impinged rather patchily on the Company. Its effects were principally financial: the loss of rent revenues and the increased cost of its employees as the cost of living rose. There was some discussion of selling freeholds at Ratcliffe and Woodham Mortimer and in 1918 an unusually severe report from the finance committee: '… the margin of income over expenditure, from which the cost of entertainment has been eliminated, is so small as to render the strictest economy imperatively necessary'.

Nevertheless, money was found to celebrate the peace in style. The Lord Mayor launched a fund, to which the Company contributed, to receive troops of the City's regiments in a march-past of 50,000 men. In July 1919, the company volunteered to entertain 62 out of 4,000 sailors who were the City's guests. There was an intense desire to return life to normality with the round of Court dinners, the Livery dinner and young soldiers returning to work or to study.

On the initiative of the Society of the Livery, there was a renewal of interest in forming links with the trade of coopering. It was felt that there was a revival of interest in apprenticeship and there might be some preference offered to sons of coopers at the school. In May 1920, proposals were put to the Court from the society by a deputation, which included Percy Gilling, Harold Griffin, James Davies and James Edward Putley. They wanted to set up a Registered Coopers' scheme. Percy Gilling had campaigned for this since 1897 but only since the last years of the war had he found substantial support among fellow liverymen. The proposals were for the indentures of apprentices, approved by the employers' Joint Council, to be registered at the Hall. At the end of the binding period of not less than five years, the apprentices would be examined and if successful gain the certificate of Registered Cooper. In support of their proposals, the deputation, which represented the master coopers in the Livery, referred to a revival of trade links between other City companies — the Spectacle-Makers, Plumbers and Farriers — and their crafts. 'Since the war', the group argued, 'there has been a great shaking of dry bones … the institutions of London have an innate strength and vigour ready for new birth'.

While giving its support to the scheme in principle, the Court remained cautious. When the Joint Industrial Council of the Coopers' Industry for London and District finally approved the main part of the plan, the Court agreed to register the apprentices, to provide examiners for the Joint Council and to award certificates. However, the Court minuted its reservations in October 1924; while the scheme would bring into the Company such practical liverymen as it may choose, the scheme must be 'at no cost to the Company' … and it must not give 'any opportunity to the craftsman-class to dominate the direction of the Company's affairs'. In a more egalitarian society, such views came to be less acceptable, although they might be privately held. But at the time, against a background of labour troubles, the collapse of Russia into violence and Bolshevik rule, communist mutterings in Berlin and Budapest, the preference for a society held in equilibrium by the maintenance of a traditional class structure becomes more understandable.

The political unease of the post-war world was echoed in the uncertainty of the property market. The Company's dependence on rental income was much reduced and, at the same time, still very important. The effects of war were to increase many property values but to drive up labour costs, so that repairs were much more expensive. Unfortunately, too much of the Company's property was in need of substantial repair or replacement. For three years, the surveyor's advice on urgent repairs to the Hall was ignored. But, when opportunity arose for redevelopment, the Court took its chance. Miles Lane was sold for rebuilding in exchange for property in Harp Lane which yielded a better rent. At Ratcliffe, the Free Trade Wharf lease was renewed in 1933 for a 99-year lease, which gave the shipping company security to rebuild, just as Broad Street was being widened. The old eighteenth century stonework with the Company's arms was retained to form an imposing entrance. In 1938, the sale of Ceylon House in Eastcheap and Cosh's Buildings in Ratcliffe allowed investment in more modern property, flats in Beckenham, ground rents in the Edgware Road and Hazlitt House in Holborn. This gave a more balanced portfolio with the balance from the sales being invested in Consols.

Woodham Mortimer's debt was at last eliminated in 1919 and the first pension on the account for 30 years was granted. Farming remained difficult with high labour costs. There was unease in 1925 when Hilliards reported almost one third of the land was growing peas and they recommended more fallow to allow the fields to be cleaned. Within two years, the tenant was bankrupt and for a few months the chairman of the creditors administered the farm while a new lease was found. The new tenant, a competent, non-resident farmer, Mr Oldfield Ratcliff, persuaded the Company to buy an adjacent farmhouse, Brookhead, with 17 acres, to provide accommodation for workers. The main house was let separately but was found to have dry rot in 1940. With wise caution, the lease was for a three-year term.

In 1942, the finance committee investigated the return on investment over the previous 25 years and found the average profit was £109. The Committee considered that the proceeds of a sale would yield 50 per cent more if invested in gilts. This conclusion was coloured in part by the good price obtained by Guy's Hospital for 3,000 acres in Essex. The tenant, Ratcliff, offered £6,000 but a counter offer of £6,300 compelled the Court to refer to the Charity Commissioners. Ratcliff angrily responded that the higher offer could only have come from someone on the Court with knowledge of his bid.

The Upper Warden, Robert Gilling, accepted the charge and argued rightly, that he had not acted illegally. However, many on the Court felt uncomfortable, particularly as Gilling was one of a forceful minority who opposed the sale. The matter was solved on the Commissioners' advice by an advertisement to which Ratcliff responded with an offer of £6,500, which was accepted. The monument to William Alexander's generous donation in 1725 was excluded from the sale. Bereft of its splendid avenue of elm trees, it stands by the roadside on a little eminence, looking like, and often mistaken for, a war memorial.

The inter-war years were marked by growing awareness of the Company's past. Perhaps it was natural, as the future seemed so uncertain. The number of groups visiting the Hall and requests for loans of treasures, particularly plate, for exhibitions, grew remarkably. For the first time the two schools, Coopers' and the Coborn Girls', brought groups to learn about their connections, and in 1937 the pupils took part for the first time in the New Year's Day service to commemorate Henry Cloker's gift and to hear the reading of his will.

Donations from members with family links from the past enhanced the Company's growing collection. John Jackson presented a water-colour portrait of his grandfather, William Landell, Master in 1886, who died aged 92 in 1888 and remained a regular attender at Court meetings until his death. In 1923, Robert Carter, Master 1922, gave portraits of his father, grandfather and great-grandfather, all past Masters. P. M. Wellock, a grandson of Henry Capel, Master 1868, who was himself a collector and recorder of Company lore, gave Capel's portrait and a snuffbox made from the timber of the 1672 Hall. Prints, medals and plate, some of the latter being handsome examples of contemporary silverware, were added in the 1930s.

The Company still lacked a history. When George Elkington retired after 30 years as Surveyor, he wrote a miscellany of his own memories with some selections from J. F. Firth's research. His *Coopers' Company and Craft* includes a section on the history of the trade. A more weighty, thoroughly researched history, was written just before the outbreak of war in 1939 but not published until 1943. This was the work of Sir William Foster, Master in 1919 and 1935, who had a lifetime's connection with the Company. His father had advised the Company on suitable sites for the school when the move from Ratcliffe was being planned in 1886. Foster himself had attended the school, won a Gibson scholarship and began a distinguished career in the India Office. His wife was headmistress of the Coborn School until her marriage and his sister won a Jubilee scholarship from the Coopers' Girls' School to study at the North London Collegiate School.

Historical matters faded into insignificance with the outbreak of war in September 1939. Unlike 1914, there had been more warning and there was greater awareness of the front-line position of London in air-warfare. In November 1938, the surveyor explained air raid precautions and in August 1939 Woodham Mortimer became a searchlight station. Two days before war was declared on Germany, the pupils and staff of the two schools were evacuated, the boys first to Ramsbury, Wiltshire, and then to Frome, Somerset, and the girls to Taunton where they used the buildings of the Bishop Fox Girls' School. Strode's remained in Egham, but shared its accommodation with two London schools in succession. The old cellars became temporary class-rooms during air-raids and all-night shelters for townspeople in Egham.

As in 1914, the Company responded quickly to the Lord Mayor's appeals for the war effort. A thoughtful, more domestic gift was £25 to the Coborn school to help with Christmas spent away from home. The first Company properties to suffer bomb damage were the houses in Thessaly Square, Battersea, given in 1937 by Harold Griffin, Master in 1932, to help elderly residents of Battersea and needy members of the Company. With characteristic generosity the donor offered £500 in war bonds to pay for the repairs. Two of the six had been completely destroyed but the others were made habitable.

Autumn 1940 was a harrowing time, as the German air offensive reduced homes, offices and public buildings to rubble in a swathe along the Thames. Thessaly Square received its second hit. Free Trade Wharf, properties in Thames Street, St Dunstan's Hill, Leadenhall Street, Crutched Friars and part of the Beckenham apartment block were all damaged. A month later, in November, Free Trade Wharf was hit for a second time, and St Magnus Church, since 1832 the venue of the Cloker service, was severely damaged.

On 29 December 1940, the Company suffered its most grievous blow from the blitz. As a result of 'a rain of high explosive and incendiary bombs' many fires broke out around St Paul's and Wood Street and took hold in locked office buildings. The flames were fanned towards the Guildhall area by a south-westerly breeze which reached almost gale force during the night. The bombs also damaged water mains, and before the water supply was restored, almost 12 hours after the raid began, St Lawrence Jewry's steeple collapsed and set off a huge conflagration. It was from this inferno that the fire spread to Guildhall and along Basinghall Street. Heroic efforts saved much of Guildhall but the wind threw burning fragments on to the Hall and set the roof alight.

The surveyor's report concluded that, had water been available, the Hall could have been saved. The caretaker, Mrs Richards, who was 81, and her daughter, were in the air raid shelter in the basement when, at about 10pm, four hours after the first strike, the emergency services ordered their evacuation. They had to leave without any possessions, since their flat on the top floor was threatened. Poor Mrs Richards had a heart attack and was taken to St Bartholomew's hospital. She survived and lived another two years provided for with a Company pension of £65.

The Company's possessions were also largely destroyed because the Court Room on the first floor and the Clerk's office were gutted. The contents of the library survived as did the 1591 pall chest and furnishings in the vestibule. The original strong room on the ground floor and the one built in the basement in 1931 were intact so the Company's records, plate, and the portraits of Avice Gibson and her second husband, Sir Anthony Knyvett were saved.

The Cloker service, held in St Magnus' crypt three days later, took on a special significance. Someone found a copy of Cloker's will but there was no music. One of those present recalled that 'O God our help in ages past' and the National Anthem 'were sung with great vigour … and save only for the lack of music and the change of venue, the service was conducted entirely as usual'.

When the Court assembled at the Carpenters' Hall on 7 January, it was almost business as usual. For the time being, the plate and records remained in the strong rooms but by May were removed, the plate being distributed among those Assistants who had suitable safe deposits. Other Companies suffered likewise: the Carpenters', Leathersellers', Clothworkers' and Saddlers' Halls had been destroyed by May 1941. The Court's new refuge was the Vintners' Hall while the Clerk eventually rented two rooms from the Painters' Company. During 1941, the property in Fenchurch Street and Poulters' on the old school site at Ratcliffe were total losses. And the Hall was hit again. After 1941, there was a lull in the bombing, evacuees began to return and some skeletal classes were run at Tredegar Square, but when V1

Adze. Often used to cut the sloped edge at each end of the cask. Properly, the ends are called the chime and this finishing process chiming.

and V2 rocket attacks began in 1944, the Coborn school was severely damaged, the Hall was hit again and at Beckenham only 19 out of 54 flats were habitable. With the collapse of rental income, it was a time of great anxiety about the ability of the Company to pay pensions. The War Damage Commission paid some initial compensation but it was Spring 1943 before claims for losses at the Hall were settled. The main payment was £3,000 for works of art. The property claims were still unresolved at the end of the war, because tenants had the right to decide whether they would rebuild or not. Whenever possible, repairs were carried out quickly and property was re-let without difficulty.

The Company contributed, as it could, to the war effort from a sale of three dozen 1927 port, raising £38 for the Red Cross, to investing £5,000 in the 'Wings for Victory' campaign. The inauguration of the United Guilds service at St Paul's in 1943 brought together the livery companies in prayer and comradeship. Individual members made distinguished contributions on the home front and on active service. Colonel Sir Leslie Burnett (Master 1947) was awarded the CBE for his work with the Home Guard while Frank (Bill) Skelton (Master 1985 and Chaplain to the Company) achieved a remarkable record, DFC and bar by November 1944, DSO the following month and bar in March 1945.

The immediate post-war concerns of the Company were securing compensation for damaged property, maximising income from investments to safeguard the pensioners against the difficulties of an inflationary economy and eventually providing a new Hall. A generous and imaginative contribution of a hogshead of whisky from Robert Gilling, Master 1951, raised £1,000 at auction to augment the Old Coopers' Livery Fund. Investment in mortgage securities was a new venture. Otherwise, prudence in the stock market and the purchase of some newer property in place of Crutched Friars, marked the post-war trend.

After the euphoria of victory celebrations in 1945, daily life settled back into austerity which was harder to bear in peace-time than it had been during the war. Austerity also seemed even more severe when administered by Sir Stafford Cripps. Food rationing prevented the revival of Court lunches and in 1946 caused the cancellation of the Livery function which followed Common Hall. The energy and generosity of Barnabas Russell, Master 1943, provided welcome good cheer. In his year as Master, he provided lunch after the Cloker Service and continued to do so for several years. During the war he had also provided the Court room with cigarettes and cigars. An outstanding memorial to his generosity is the Coopers' window in the restored church of St Magnus the Martyr which he gave in thanksgiving for the safe return of his four sons from active service.

In September 1945, the two schools reassembled in Tredegar Square while the Coborn School was rebuilt. Closer links were eventually established with Strode's School through the energy of Malcolm Glenny who in 1950, became the Company's representative on the governing body. In 1951, the Company presented the school with a fine pair of ornamental gates and the majority of the Court attended the school's annual Founder's Day Service where the preacher was an Old Strodian, Edward Carpenter, subsequently Dean of Westminster. The offer of an annual apprenticeship to the Master for one Strodian opened up entry to the Company to a succession of young men, just as a similar arrangement had done at the Cooper's School since 1898.

In March 1951, the Coborn School marked its 250th anniversary with a visit from Queen Elizabeth. The Queen's speech contained sentiments which must have struck a chord among the members of the Company and cannot have failed to remind her of her visit, with her husband King George VI, to the bomb-shattered streets of wartime London. 'The terrible destruction which came upon you several years ago might well have seemed a mortal blow. But your endeavour outmatched disaster…' Her Majesty's words applied just as much to the Company as to the school.

CHAPTER TWELVE
Rejuvenation 1952–1980

> *Post-war optimism and full employment gave way to a series of economic crises. Britain was slow to understand the full extent of its changed position in the world — in 1956, the Suez crisis came as a shock — and failed to see its future lay as part of Europe. It demolished the Empire with dignity and joined the Common Market with reluctance. Gradually the indigenous population accepted it had become a multi-racial society. During the 1960s, authority in all its forms was challenged and legislation on betting, divorce, abortion, capital punishment and homosexuality challenged traditional values. Women asserted their right to have careers outside the home and equal pay. The 1970s began and ended with severe inflation and the industries which created Britain's nineteenth century wealth — textiles, coal, iron and steel — in crisis.*

A NEW REIGN and a young queen, in 1952, seemed to herald a new age. The symbolism of the second Elizabethan age was echoed nationally in the desire to step out from under the long shadow of wartime destruction and the misery of prolonged austerity. The Company, too, embarked with optimism on rebuilding. It was determined that it must have its own Hall again. Not only did the possession of a Hall give a City livery company a certain amount of prestige, but it provided a physical focus for its work and play. A Hall was an expression of the corporate existence.

The search for a new Hall was held up until demolition on the Basinghall Street site was completed and compensation for bomb damage had been agreed. A Hall Committee was set up to oversee this process and to begin to look for a site. There were several options to be explored. For a year or so, the front-runner of these was a scheme to share a building with the Painter-Stainers and Cordwainers in order to secure a building large enough to accommodate gatherings of the Livery, such as Common Hall, while at the same time sharing the high overheads, which such a building would impose. By November 1956, it was clear that such a scheme would not work and the Court decided not to proceed further. At the same time as these discussions, and gaining support as the joint-venture flagged, the City Corporation offered to grant the Company a 99-year lease on a wing of Guildhall. This idea was also abandoned, in 1956, on grounds of cost and the small size of accommodation offered.

So the Court was patient and decided to await the compensation which would eventually be awarded by the War Damages Commission. Meanwhile the City Corporation wanted to buy the Cooper's site so that it could enlarge its Guildhall offices. Some delicate negotiations went on during 1956: the City Corporation offering £47,000, the Company seeking £50,000. Completion was agreed in June 1957 with the difference split and £48,500 of Treasury bills were transferred to the Company's account. Some other sites for a new Hall were considered during spring 1957, including 85/88 Minories and 21 Wormwood Street. The latter was strongly favoured by a number of the Court, but the surveyor had other views and they prevailed. He recommended a late seventeenth century merchant's house at 13 Devonshire Square and sought leave to bid at auction. Permission was given up to £26,500. The property was in need of serious repair, even doors and windows needing to be secured. The surveyor thought about £6,000 would then be required for further repairs and redecoration. It was a conservative and tactful estimate.

The Devonshire Square house was secured for £24,000. The lowest tender for refurbishment was over £9,000 for 32 weeks' work. That proved optimistic and it was not until February 1959 that the Court held its first meeting in its own Hall since December 1940. The new Hall was one of two survivors of the original square built on the Earl of Devonshire's garden by Nicholas Barbon in the years after 1678. Although listed as a Georgian building and described in Pevsner's *Buildings of England* as mid-Georgian, the house is a timber-framed structure and apart from its later facade, sometime after 1728, it belongs properly to the seventeenth century. In its hey-day, the square was 'inhabited by Merchants and persons of Wealth' who included many of the leading merchants of the Levantine Company. They dealt with Aleppo and several travelled and lived there for a time.

The Company could not quite match the eighteenth century affluence of the square: it was enduring one of its periodic spells of economy, when even Court lunches had, for a time, been suspended. It decided it could afford to use only one floor of the six-storey house but the Assistant Clerk had an office on the second floor and one of the two basement rooms was allocated for use as a wine-cellar.

Furnishing the Hall generated much activity and generosity among members. The 19-foot mahogany Court-room table with 16 chairs and three elbow chairs came from Maples. They were leather-upholstered and embossed with the Company's Coat of Arms. Barnabas Russell found the Master's chair which was donated by his brother-in-law, Vivien Elkington (Master 1944). It was damaged in the bomb blast in Bishopsgate in 1993 but repaired as good as new. A bequest from A. W. Turnbull, (Master 1925)

13, Devonshire Square, which became the Company's fourth Hall in 1957.

provided two embossed Victorian Embassy chairs. T. W. Saint (Master 1952) marked his 50 years as a liveryman by donating a pair of early Georgian candlesticks. Four cocktail parties for the Livery were held in the spring of 1959 to introduce the Company to the new Hall. Sadly the surveyor, A. S. Ford, whose 22 years in the post had spanned a particularly difficult period, died in 1959. A plaque in the entrance hall commemorates his work, and that of the two Masters, G. H. Hall and H. F. Curtis (1957, 1958) in acquiring and renovating the Hall.

With only modest resources and with new commitments, there was pressure to maximise income. The aims were clear, but willing the means to achieve them proved more laborious than many might have expected. Change came very slowly. There was, until 1959, very little structure in the conduct of the Company's finances. There was still a Finance Committee but it lacked continuity in membership and from the evidence of a 1959 Court meeting it seems to have had casual arrangements. It was asked to appoint a permanent chairman, to submit an annual budget and to produce a monthly cash statement of expenditure under each budget item. Investments appear to have been made *ad hoc*. Too much cash was kept in current accounts and much of the stock was old and characterised by low yields and reduced capital values.

Slowly the situation was improved. In the first phase of change the committee structure was overhauled 'with a view to the business of the Court receiving more detailed and continuous attention'. Membership was to be for three years, with those not *ex officio* retiring in succession so as to achieve both continuity and fresh thinking. Three committees were proposed: Finance and Property; Charities; General Purposes. (The latter, to oversee social activities, apprenticeships and membership, was not set up.) The new Finance and Property Committee had power to act quickly in switching investments but, by 1965, it was felt that there were so many areas of overlap between it and the Charities Committee, that the two were merged.

The experiment was useful in bringing a sharper focus to the planning of financial management. Two other valuable developments were the practice of co-opting committee members from the Livery and the new office of Treasurer. The latter provided continuity and direction for the Company's financial policy. The Treasurer served for at least three and up to five years. From 1970, the custom was established for there to be an overlap in the appointment of a successor.

Meanwhile, the effects of inflation and shortages on the property market forced changes in the Company's policy. It took time to develop coherence in investments and, for a while, external pressures were the origin of change rather than a pro-active approach. Long-term leases and ground rents were no longer viable. However, it was not until 1977 that ground rents in Edgwarebury Lane and Mowbray Road were sold. The six houses in Thessaly Square, which were the endowment of the Harold Griffin Charity, produced compensation of £1,133 for bomb damage on two. The process of sale began in 1955 and was completed in 1960. In 1959, Chelsea Borough Council wanted to re-develop Blantyre Street where the Company held the ground rents of Numbers 19 to 23. These were sold to the Council for £2,100.

The pressure for re-development across London, as bomb damage was cleared, brought about more changes, in particular among the properties of the Ratcliffe Pension Fund and the Stepney and Bow Foundation. Re-development of bomb-damaged sites did not tempt the Company. It seemed too risky and, as trustee, the Company felt it had to be cautious. In 1956, it sold the property in Harp lane, which represented the Cloker gift, for £22,000, the proceeds being shared as determined by the Court of Chancery in 1828, three elevenths going to the Company, the remainder to the Stepney and Bow Foundation. Other Ratcliffe property in Thames Street consisted of a bombed site destined to become a car park in the City Corporation's development plan. There were protracted negotiations 'as a result of which' commented the new surveyor, Murray Fox, 'the Company might henceforth expect the humble rent of £26 10s per annum', for car parking spaces.

Murray Fox's appointment in 1959 gave a new dynamic to the process of modernising. He strongly recommended the sale of the remaining properties in Ratcliffe, the old school site and Free Trade Wharf, but both were problematic for different reasons. The Free Trade Wharf had some sentimental value to the Company and had for long been considered the ideal site for a larger Hall, which would accommodate the whole Livery. By 1970, the surveyor's advice was to sell but then a new consideration caused delay, that of waiting until a suitable property came on to the market. Inflation after 1971 became another reason to delay. With prices averaging ten per cent increase a year in place of the three per cent average in the previous 20 years, there was a strong temptation to wait. The eventual sale was completed in June 1977. The price offered in May 1971 was £30,000. It had doubled by 1977.

The old school site posed more problems. The Court accepted that it was, in the surveyor's words, 'completely the wrong sort of property for a charity to hold'. The site covered about half an acre with frontages on The Highway (the former Broad Street) and Cable Street, to the south and north respectively. Bomb damage was repaired in 1955 and the property was insured for £28,000, increased in April 1956 to £47,000. Agreement to sell was reached in

1970 but then came a number of hitches. The leaseholders had gone bankrupt but the Company was unable to terminate the lease on a technicality: its agent had accepted rent. By 1975 the property was in a very dilapidated state; squatters moved in with 16 caravans, some of which were enterprisingly linked up to the street lighting for a free supply of electricity. When the caravans were eventually removed under a Court order — it took two attempts — the area became a dumping site, because it was not immediately fenced off. That, at least, had the advantage of keeping out the squatters. When agreement was reached in 1980 to put the site on the market jointly with an adjacent property belonging to the Greater London Council, a successful sale was reached within months. It achieved £107,000 for the Company.

The first major post-war investment policy review coincided, in 1961, with the more orderly management of the property portfolio. The Finance Committee proposed to reorganise investments, increasing the proportion of insurance stock to 32 per cent of the total, reducing banks to eight per cent and allocating the remainder in the proportion three, two, one between good class equities, gilts and high yield debentures. The Court accepted these recommendations but added that the Company should acquire more real property to achieve a balance between stock market investments and property yielding good rents. It would need to move gradually. In some respects, the caution was extreme and good property investments were missed. It was a frustrating situation: holding on to existing property until a suitable alternative appeared and then being unable to realise the existing asset in time to buy the new one.

The 1961 policy was reiterated in 1965 at a time when Murray Fox was actively seeking to purchase property which would yield six to seven per cent in rents. In 1966 two commercial properties were purchased in Watford and by 1969 were returning ten per cent.

The Finance committee felt encouraged by the signs of success coming from the application of the new policies. In 1968, the committee pressed ahead and appointed a firm of portfolio managers to help achieve a sharper reaction to the state of the market. The full Court, however, preferred that a firm of stockbrokers be used and probably reacted rather strongly to the Finance Committee's initiative because it feared losing control. It insisted that the agreement already made should be for a year only. It should be subject to review and two members of the Court should consult with the portfolio managers. In May 1969, stockbrokers Beamish and O'Kelly were appointed to advise, to provide quarterly reports and an annual valuation of the Company's portfolio. They were given power to act quickly, in consultation with the Master and Treasurer.

During 1969, low-yielding company shares were switched to treasury stocks, some paying as much as ten per cent. Balances on the charity funds and the Company's own corporate funds were invested in short-term loans. With the concurrent property changes, the Company was more comfortably able to provide the income which was essential, estimated at £7,500 a year, and build a hedge against the gathering storm of inflation.

In December 1969, H. W. Norris (Master 1973) and E. P. Hatchett (Master 1981) were co-opted from the Livery to the Finance Committee. Thereafter, a greater sense of urgency was felt to get the balance of investments right. Edward Hatchett, in particular, brought great expertise as well as methodical practices into the whole of the Company's financial activity. The deteriorating state of the national economy and fears of runaway inflation served to concentrate minds, though not to remove entirely the delays in Court decisions which persisted in hindering their ability to be ready to invest. Just as frustrating must have been the haphazard administration, which had no proper filing system, no archiving, no regular stocktaking or audit of deeds. In October 1972, there were serious delays caused by the disappearance of some stock certificates and property deeds. The Company was no worse than many businesses and probably better organised than many charities and social clubs. Nevertheless, it needed to be sharper to survive unscathed the uncertainties of the markets as inflation mounted and a third Middle Eastern war in 1973 produced a world-wide oil crisis.

The reformers on the Finance Committee pressed ahead, redefining the Company's capital, merging separate funds in order to introduce effective forecasting of cash flow and looking constantly for economies and greater efficiency in the administration. Edward Hatchett set an example: he always used the bus (never a taxi) to travel to the Hall from his offices in Holborn. In 1973, a subcommittee was set up to look at property management and find the most effective way of collecting the Company's rents. When rent reviews were due, there was tough bargaining to ensure the Company's income increased. The commercial leasing of parts of the Hall yielded a five-fold increase in 1973.

The first major review of the Company's portfolio, presented by Edward Hatchett in 1972, recommended major changes which eventually improved the charities' incomes. When matters worsened nationally through 1973 and led to the three-day week and the 1974 bank crisis, the Company was assured that its investments were sound. Though there were frequent and anxious consultations, Edward Hatchett remained calm throughout. He advised no changes. The reinvestments had been made wisely and just in time to ride out the storm.

A welcome and to some extent unexpected benefit was the sale of a Bevis Marks property in 1973 for £262,000. It had been bought for £16,000 in 1961, and then become the subject of compulsory purchase for road-widening in 1970. When that threat evaporated, it was recognised as a prime site for redevelopment and valued at £150,000. Its eventual sale price indicates the explosive nature of the London property market at the time and why it was so vital for the Company's experts to take decisions with some speed. For the time being, the proceeds of the sale, together with £21,000 realised on the sale of a Leadenhall Street property, were invested in various short-term loans to take advantage of double figure interest rates. This action had the virtue of funds being available for purchases if something suitable came on to the market. During 1976, properties as far afield as Winchester and West Bromwich were considered. For the first time since the war, the Company was in the advantageous position of having cash easily available.

Another review in 1977 resulted in a decision to reduce investments in banking and insurance and move to high-coupon gilts. The policy had been first agreed in 1961. The charities' position improved again when their funds were moved to companies approved by the Charity Commissioners, namely to Charinco and Charifund. The investment team was strengthened by the appointment, as Treasurer, of Allan Grant (Master 1984). With Edward Hatchett and eventually John Howard, (Master 1986), the Company had a first division triumvirate of investment experts.

The notion of a new, larger Hall had not entirely been dropped and may well have been revived by the improving financial position. In 1971, there was a proposal to buy a redundant church. The idea was abandoned when it was realised that only one remained on the market and that was a singularly unattractive building in City Road. The Court contented itself with registering with the Church Commissioners in case other churches should become available. In 1974, the Master, Harold (Bertie) Norris, wrote, 'It would be wonderful if we could, one day, obtain a Hall large enough to entertain the whole Livery and this hope is in the minds of the Court members [that] at some future date … this dream of our own large Hall may become a reality'. Another approach was to expand from No 13 Devonshire Square by purchasing No 14. Negotiations lasted several months without reaching a satisfactory conclusion.

Although the Court never took a decision not to proceed, the idea of a new Hall died away in the 1970s. In part, this may have been because of the opportunity arising from the ending of leases to the Hall's tenants. The transformation of the Hall began in 1973 with the creation of a waiting-room

Exhibition in 1976 to mark the opening of the museum at the Hall. Leonard Sharpless, the first honorary curator, is on the far left; the Master, Ian Norman, centre; and Bunny Palmer, far right.

on the ground floor. Then there followed a new ground floor Court room and a strong room in the sub-basement. The basement, vacated by tenants, was converted to accommodate cloakrooms, a museum and exhibition room to celebrate the craft of coopering as well as house memorabilia and treasures. These renovations were first estimated to cost £15,000 but re-decoration and an extension to the kitchen brought the amount up to £20,634. The design and execution of these changes was the work of E. P. (Bunny) Palmer (Master 1974). The result is the current arrangement (1999) with the Court room and offices on the ground floor and elegant entertaining rooms on the first floor, much as the building would have been used in the eighteenth century.

As important in its way to the corporate health and reputation of the Company as sound investment and modern management was to its stability, was the renewal of its membership. Many senior members could easily become eloquent on the subject of ensuring that the 'right kind of candidates' came forward to take the Freedom and Livery. During the 1950s, recruitment appeared to be haphazard with no system for introducing and interviewing prospective candidates. After one or two embarrassments, it was stipulated in 1959, that if neither the proposer nor seconder were members of the Court, then an interview was necessary. Fees for the Freedom and Livery were also in need of revision, if only to remove the anomaly that it was cheaper to enter the Company by servitude (apprenticeship) than by patrimony. Hence, during the 1950s, servitude was chosen by many liverymen as the route for their sons. Changes implemented in 1961 kept the patrimony fees unchanged but increased those for entry by servitude (apprenticeship) and redemption. Unfortunately, 18 apprentices were caught in this trap and had a pragmatic decision not been made to charge the Freedom and Livery fees in existence at the time they began their apprenticeships, their fees would have been double the amount they originally expected.

The matter of fines and fees was dealt with on an *ad hoc* basis; for example, in 1947, it was decided to have them unaltered for one year. Then nothing was done until the changes in 1961. Further revisions in 1967, 1969 and 1973 were intended to recognise the pace of inflation but it was not until 1978, that proposed increases were carefully compared against the retail price index and one or two other livery companies. Thereafter, fine judgement was applied to what the market would bear. It was imperative to maximise all sources of income to the company and, with a waiting list for admission, it seemed a favourable time to apply increases. At the same time, a quinquennial review was agreed.

The size of the Livery and the regulation of its intake was tackled with determination and imagination. In 1959, the number of liverymen was 174 and a limit of 210 was imposed in 1961. This marked the end of the surge of admissions by redemption and led to a more controlled admission procedure. An attempt was made, not always adhered to, to ensure elections to the Livery were held annually, just before Common Hall (Election Day). Paperwork was improved. Formal application, using new forms, was required and interviews with candidates were conducted by three members of the Court or two and the Clerk. Admissions were buoyant throughout the 1960s to the extent that the maximum number was raised from 210 to 230 in 1967. In addition, a more balanced intake was sought by imposing an annual limit of three admissions by servitude, ten by redemption and no limit on patrimony. The waiting list of Freemen grew in spite of these rules so that, in January 1975, it was decided to rescind the limit temporarily and invite all Freemen waiting for admission to take up the Livery and thus remove the waiting list. Out of 18 on the list, 15 accepted the invitation. This increased the Company to 255.

By the end of the 1970s it was felt that 255 was enough to provide the Company with a pool of varied talent and opportunities for all to find fellowship. It was still small enough to retain a sense of belonging, a sense of responsibility for corporate affairs and a sense of brotherhood in the long tradition of the Company. No limit was placed on the grant of the Freedom. Used as a staging post, but conferring no automatic right to the Livery, it proved a useful and flexible device.

A new committee of the Court, first chaired by M. J. Glenny (Master 1965) was set up to deal with Freedom and Livery matters. It gave considerable thought to the qualities the Company needed in candidates and initiated a thoughtful debate. Malcolm Glenny argued for proper guidelines and a stringent set of rules 'to ensure the right type of person [was] admitted... who [would be] likely to have the qualities required for the future welfare of the Company'. He insisted that all applications should go before the committee irrespective of sponsor. The practice in recent years of admitting, rather indiscriminately, those who wanted to be liverymen, appeared to be 'good chaps' but stood no chance of being elected to the Court, had, he believed, had a harmful effect. He argued that the Company had taken their money, believing that their presence in the Livery would not affect the chances of able, younger liverymen gaining promotion. It had had the opposite effect 'in that the Company will run out of suitable people for promotion in future'. Entry by patrimony was at an all-time low by contrast with 'the old days, when much of the Livery was made up of family connections'. The Court agreed that entry by patrimony should be allowed irrespective of the numbers on the Livery list.

A contrasting view was expressed by Bertie Norris. He disagreed with stringent rules. The committee might well work to a broad basis of guidance 'but you cannot endow the committee with wisdom, clairvoyance or perspicacity... we are looking for age, social background, family connections, social skills plus other attributes as make a person "suitable"...' He may have believed his own rhetoric but in challenging a more prescriptive method of selection and recommending a vague criterion of 'suitability' he was arguing for the *status quo*. The qualities required were ones which contained the potential for ensuring the advancement and prosperity of the Company and good fellowship among its members. Knowledge, expertise, integrity, untiring concern for the schools and charities, as well as a particular interest in the social affairs and collective needs of the City were further attributes which, Bertie Norris argued, the committee should seek out. Perhaps the essence of all this is the recognition that, no less than any business, the

Company depended as much on its human as on its financial resources. Above all, it needed to retain 'its deep interest in the humanities'.

The renewal of vigour in the Company's leadership was a matter in need of as much passionate debate as entry to the Company. In the 1950s, the Court was dominated by old men. There had never been any age limit on membership. In the past it had been unnecessary. Plague, fever, influenza, appendicitis were all killers. Until the late nineteenth century, natural causes culled the Court and ensured that it was only the odd one who lived to complete his natural span of three score years and ten. Improved hygiene, nutrition and medical advances ensured longevity and created a problem of managing retirement and renewal in the twentieth century. The only limitation on Court membership was an inability by reason of old age, frailness, or illness to attend meetings regularly. Vacancies, therefore, occurred on death or voluntary retirement and there was often little time for the newly-elected Assistant to become accustomed to his new responsibilities before his turn came for election as Master. The problem was compounded by the passion with which some members defended seniority in election to the Court. Lest any newly-elected Warden be in any doubt about the power of seniority, it was the custom for the 'father of the Court' to sit next to the Under Warden to guide and advise during meetings.

Some of the frustration in reforming the Company's practices and finances during the 1950s, was born of the perception that old men resist change. The first major post-war change was the decision in 1966 to appoint the Master presumptive as Renter Warden instead of the existing custom of the post going to the immediate past master. The change, at least, allowed a new member of the Court a year of experience in office before becoming Master. It also stimulated debate about other aspects of the constitution. Seniority, as a principle, was again re-affirmed but there was support for flexibility and evidence in practice, when two new members of the Court were elected 'out of turn'. There was even a discussion about 80 as a retiring age but nothing came of it until, in 1973, it was agreed that 75 should be the age of retirement from the Court. This decision caused three immediate retirements. Fears were immediately raised that with eight vacancies occurring in the next five years, the tradition would be lost of Wardens retiring to the ranks of the Livery and for a few years and helping bridge the gap between Court and Livery. The majority view was that sufficient change had been absorbed for the time being. Not even a sensible proposal, to meet at 11.30am rather than after lunch, could be entertained. The Master's motion was defeated.

Improving links between Court and Livery was a recurring concern. For years, apart from Common Hall and the Livery dinner, there was little contact. The opening of committees of the Court to co-options from the Livery, as well as encouragement to become associated with the Company's charities, were valuable initiatives, in tune with the times but in reality touching only a handful of liverymen. Opportunities for the membership to come together were always being sought. The Court viewed the annual service at which Henry Cloker's will was read as one such and annually bemoaned the tiny attendance. The service had the great disadvantage of being held on New Year's day, as inconvenient as a working day in the 1950s and 1960s as when it became a Bank holiday in 1974. Attempts to attract a higher attendance were made by arranging a luncheon after the service; adding a display of silver in 1969 and then providing the meal at the Hall. On the first occasion, it attracted 119 liverymen and guests. The following year, 1973, a thoughtful addition was inviting liverymen's widows as the Company's guests. An experiment with an afternoon service followed by tea proved much less successful. Once the decision was made to move the date to October, to regulate the attendance of the Coopers' and Coborn School choir, newly amalgamated at Upminster as one co-educational school, and to include representation from Strode's school, the Cloker service came to be regarded as a major Company event. It became more inclusive, not only observing Henry Cloker's wishes by reading a branch (section) of his will, but as a commemoration of and thanksgiving for all the Company's benefactors. It provided an example of blending old and new in the Company's traditions.

An experiment at Common Hall in 1979 was a question and answer session which revealed the extent of the Livery's ignorance about the Company's affairs. The subjects included the schools — what responsibilities had the Company?; who appointed governors?; the wine cellar — was it true it was the best in the City? where was it? who buys the wine and looks after it?; trade and industry — what links exist and with whom?; admission by patrimony; and lastly, the nature and extent of charity work. The event revealed the thirst for more dialogue.

Social activities remained one of the prime purposes of the Company, as they had been from its earliest days. Livery dinners, Court luncheons and cocktail parties were easy targets for critics who saw the modern livery companies as mere social clubs propping up an arcane and archaic system of City government. In fact, the social functions held the Company together and enabled it to sustain its schools and charities. The opening of the Hall and later its renovation in 1977, provided the occasions for receptions for the

Livery and their ladies. The annual United Guilds service at St Paul's provided the occasion for a Livery luncheon at Painter-Stainers' Hall. In 1969, this service was marked and, nearly marred, by a screwdriver, which fell from the cathedral dome and narrowly missed the Under Warden. W. B. Holden, the Master, commented, 'It nearly ended in tragedy [which] would not only have been sad... but also ironic, for during the war, the Under Warden had spent many hours protecting the dome from fire'.

The discovery, in 1960, that the Australian ambassador to the USA was entitled to the Livery by patrimony, gave the Court an opportunity to honour a distinguished diplomat, Harold Beale, with an extraordinary Court meeting and luncheon in June 1961. His Excellency's grandfather, a cooper, had emigrated to Australia. The gifts exchanged were a piece of new world silver, designed by C. Ericson Gardner of Boston, and, a silver champagne cup, a replica of one given to the Company by Sir David Salomons.

The annual Livery dinner, at which the Lord Mayor was the chief guest, settled into a routine in the 1960s when the Company established the tradition of being the first livery company to entertain the new Lord Mayor in the Mansion House. During the 1950s, the occasion was held in a variety of places and in 1959, there were many complaints about the standard of catering. Subsequently, a cocktail party on HMS Wellington was given as compensation for the disappointing Livery banquet.

The decision to allow ladies, one guest per liveryman, to attend the Livery dinner in 1970 was promoted by the Master, J. L. Reed, but was too radical for many senior members. It was decided that the matter of inviting ladies would, in future, be determined each year. The vote went against their presence in 1971, for in 1973 and against in 1976, which was the year of Sir Murray Fox's Livery banquet. The solution that year was a separate ladies' dinner, hosted by Lady Fox, after which the ladies listened to the men's speeches. The forces to maintain the status quo remained strong and were aided in their determination to keep the ladies out of the main Livery function by the drive for economy. There was a deficit on the accounts in 1978–79, largely because of the high level of corporation tax levied at 52 per cent. The decision about the banquet was left to the Master, A. Newton Husbands. The ladies were excluded but tickets did not sell sufficiently well to fill the Egyptian Hall at the Mansion House. There was some irony, in that the emergency plan to hold the banquet at Coopers' Hall, resulted in a splendid feast, one of the best, but did little for domestic economy. The Company felt it had to pull out the stops, lest it should seem ungracious towards the Lord Mayor and its other guests.

The Company's charities were increasingly administered in ways which were thoughtful, tactful and above all, personal. The custom grew of the Master visiting as many as possible during his year in office and individual liverymen were encouraged to become involved in visiting those to whom the Company now made grants. In Egham, Commander C. R. Perrin (Master 1987) looked after these grants from the Strode's funds and their recipients for many years until his retirement to Cornwall. His local knowledge meant he could work closely with other local charities. During the 1950s, there were many people in Stepney and Egham who were in their eighties and who did not qualify for the state pension so the Company's grants were of great importance. The Ratcliffe recipients were chosen after advertisement and interview. Their grants were usually of £100 a year and subject to three-yearly review. In 1958, it was reported that all recipients had incomes of under £5 a week.

The Old Coopers' Livery Fund and the William Alexander Fund were both quite small and used at the Court's discretion without any advertisement or means test. The Harold Griffin Fund continued to be administered by his family and had the great merit of being flexible. As a result of a review of the Company's charities in 1963, it was recommended that the Ratcliffe and Egham charities, whose purposes were so similar, should be merged. The Egham Charity was fully used while the Ratcliffe had surplus funds. The Charity Committee argued that by merging there would be more scope for reinterpreting the charities to suit contemporary conditions. It considered that provision of good housing might be more beneficial than small money grants. The Charity Commissioners were approached and, though the merger did not take place, a modified scheme was introduced in 1966 which took account of the reorganisation of London boroughs and gave the Ratcliffe Fund scope to work in Tower Hamlets. The idea of housing provision was dropped in favour of sponsoring pensioners in sheltered accommodation. This allowed the Company to learn at first hand what were the real costs of housing assistance. By September 1968, a new scheme was launched. Eight people were chosen, each to receive £52 a year in grants. Local and professional advice, in particular through the agency of Toynbee Hall, was sought to maximise benefits. Often these included provision of household equipment, such as new vacuum cleaners, or refrigerators.

The Company's own charitable gifts, as distinct from the charities of which it was trustee, were resourced by its Benevolent Fund, which was created by covenant from corporate funds and topped up as necessary. It provided regular Christmas donations to City churches, settlements and charities as well as hampers for the Ratcliffe and Egham grantees. A result of the overhaul of investments in the 1970s was greater income for the charities. The total income of £4,000 in the late 1950s had become £25,000 by 1978. There were more gains when the Company decided to use in-house accounting and to collect its own rents. In 1977, the Queen's Silver Jubilee was marked by an additional £10 gift to each grantee, a donation to the Prince's Trust and a contribution to the Jubilee garden on the south side of Devonshire Square.

A new charitable foundation was set up by the will of Bunny Palmer (Master 1974) in 1979. The fund included the Company's own charitable donations, the former Benevolent Fund and the dividends from Bunny Palmer's property company, Waverley Court Ltd, which he bequeathed to the Company. Half of this latter income was for the Cooper and Coborn Educational Foundation and half was for the Palmer Foundation. The Foundation enhanced both school and college provision of prizes and books at a period when cuts in their state grants affected necessities such as books.

The Jubilee scholarships at the Cooper and Coborn School were increased to £500 in 1977 as an appropriate way of marking Queen Elizabeth's Silver Jubilee. Their distribution was left to the discretion of the chairman of governors and the headteacher and their purpose remained to help students to go on to further study. Strode's College boat club, which was proving one of the most successful in England, was helped by the provision of equipment. In 1964, when an appeal for a new boat house and sports pavilion fell short of also providing a new cricket square, the Company contributed most of the cost. Even more sportingly, it fielded a team captained by Neville Atchley (Master 1979) to play Strode's in 1970 — and was defeated.

Between 1966 and 1976, the Company's schools went through great changes. The Coopers' School and Coborn Girls' were already poised for change and a move from the East End, when plans for comprehensive reorganisation were issued in 1965. The post-war shift in population from the East End of London to Essex resulted in over half the schools' population travelling in from Essex. It was a situation which recalled that of the Ratcliffe school in the 1880s. In 1966, the decision was taken to move to Upminster in the Borough of Havering, where the schools were amalgamated and a degree of selection was preserved. Throughout the next eight years of preparation and building, the amalgamation was kept on the Court's agenda and the chairman of governors, Baron Burn, was invited from time to time to give a briefing on developments. The Court wanted to ensure that it would have adequate representation on the new governing body of the combined schools but it showed a little reluctance about lady governors. The local education authority's insistence on this matter produced a minute in 1971 that at some date it might become necessary to appoint lady governors among the Company's allocation of places. In fact, two were appointed in 1974.

Strode's transformation from a selective boys' grammar school to a co-educational comprehensive sixth form college was achieved in 1975 as part of Surrey County Council's reorganisation of secondary schools. The Company's links were limited to a representative on the board of Trustees of the Strode Foundation and one governor. This did not prevent the Court as a whole regretting the upheaval, and in particular the abandonment of academic selection. It was the wisdom of individuals on the Court and within the governing boards of the college and the school, which helped the majority to come to terms with these changes. If anything, the links became closer as both Company and schools recognised they had to work with determination to keep their contacts alive.

Some of the tools of coopering displayed in the Company's museum.

The Company's links within the City developed and were renewed according to the commitment of senior members to City organisations. In 1954, C. F. Glenny (Master 1940) became Chief Commoner, when he was elected chairman of the City Lands Committee. The position was a 'first' for the Company. Special links were made with the Honourable Artillery Company and with the London Division Royal Navy Reserve. In the exchange of gifts, the Company produced a rum ration tub made by the Under Warden, M. H. Gorsuch Browne, with silver decoration by Major J. N. Russell (Master 1961). The latter's skill as a silversmith resulted in a number of fine pieces of plate for the Company and a tradition of a silver cup for each past Master.

In 1961, the Company's surveyor, Murray Fox, was elected Alderman for Bread Street Ward. His increased commitments to the City Corporation led to his resignation as surveyor but he was elected to the Court in 1969. There he continued to advise on the Company's investments in property. He was due to serve as Renter Warden in 1973 but as this clashed with his election as Sheriff, he gave way to Bunny Palmer. Murray Fox's position brought the Company 'very much closer to the City', in the words of a senior member. His election as Lord Mayor in 1974 produced great activity at the Hall. The Company planned to have a float in the Lord Mayor's procession but this was altered to a carriage for the Master, Wardens and Clerk accompanied on foot by 20 liverymen carrying the tools of the trade. The gowns worn by the Court were refurbished, and a special luncheon was arranged to follow Common Hall at which Murray Fox was elected Lord Mayor. There was also a Court dinner at the Mansion House. One of the Lord Mayor's duties was inaugurating the sixth form college at Egham.

In June 1976, Murray Fox was duly elected Master of the Company and immediately made history by presiding over Court meetings which began at 11am. Other signs of a brisk, modern approach included drawing up job descriptions for the chief officers to avoid gaps and overlaps, broadening the search for property investments, introducing economies and rationalising the Company's hospitality. He also made an important contribution to the Company's museum with the gift of a set of Cooper's tools which he acquired from the Port of London. To mark the distinction he had brought to the Company, his portrait was commissioned from Leonard Boden. It was unveiled in May 1978 by the Lady Mayoress.

Towards the end of the decade, there was a groundswell of activity in the Company directed towards making the management of all its affairs more efficient and effective. There was a healthy combination of greater professionalism in the administration with self-help among the members. The Hall Committee organised regular working parties of volunteers to keep the building in a good state of general maintenance. The importance of continuity and expertise in the Clerk's office was brought home dramatically, in autumn 1976, when the Assistant Clerk and Beadle, Mr Harrod, had to retire because of sudden illness. Until this crisis, the Court had employed a part-time Clerk and therefore had relied on the Assistant Clerk for all day-to-day matters. D. G. Baker (Master 1971) stepped in temporarily to 'hold the fort' as Assistant Clerk until the appointment in June 1977 of J. A. Newton. The latter's arrival to work for a time in tandem with the Clerk, J. W. S. Clark, seemed to give encouragement to the modernisers on the Court to push ahead on all fronts with streamlining the Company's affairs. The change of pace was very necessary if the Company were to withstand the economic pressures of the time and maintain, even extend, its commitments. For one member, it was all too much. When, to meet the timetable of the new accounting system, the Court day was moved from the first to the third Tuesday in the month, he protested it was going too far to interfere with a custom which had lasted unchanged since 1653. It was, however, a minority view.

Chapter thirteen
Into the Future 1980–2000

> *The Thatcher government unsentimentally destroyed the old capital industries and the power of the Trades Unions. Local democracy was attenuated. Power was concentrated at the centre to ensure radical policies were put into action in Education, Health and Social Services. Private enterprise triumphed, electronic technology transformed every aspect of life. Wealth was distributed less equitably and used more conspicuously than for a century. The electorate swept New Labour to power in 1997 to rebuild basic public services, to temper individualism with more concern for social and environmental improvements, and to replace confrontation with consensus in public life.*

'WE LIVE IN AN EVER-CHANGING WORLD and the future should be addressed with spurs not laurels.' This injunction to the Livery from a Master of the Company catches the mood of the 1990s. Any lingering complacency, if not banished, was, at this period, in the process of being challenged, as were some cherished traditions. Where long-established practices and customs were considered to be a hindrance to improvements, they were subjected to examination and often were amended.

One change which may eventually prove to have had a great impact on the Company was the decision, in 1973, to introduce an age limit of 75 on membership of the Court. But an abrupt application of this limit might have compelled four retirements in a single year. Retirements were introduced on the basis of one each year. When, eventually, all members of the Court are those elected under new provisions, they will serve a maximum of 18 years. The pace of change in business, manufacturing and the professions was accelerated as never before by the computer revolution. As a result, government of the Company, mainly by men who had retired from business, threatened to divorce the Court from new trends. That threat, too, receded as the principle of election to the Court by seniority, challenged and often disregarded before the 1980s, gave way to the election of younger liverymen who could bring new, or special or complementary skills to the Court. However, the great pressure of work on the time and energies of those in full-time employment in the 1990s, ensured that its older, retired members continued to play an important part in Company affairs, perhaps more than the reforming members of the 1973 Court expected. The move was undertaken with caution and awareness of the dangers of a self-perpetuating oligarcy once the old rules had been abandoned.

As important and radical a change, in the view of many members, resulted from the decision, in 1992, to abolish the Finance Court, which had been meeting infrequently with little business to discuss, and to replace it with an Advisory Group. The purpose of the new group of five members was to promote 'the continuity and oversight' which were thought to be missing from the Court and difficult to provide by a group of 20 members meeting 10 times a year. The work of reviewing Court policies and procedures and the preparation of recommendations ahead of Court meetings, have contributed to the Court's effectiveness. The group's production of a Court handbook 'detailing the duties, obligations and responsibilities of Court members', points to a continuing aim of efficiency and adopting the best practices of modern management. Little sign here of resting on laurels!

Without a decision to appoint John Newton, the Assistant Clerk, as full-time Clerk in 1981, (the first full-time Clerk for over half a century), these and other schemes to modernise the Company and extend the scope of its charities, could not have been successful. With the help of successive Assistant Clerks, Beadles and some Court members, he was able to provide the necessary administrative structure and adopt up-to-date office technology.

Such changes were not common among livery companies. The Coopers had reason to feel some satisfaction that in modernising their ways, striving to keep abreast of change, and to be responsive to the needs of the City, they were doing their best to shed the popular (but inaccurate) description as one of the many dining and wining clubs in the City, and little else.

In one respect, the Court was not ready to 'move with the times'. This was the issue of admitting women to the Livery. The matter was first raised in 1983 with the presentation of Alice Hoare, a student at Strode's College, as apprentice to the Master. There was no problem in a girl apprentice being admitted to the Freedom after four years (or by patrimony) but thereafter her path was blocked. There were those who argued that girls should not be selected for the apprenticeship since they would be barred from the real prize, admission to the Livery. However, for more than a decade, more girls than boys at Strode's College were keen to put forward their candidature for the Master's apprenticeship, many believing the Freedom of the Company and of the City were worthwhile objectives. Some also thought that their presence in the ranks of Freemen was a reminder to the Company that in the world at large women were no longer content with small consolation prizes. They were winning their way into senior ranks in the professions, business and politics. The first woman prime minister was elected in 1979 and the first Lady Mayor of London in 1983. By the 1990s, even the armed forces were allowing girls into to careers involving active service.

In 1986, the Master, John Howard, referred the matter of admitting women to the Livery to the Freedom and Livery Committee. As a result it was agreed that the Court's decision on such a fundamental change should be by a two-thirds majority. The outcome was a decision to maintain the status quo and not to return to the issue within ten years. Research among the other 22 minor companies which had their own Halls, indicated that women were in the Livery in one only (the Apothecaries), where full membership was a means of access to the particular profession. On this occasion, the Court was 'not minded' to give a lead. It felt that the best policy was caution, and keeping in step with the rest. But at least the issue had been carefully and thoroughly discussed and a straight majority (not the required two-thirds) had voted in favour of admitting women.

There matters rested until 1999. By then, the admission of women to the livery of many other companies made the issue rather less contentious. The Master, Michael Howell, was in favour of testing the Company's view. After careful consideration by the Court and consultation with the Society of the Livery, the Court voted to overturn the custom of centuries. Women were to be admitted on a equal basis with men, by servitude, redemption and patrimony. The logic of equality also meant that children of women in the Livery would qualify for admission. The Company was once again brought into the mainstream of changes in the City, better able to reflect and benefit from the transformation of business and professional life.

The Court promoted the Company's charitable work with great conviction and vision. The finances and annual accounts of the various charities were made more easily available; and the Company's own charitable gifts were regularly channelled into the newest charity, the Palmer Foundation. The Company's Charity Committee under successive chairmen—Digby Smith, Ian Norman, 'Bill' Skelton and Peter Allington—involved the Livery to a greater extent and became more structured and systematic in its approach. Its guidelines were formalised and information about its activities was publicised among the Livery. With the help and advice of the social services department in the borough of Tower Hamlets, the Charity Committee was able to focus its activities effectively. Tower Hamlets, which was created in the reorganisation of local government in 1974, encompassed Ratcliffe, Stepney and Bow, those areas of east London where the Company had sustained charitable work since 1554 and which had been the location, until the last decades of the twentieth century, of many cooperages.

The need for voluntary help increased in the decade of the 1980s as government cuts in social service budgets became increasingly severe. The Company's response was to seek an alteration in the allocation of the income of the Ratcliffe Trust made in 1891 when the school at Ratcliffe was about to move to Tredegar Square and the almshouses were replaced by pensions. (For a full explanation of this matter, see Appendix 3). This resulted in much larger income for distribution. A snapshot of the Ratcliffe Trust in 1993 showed it allocated over £24,000. In addition to support for 13 grantees, the charity made grants to benefit young people (NSPCC; Attlee Adventure Playground), the homeless, the disabled and the elderly. Organisations such as the Whitechapel Mission, the Bow Community Trust, Age Concern and Oxford House were used to channel support as effectively as possible. The detailed local knowledge of 'Jo' Joughin, Master in 1992, was the source of much of the advice received by the Charity Committee.

The Palmer Foundation (see p. 236), which the Company used to convey its own corporate gifts to charities, became the largest of the Company's six charities. 'Bunny' Palmer's generosity became the inspiration and the vehicle by which the Company's whole approach to charities changed. A new commitment to corporate giving was the result. Among its recipients in 1993 were charities helping the homeless, the Citizens' Advice Bureau in Tower Hamlets, Centrepoint and the Salvation Army. The Company's school and college, were also recipients each year of support through the Palmer Foundation. Though not in any way replacing cuts in government and local authority funding, these grants came at a particularly fortuitous time to enhance much needed technology and media facilities. The Egham Charity supported ten 'grantees', the Harold Griffin Charity supported three in Battersea, and the William Alexander and Coopers' Liverymen Fund continued to be available to help members of the Company and their families.

Impressive as the reforms and improvements were in the Company's charitable work, it was the personal commitment of individual members of the Court and the Livery which best defined and characterised the collective effort. The regular visits by members to grantees ensured that the Company's tradition of care did not become submerged in the mechanics of fund-management or lost in the complexity of state and local government administration. The personal link ensured that individual needs and priorities were known and the right kind of help could be found. In 1989, one grantee, an 80 year-old amputee became house-bound because she was frightened to use a wheel-chair designed only for the road. The Company was able not only to secure a chair suitable for mounting pavements, but the patient research and persistence of 'Jo' Joughin unlocked social services funds and she was granted a mobility allowance. Her letter of thanks included a fine testimonial: 'For years I have struggled to pay for anything that I needed and when I need a chair there (are) kind people like The Worshipful Company of Coopers about, who help honest people'. Another personal touch, which over the years from 1981 brought great pleasure to hosts and guests alike, was a garden party at Edward Hatchett's home at Henley for grantees who used Toynbee Hall as a day centre. Even after his death, his widow, Peggy and his family ensured that the event, with its popular river-trip, continued.

By 1998, the Palmer Foundation and the Ratcliffe Charity enjoyed much improved incomes of £75,000 and £45,000. The policy of distributing a few larger sums to groups of charities on a cyclical basis was well-established. In 1998, charities for the frail and elderly and sufferers from Alzheimer's disease were the main beneficiaries. The Ratcliffe Charity had developed a method of quick response to critical needs in Tower Hamlets by using the local knowledge of borough officials, working closely with 'Jo' Joughin. By having available an emergency fund to use where there were no appropriate government funds, and having discretion to use up to £100 for each case, the local officers were able to give help where it was most needed.

In the 1990s, the Company was energetic in its attempts to keep pace with the changes which were transforming businesses in the City. The jargon and methods of business management crept in, at first stealthily and then with a rush. Some of the older Assistants were among those keen to move the Company into the electronic age. By comparison with the recent past, there were more committees, sub-committees and working parties. Changes were agreed, implemented and then, kept under review. The Company reaped the benefit of finances which were sounder and more professionally managed than at any time in the past. In a bid to bring income from property up to the efficiency achieved by investments in equities, the long lease on Hazlitt House in Southampton Row was bought back and as the millennium approached, the Company was poised to develop the property.

The domestic affairs of the Company ran less smoothly. The Hall suffered a flood from tenants' quarters on the upper two floors in August 1989. The water overflowed during a week-end and brought down the plaster ceilings at the rear of the building. It was seven months before the

Company could re-occupy its Hall. On 10 April 1992, a bomb planted at the Baltic Exchange as part of the IRA's campaign of terror, exploded and caused extensive damage, smashing windows and cracking plaster. But it was the bomb in Bishopsgate on 24 April 1993, which caused the greatest damage of these three catastrophes. The narrow street from Bishopsgate to Devonshire Square funnelled the blast all too effectively. All the windows of the Hall were smashed, the front door and three security doors in the basement were blown in and their frames severely damaged. The heavy interior doors to the Court room and the dining room were blown off their hinges and were found lying damaged together with their frames. Once again walls and ceilings were cracked. Flying glass damaged furniture and the first members on the scene found they were ankle-deep in broken glass. Those who arrived to clean up on Sunday morning, including two who had returned early from holiday, found the fax machine still working and bearing a message of sympathy from the Company's surveyors.

Hardly had the paint dried on the restoration work, than the Court started to plan the Company's celebrations for the quincentenary of the grant of the first royal charter in 1501. The special committee appointed for this purpose determined to mark this milestone in the Company's history by setting up a new charity to provide sheltered housing for the elderly in the Borough of Tower Hamlets, appropriately the area where the Company's first charity, founded by Nicholas Gibson, had its origin (Ratcliffe is one of the 'hamlets'). The scheme which was adopted showed imagination and ingenuity. A new charity, the Coopers' Livery Housing Fund raised substantial initial funds from the liverymen and sought further donations from trusts and individuals with connections in the City. The first project was in partnership with the Shaftesbury Housing Group, which already had provided and managed 17 schemes for sheltered housing in Greater London and worked on other schemes with a large number of local authorities. Its major contribution was the management of the property. The third partner was Tower Hamlets. It faced a major challenge in the 1990s as affluent workers from the City moved east to new developments by the river and elsewhere in the borough. These changes contributed to a rise in the cost of housing and a scarcity of homes for rent at reasonable charges. The borough helped in two ways. It brought to the scheme its experience of providing 1,000 new homes for rent between 1994 and 1998. It also provided the land. This partnership of Company, housing association and borough attracted a government grant for 'social housing'.

The ingenuity of the scheme is that the Company's financial contribution will be regarded as an interest-free loan, (though there is provision for interest to be charged). Once the 40 self-contained homes in Coopers' Court, on the Mile End Road, are fully occupied, the Company's 'seedcorn' money will be repaid by the Shaftesbury Housing Group and so made available for another scheme. In this way, not only can charitable funds be recycled, but each scheme will be capable of responding to current needs and conditions.

The Company might have expected to have one of its Assistants as Lord Mayor early in the new millennium, when Malcolm Matson was elected as Alderman for Bread Street Ward in 1994. His manifesto programme was one of reform of City government. His subsequent rejection by the Aldermanic Court, a right maintained since the twelfth century, and his pursuit of natural justice — to be told the reason for his rejection — led on to a personal campaign to reform City government. During the next few years, some loyalties in the Company became strained. To some members, the campaign seemed too strong an attack on the Corporation to which livery companies traditionally offer respect, even deference. Others took the view, which was echoed in other companies, that reform of the franchise was overdue.

Many of the traditional City practices were also being called in question by the New Labour leadership, hopeful, even confident, of victory in a general election due in 1996 or 1997. There was widespread agreement that the City needed more openness if it were to pursue its aim of retaining pre-eminence in the European and world financial markets. By appearing to silence debate on a reform of the City franchise; by maintaining a tradition that an Alderman who does not receive 70 per cent support in the Aldermanic Court should 'fall on his sword' and resign, by such procedures the Corporation seemed out of tune with the times. When the New Labour government published its Green Paper on London government, the City Corporation was told to improve its procedures. This it sought to do in a Private Bill, 'City of London (Ward Elections)', which proposed a franchise based on rateable value. This gave businesses in the City the leading role in determining future elections, but it left the ordinary residents of the City, (about 5,000 as against 34,000 businesses), to remain an unheard minority.

Having been deprived of an opportunity to press the cause of reform from within the City Corporation, Malcolm Matson campaigned, in a personal capacity, from without. He wrote a pamphlet for the Fabian Society *The last rotten borough* and opposed the Bill at Westminster, giving evidence before the Select Committee and championing the rights of the ordinary citizens.

Malcolm Matson may not achieve his goal of a fully democratic franchise. (In the unique circumstances of the City, with a daily population of half a million and a resident population of 5,000, it would be difficult to achieve). He may, however, be counted with the small band of Coopers, (some acting as individuals, others giving a lead in the Company), who, over the centuries, have dared to challenge established methods, traditions and prejudices.

As the Company approaches its quincentenary, it can feel satisfaction in being abreast of the times. The last few decades of the twentieth century were as remarkable for the speed of change within the Company as for the technological and social revolution all around. Building on much more solid and lasting financial security than in the recent past, the Company can foresee an important, and perhaps key role for itself. That is as a provider of support and help through its charities of its many neighbours who are disabled, disadvantaged and only partially helped by the State. Above all, the Company's help is personal. All who are able to help are encouraged to do so.

This fact has done much to break down any perceived gap between the Livery and the Court. The Society of the Livery also played its part. It provided a focus of interest and involvement for the Livery and a preparatory arena in which future Wardens and Assistants can find scope to develop. In its turn, the Court gave financial help to the Society so that it could organise a lively social programme for the Livery. With changes in the relationship between the City and the livery companies very likely in the near future, it is appropriate that a working party, charged with planning the objectives for the future of the Company, should already be at work to prepare for a new situation. The Livery is represented on the working party by three of its members and all liverymen have the opportunity to contribute their views on the Company's future as it prepares 'to enter the new Millennium and start the second 500 years of … corporate existence'.

Captions, Appendices, Glossary, References and Indexes

Captions to Colour Plates

Appendix one: Casks and their Capacities

Appendix two: Apprentices: social and geographical origins

Appendix three: Revised Income of the Ratcliffe Pension Charity

Glossary

References

Index of People

Index of Subjects

Captions to Colour Plates

Plate 1   Dame Avice Knyvett *c.* 1540. Her first husband, Nicholas Gibson, founded the Ratcliffe Charity. She ensured it passed into the care of the Coopers' Company on her death (1554).

Plate 2   The Egham Charity founded by Henry Strode (Master 1703). This watercolour dating from 1812 shows the original 12 almshouses and schoolhouse dating from 1706. The painting was submitted as evidence in a dispute between the Company and the schoolmaster on the one hand and Egham tradesmen on the other.

Plate 3   Woodham Mortimer Hall, which, with over 300 acres, was bequeathed to the Company in 1725 by William Alexander. It was intended to provide pensions for needy members of the Company. The mid-seventeenth century facade conceals a much older building, parts of which are mediaeval.

Plates 4 & 5   Memorial and inscription to William Alexander erected in 1826 on the initiative of Robert Carter (Master), and James F. Firth (Upper Warden). It stands opposite Woodham Mortimer Hall by the side of the main Chelmsford to Maldon road and is often mistaken for a war memorial. When the hall and land were sold in 1943, the Company retained possession of the memorial. Originally, it was the focus of a double avenue of elm trees.

Plate 6   Plan of the Egham Charity's lands at Staines based on a survey made by John Dugleby for the Company in 1798. The green patches are the mediaeval strips, each of one or two acres, which were consolidated into fields in 1817.

Plate 7   Drawing the lottery in Coopers' Hall in 1803, an engraving by W. Charles. The two wheels contained the numbers which were drawn by boys from Christ's Hospital. These were checked by the Commissioners seated at the raised table, recorded by three clerks and witnessed by a jury. The clock beneath the royal arms was later lost and recovered by chance in the 1950s by Liveryman Major John Russell.

Plate 8   Sir David Salomons (Master 1841), in his mayoral robes, 1855, by Solomon Alexander (1806–81). He was the first Jew to become Lord Mayor of London as the result of a ten-year struggle to repeal the law debarring Jews from taking office.

Plate 9   Henry Capel (Master 1868); a portrait presented to the Company in 1936 by his grandson, Mr Percy Wellock. Capel was a wine merchant and from the 1820s a tenant of the Company. His commonplace book about the Company and London contains the Coopers' song which he probably wrote and which may have enlivened the long dinners of his day. His interest in education included the Ratcliffe School and the City and Guilds Institute.

CAPTIONS TO COLOUR PLATES

Plate 10   Chapel in the Ratcliffe Charity, 1898, a watercolour by J. P. Emslie. This is one of several watercolours which recorded the Charity just as its buildings were about to be demolished.

Plate 11   Dining Room in the third of the Company's Halls, 1900; wash and ink by William Luker, junior (1867–1951). This Hall was destroyed in 1940 with the loss of many of the Company's pictures.

Plate 12   Sir Henry Murray Fox (Master 1976). He was Lord Mayor in 1975. Oil painting by Leonard Boden.

Plate 13   Dining Room at 13 Devonshire Square, the Company's fourth Hall. This first floor room is decorated in the early eighteenth century style. Above the fireplace is a finial from the Company's eighteenth century barge, painted and gilded with the Company's arms. The portraits by Godfrey Kneller depict Joseph Taylor (Master 1732) and his wife.

Plate 14   Coopers' Court, Maplin Street, Bow, 1999. The quincentenary sheltered flats: a computer-aided impression.

Plate 15   Last brewery apprentice of the twentieth century, Jonathan Manby, after the traditional 'trussing-in' which marks the end of a coopers' apprenticeship. The apprentice is placed in a hogshead which he has made; then hops, surplus yeast and shavings are poured over him. Next, he is rolled round the brewery yard, sacked by his employer and reinstated as a qualified, journeyman cooper. Finally, he is allowed to drink as much ale as he can for the rest of the day.

Plate 16   Cooper Lew Jones at work preparing a cask for the head to be fitted. He is one of only eight brewery coopers in Britain, although the craft flourishes in distilleries.

Appendix One:
Casks and their Capacities

Cask is the generic term for the whole range of wooden vessels made by coopers.

The modern standard cask capacities are those for beer.

CASKS	GALLONS
Pin	4.5
Firkin	9
Kilderkin	18
Barrel	36
Hogshead	54
Puncheon	72
Butt	108
Tun	216

There was variation in capacity according to the contents. For example, in the seventeenth and eighteenth centuries, an ale barrel held 32 gallons and the half barrel, or rundlet of ale held 15 gallons. A wine butt was called a pipe and held 105 gallons and a wine tun held 252 gallons.

APPENDIX TWO:
APPRENTICES: SOCIAL AND GEOGRAPHICAL ORIGINS

The following sample is taken from records of the apprentices bound between January 1586–87 and December 1589; and March 1591 and May 1594.

Geographical origin	number	%
Midlands	147	36
North	91	22
South East	54	13
South West	57	14
London	37	9
Wales	14	3
East Anglia	14	3

Social origin (father's occupation)	number	%
Gentleman	1	–
Yeoman	46	11
Husbandman	180	44
Labourer	17	4
Trades	162	39
Clerk	8	2

KEY:

MIDLANDS: Bedfordshire, Berkshire, Buckinghamshire, Hereford, Huntingdonshire, Leicestershire, Northamptonshire, Oxford, Shropshire, Staffordshire, Warwickshire, Worcestershire.

NORTH: Cheshire, Cumbria, Derbyshire, Co Durham, Lancashire, Lincolnshire, Northumberland, Nottinghamshire, Westmorland, Yorkshire.

SOUTH EAST: Essex, Hertfordshire, Kent, Middlesex, Surrey, Sussex.

SOUTH WEST: Dorset, Gloucestershire, Hampshire, Somerset, Wiltshire.

EAST ANGLIA: Cambridgeshire, Norfolk, Suffolk.

Appendix Three: Revised Income of the Ratcliffe Pension Charity

Towards the end of the nineteenth century, the Company had incurred the displeasure of the Education authorities and the Charity Commissioners by setting up a girls' school in Bow and deciding to move the boys' school from Ratcliffe, without first seeking their permission. Changes in the Education Acts led to the transfer of the girls to the Coborn Girls' School and made the Company responsible for both schools. The funds which the Company had accumulated for educational purposes were transferred to the Foundation governors. Those which related to the almshouses or to pensions formed the basis of the present Ratcliffe Pension Charity (R. P. C.) This left a small balance of funds (the Ratcliffe Trust), which did not specifically relate to either, and which produced an annual income of £4,200. The Charity Commissioners decided that one third of this income belonged to R. P. C. and two thirds to the School. But despite protests from the Company, they decreed that the fixed sum of £1,400, (rather than one third of the income) should go to the R. P. C. and the remainder (rather than two thirds), should go to the school; and that this decision would not be subject to review.

By the 1980s, the income to the school had risen to more than £60,000 per annum whilst R. P. C.'s share remained at £1,400. The Charities Committee, after several years of research and a detailed study of the Company's records, decided to challenge the decision made in 1891. Discussions with the Foundation governors led to a joint approach to the Charity Commissioners by the school and the Company, resulting in a change to the one-third/two-thirds split originally proposed by the Company in 1891. A snapshot of the R. P. C. funds in 1993 shows that it had £24,000 for distribution. By 1995, it had risen to more than £40,000.

L. Joughin (Master 1992)
August 1999

Glossary

Apprentice   usually was a teenager, bound by a formal agreement (an indenture) to a master, to learn a craft. The minimum term of service was seven years, during which the master taught, fed, clothed and boarded the boy.

Assistant   one of 17 senior coopers who constituted the Company's governing Court under the terms of the 1661 Charter; an assistant to the Master and Wardens. Before 1661, the term had no legal force but was used to describe senior coopers who gave the officers help and advice.

Beadle   the Company's officer responsible for summoning members to meetings and to answer for their behaviour or work before the Court. He was often the source of information about breaches of Company rules and he kept order at the Hall and on public occasions. In the twentieth century, his duties often included those of assistant to the Clerk. He attends the Master on official occasions, and must be a Freeman of the Company.

Cask   the term used by coopers for all sizes and capacities of wooden vessels. A barrel, for example, is a cask with a capacity of 36 gallons.

Clerk   the Company's chief administrator, scribe, book-keeper and legal adviser. He was often, but not necessarily, a liveryman and was originally paid a small salary which was augmented by legal and other fees. In the twentieth century, the Clerk became the Company's chief executive.

Clothing   the livery or distinctive hood and gown which liverymen were entitled and expected to wear when attending the Hall on business. To be 'of the cloathing' meant to be a liveryman.

Court   since 1661, the governing body of the Company comprising 17 Assistants, a Master and two Wardens. Before 1661, the Court was the formal and, usually, monthly meeting of some or all the Livery to carry out the Company's business.

Fine a)   a financial penalty imposed on members for breaking the laws or ordinances of the Company. The ordinances provided a tariff of fines which was used as a guideline and not normally exceeded. Members could be fined for poor work, dishonesty and unruly behaviour.
b)   a payment to the Company in default of holding office as Master, Warden and Steward.
c)   a payment on being admitted to the Livery and to the Court.

Freeman a member of the Company who had completed his apprenticeship and at the age of 21 was admitted to the freedom. Freemen enjoyed some, but not all, the benefits of membership. They became eligible, because they were freemen, to be admitted to the Freedom of the City of London and were then allowed to practice their craft within London and the suburbs.

Householder a Freeman who had been given the Company's approval to set up in business independently. He could employ other coopers and take apprentices. His work was identified by his 'mark', granted and registered by the Company.

Informer originally the Lord Mayor's officer whose task was to investigate and bring to the Lord Mayor's Court breaches of City ordinances in the size and quality of casks. He usually accompanied the Court at a general search. By the late sixteenth century, he was paid a fee by the Company to provide more information about coopers who were breaking the rules than could be obtained by the Beadle.

Journeyman a freeman who worked as a day labourer, employed by a householder or a liveryman.

Livery originally the food and clothing allowance for members of great households. The term then came to mean the distinctive clothing of retainers. In craft guilds, it was adopted as the special hood and gown which voting members of the Company were allowed to wear when they were admitted to full membership and which, on public occasions, distinguished each Company.

Mark   the distinctive sign which was bestowed on a freeman when he was admitted as a householder. It had to be branded on to his casks and was the means by which the Company's officers, in particular the Sealer, identified each member's work.

Master   the Company's chief representative who presided over Court meetings. The office was created by the 1501 Charter. Since 1661, the Master must be chosen from the Court of Assistants. He was elected to serve for a year by the liverymen meeting in Common Hall on the Sunday (from 1654, Monday) next before Pentecost.

Proof work   a piece of coopering set as a test for a freeman under special conditions and then judged by senior coopers. It was to ensure that the freeman was worthy of being granted his mark and be allowed to set up his own business.

Quarterage   the subscription of ten pence a quarter paid towards the running costs of the Company by each member. Freemen, who were not householders, were allowed to pay at the lower rate of eight pence.

Quarter Days   25 March, (Lady Day), 24 June (Midsummer), 29 September (Michaelmas) and 25 December (Christmas). Days when rents were due, accounts settled, stipends paid and when leases began and ended. Lady Day was the beginning of the new year until 1752 when England also adopted the Gregorian calendar, which entailed 'losing' 11 days. (3 September became 14 September).

Renter Warden   the junior Warden responsible for collecting the Company's rents. The post was introduced in 1563 and lapsed between 1584 and 1619. More recently, the Renter Warden became responsible, with the Treasurer, for the Company's expenditure. The post is normally held by the Master Presumptive.

Sealer   a Company official, always a liveryman, who paid a rent to use the Company's seal, a branding iron in the form of T, (St Anthony's cross), on all true, well-made casks. He could charge one farthing a cask and when business was brisk made a profit after he had paid the rent. By the late sixteenth century, there were usually three Sealers, each with their own district and often employing a deputy to do the leg-work.

Steward a senior liveryman, one of three, chosen by turn each year to bear the cost of the Livery feast on Election Day (later moved to Audit Day). It became customary to pay a fine in lieu of bearing the cost.

More recently, if the fine is refused, it is taken as an indication that the member does not wish to serve as Warden or Master and he will not normally be invited to become an Assistant.

Warden the keepers or guardians of the Company, and its chief officers until the 1501 Charter added the office of Master. From the earliest times in the Company's history, there were two, Upper and Under Warden, each elected to serve for a year. It became usual, in the nineteenth century, for the Under Warden to succeed to the office of Upper Warden.

Before 1827, the Wardens were normally chosen from the Assistants. Since then, they have been chosen from among able and assiduous liverymen. They return to the Livery after their year(s) in office. Traditionally, their duties were to govern the Company, enforce the ordinances, protect the trade and punish wrong-doers. Since 1827, they have become representatives of the Livery.

REFERENCES

THE MAIN SOURCE OF MATERIAL for this history is the collection of the Company's rough minutes (37 volumes) and official minutes (33 volumes) deposited in the Manuscript Department of Guildhall Library. These begin in 1552 (rough minutes) and 1567 (official minutes), and have scarcely any gaps. The earliest account books, which begin in 1528, are particularly valuable for the sixteenth and early seventeenth centuries for their detailed descriptions of expenditure. The Company's oldest surviving record, known as the Vellum Book (Guildhall Manuscript L37 5614A) was discovered, in 1842, by James F. Firth (Master 1847 and 1848). It has been described as the Warden's account book, but is the subscription book showing members' names year by year and recording their payment of quarterage. It begins in 1439 and concludes with a set of accounts for 1523–24. Firth was archivist to the Corporation of London and compiled a collection of abstracts, transcripts and translations of key documents relating to the statutes and ordinances governing the Company, its benefactors and bequests and its property, both corporate and charitable. An earlier collection dealing mainly with bequests was made by Joseph Browne, Clerk from time to time between 1673 and 1716. These two collections are catalogued as 7696, Firth, and 5633, Browne.

There are three histories of the Company. Earliest is James F. Firth's *Historical Memoranda of the Coopers' Company* which is based on Ms 7696, to which has been added lists of Masters, Schoolmasters, Clerks and Beadles. It contains no narrative and no commentary. It takes the extreme nineteenth century view of history that the facts must speak for themselves. It is very rare: not even the Company possesses a copy. George Elkington (Master 1931) *The Coopers: Company and Craft* quotes extensively from Firth and uses other (unnamed) sources. The most recent history *The Coopers' Company* (1944) is by Sir William Foster (Master 1918 and 1935). I have referred to it throughout, although, apart from a postscript on the blitz in 1940, it virtually ends in 1870. It deals thematically, rather than chronologically with the Company's history and refers to the main charities separately as appendices. Two recent accounts, which I have also referred to throughout, deal with the Company's schools: *The Coopers' Company and Coburn School* by Colin Churchett (1986), and my own *Henry Strode's Charity* (1994).

Abbreviations

G. L. Ms   Guildhall Library, Corporation of London manuscript
op. cit.   *opere citato*, which means 'in the work cited'

Prologue and Chapter one

Manuscript sources:
Coopers' Company Papers in Guildhall Library, Corporation of London:
    Rough minute book G. L. Ms 5603, vol. 1
    Quarterage book G. L. Ms 5614A
    Will book G. L. Ms 7549
    Account book G. L. Ms 5606, vol. 1
    Charter (1501) G. L. Ms 5805
    Memorandum book G. L. Ms 5633

Printed Primary Sources:
R. R. Sharpe, ed., *Calendar of the Letter Books of the City of London* (1907)
Calendar of Wills proved and enrolled in the Court of Hustings 1258–1688

Secondary Works:
Cook, G. H., *St Paul's* (1955)
Duffy, Eamon, *The Stripping of the Altars* (1992)
Haigh, Christopher, *English Reformations* (1993)
Heard, Nigel, *Tudor Economy and Society* (1992)
Holt, Richard, and Rosser, Gervase, eds., *The Mediaeval Town* (1990)
Jack, Sybil M., *Towns in Tudor and Stuart Britain* (1996)
Mackie, J. D., *The Early Tudors* (1951)
Mattingley, G., *The Defeat of the Spanish Armada* (1959)
Pendrill, C., *Old Parish Life in London* (1937)
St. Clare Byrne, M., *Elizabethan Life in Town and Country* (1950)
Stow, John, *A Survey of London* (1603)
Weinstein, Rosemary, *Tudor London* (1994)
Williams, Neville, *The Cardinal and the Secretary* (1975)
Youings, Joyce *The Penguin Social History of Britain: Sixteenth Century England* (1984)

CHAPTER TWO

Manuscript Sources:
Coopers' Company Papers:
   Rough minute book G. L. Ms 5603 vol. 1
   Minute book G. L. Ms 5602 vol. 1
   Account book G. L. Ms 5606 vol. 1
   Memorandum book G. L. Ms 5633

Printed Primary Sources:
Calendar of Wills *op. cit.*
Prockter, A., Taylor, R. and Fisher, J., *The A to Z of Elizabethan London* (1979)

Secondary Works:
Duffy, E., *op. cit.*
Fletcher, A., *Tudor Rebellions* (1973)
Foster, Sir William, *Nicholas Gibson and his Free School at Ratcliffe* (1936)
Foster, Sir William, *The Ratcliffe Charity* (1936)
Hatcher, J., *Plague, Population and the English Economy 1348–1530* (1986)
Jack, S. M., *op. cit.*
Levey, Santina M., *An Elizabethan Inheritance: The Hardwick Hall Textiles* (1998)
Mackie, J. D., *op. cit.*
Sharpe, R. R., *London and the Kingdom* (1894)
Slack, Paul, *Poverty and Policy in Tudor and Stuart England* (1988)
Smith, Alan G. R., *The Emergence of a Nation State* (1984)
Williams, N., *op. cit.*
Youings, J., *op. cit.*

CHAPTER THREE

Manuscript Sources:
Coopers' Company Papers:
   Rough Minute books G. L. Ms 5603, vols 2–4
   Minute books G. L. Ms 5602, vols 1,2
   Account books G. L. Ms 5606, vols 2,3
   Quarterage books G. L. Ms 5614, vols 3,4
   Henry Cloker's will G. L. Ms 7533/1

Will book G. L. Ms 7549
London Ordinations 1578–1628

Printed Primary Sources:
Register of Wills proved in the Commissary Court of London
Index to the Testamentary Records in the Archdeacon's Court of London
Prockter, A., Taylor, R., and Fisher, J., *op. cit.*

Secondary Works:
Dictionary of National Biography
Outhwaite, R. B., *Inflation in Tudor and Early Stuart England* (1982)

CHAPTER FOUR

Manuscript Sources:
Coopers' Company Papers:
    Rough Minute book G. L. Ms 5603, vols 3,4
    Minute book G. L. Ms 5602, vols 3,4
    Quarterage books G. L. Ms 5614, vols 4–6
Foster, Sir William, *Coopers' Hall and other Essays* (n. d.)

Secondary Works:
Akenby, David, 'Radicals of St Stephen's Coleman Street 1624–1642' in
    Guildhall Miscellany, vol. III, no. 2 (1969–70)
Coward, Barry, *The Stuart Age* (1980)
Muddiman T. R., *The King's Journalist*
Pearl, Valerie, *London and the Outbreak of the Puritan Revolution* (1961)
Porter, Stephen, ed., *London and the Civil War* (1996)
Russell, Conrad, ed., *The Origins of the English Civil War* (1973)
Smith, S. R., 'Origins of London Apprentices 1630–1660' in *Guildhall
    Miscellany*, vol. 4 (1973)
Williams, D. A., 'London Puritanism' in *Guildhall Miscellany* 1960–68
Wrigley, E. A., 'London's Importance 1650–1750', in *Past & Present* no. 37 (1967)

REFERENCES

Chapter Five

Manuscript Sources:
Coopers' Company Papers:
    Minute books G. L. Ms 5602, vols 4–6
    Mark book G. L. Ms 5631, vol. 1

Printed Primary Sources:
Baxter, Richard, *Autobiography* (1974)
Jones, P. E., The Fire Court, vol. 2 (1966)
Mills, P. and Oliver J., *The Survey of Building Sites in the City of London after the Great Fire of 1666* (1967)
Pepys, Samuel, *Diary* (1967)

Secondary Works:
Reddaway, J. F., *Rebuilding of London* (1951)
Vann, R. T., 'Quakerism and the Social Structure in the Interregnum', in *Past & Present,* no. 43 (1969)
Wrightson, K., *English Society 1580–1680* (1987)
Wrigley, E. A., *op. cit.*

Chapter Six

Manuscript Sources:
Coopers' Company Papers:
    Minute books, vols 6 & 7
    Will book G. L. Ms 7549
Verney Archive at Claydon House:
    The Diary of Henry Strode, 1699–1700
    The Account Book of Henry Strode, 1695–1696
Foster, Sir William, *Coopers' Hall and other Essays* (n. d.)
Jephson, A., *An account of the ancestors and family of Alexander Jephson* (1708)
Vestry Minutes of St Lawrence Pountney G. L. Ms 3908, vol. 2

Secondary Works:
Jones, J. R., *The First Whigs* (1961)

Chapter Seven

Manuscript Sources:
Coopers' Company Papers:
    Minute books G. L. 5602, vols 7–9
    Default book G. L. Ms 5625, vol. 1
St Lawrence Pountney Vestry Minutes
Verney Archive at Claydon House:
    Notebook of Henry Herring
    Diary of Henry Strode

Printed Primary Sources:
The Report of the Commissioners ... to enquire concerning Charities ... relating to the County of Surrey, 1819–1837

Chapter Eight

Manuscript Sources:
Coopers' Company Papers:
    Minute books G. L. 5602, vols 9–11

Printed Primary Sources:
Sermons on Remarkable Fires in London 1715–1794: Discourse on the Dreadful Fire at Ratcliffe, July 23 1794.
The Times, 24 and 25 July 1794

Secondary Sources:
George, M. D., *London Life in the 18th Century* (1965)
Marshall, Dorothy, *Industrial England 1776–1851* (1973)

Chapter Nine, Part One

Manuscript Sources:
Coopers' Company Papers:
    Attorney General and the Company: brief to the defendants and letters G. L. Ms 7538
    Minute books G. L. Ms 5602, vols 11–18

REFERENCES

Memorandum book G. L. Ms 7538
Steward's Account book: Egham Charity 1793–1813. G. L. Ms 5812
Capel Papels: G. L. Mss 19566, 19567
Capel, Henry, *Historical Memoranda of the Coopers' Company* (1872)

Printed Primary Sources:
Report of the Commissioners … (*op. cit.*)
Winstanley, R. L., *Another Parson: Thomas Jeans* (Woodforde Society, 1978)
Woodforde, James, *The Diary of a Country Parson*, ed. John Beresford (1935)

Secondary Sources:
Barnard, H. C., *A History of English Education from 1760* (1961)

Chapter nine, part two

Manuscript Sources:
Coopers' Company Papers:
    Minute books G. L. Ms 5602, vols 11–18
    Capel, Henry, *op. cit.*
    Foster, Sir William, *Coopers' Hall and other Essays* (n. d.)

Secondary Sources:
Dictionary of National Biography
Marshall, D., *Industrial England 1776–1851* (1973)

Chapter ten

Manuscript Sources:
Coopers' Company Papers:
    Minute books G. L. Ms 5602, vols 18–24

Secondary Sources:
Orwin and Whetham, *op. cit.*
Saul, S. B., *The Myth of the Great Depression* (1985)
Webb, R. K., *Modern England* (1969)

Chapter Eleven

Manuscript Sources:
Coopers' Company Papers:
    Minute books G. L. Ms 5602, vols 24–33
    Society of the Livery Minute books
Stepney and Bow Foundation Minute books

Chapter Twelve

Manuscript Sources:
Coopers' Company Papers:
    Minute books, vols 34–37
    Annual letters of Masters of the Company

Secondary Sources:
Bradley, S. and Pevsner, N., *London 1: The City of London* (1997)
Davis, R., *Aleppo and Devonshire Square* (1967)

Chapter Thirteen

Manuscript Sources:
Coopers' Company Papers:
    Minute books, vols 37–40
    Annual letters of Masters of the Company

Secondary Sources:
Matson, M., *The last rotten borough*, (Fabian Society, 1997)

Index of People

Numbers in *italic* type refer to illustrations in the text. Cross references in SMALL CAPITALS refer to the INDEX OF SUBJECTS (page 272 onwards).

Adams, John: 137
Alexander, William: *116*, 117–18, 163–4, 215, 235, 244 (*see also* WOODHAM MORTIMER; OBLELISK)
Algar, Abraham: 147–9, 164, 174
Allen, George: 68
Allen, Henry: 68
Allen, James: 68
Allen, Richard: 68
Allen, Robert: 68, 83, 84
Allen, William: 68
Allington, Peter: 243
Allington, William: *116*
Andrewes, Lancelot: 46
Archer family: 153–4
Ashbee, C. P.: 198
Astley, Mrs Waldo: 181
Astrey, Luke: 99–100, 105, 118
Atchley, Neville: 236

Baker, Agnes: 3
Baker, D. G.: 238
Baker, John: 1–3, 5, 7, 11–12, 17, 21–22, 27, 29, 35, 105
Baker, Richard: 65
Baker, William: 3
Baldwin, Peter: 108
Bartlett, Arthur: 192–3
Bartlett, Mr: 190–2
Bartlett, Richard: 21
Basley, John: 18
Bate, William: 10
Baxter, Richard: 89
Beale, Harold: 234
Beattie, John: 166, 194–5, 202
Bedwolff, Thomas: 52
Bethell, Sir John: 204
Blake, Caleb: 114
Blake, Thomas: 15
Bleek, Anthony, *18*
Bleek, Thomas: 21, 26
Boden, Leonard: 238

Boleyn, (Queen) Anne: 23, 33–4
Booker, Edward: 101
Boughey (à Bough), Ralph: 26
Boyer, Edward Lawrence: 211
Boyer, Henry: 192
Boyer, Henry Pelham: 197, 210
Boyer, James: 164, 168, 195
Bray, Arthur: 22, 57, 65
Bray, Arthur (the younger): *110*
Bray, John: 22, 25
Bray, Thomas: *23*
Bray, Warden: 103
Bray, William: 67
Breffit, Edgar: 179–81, 187–8
Brende, Thomas: 45
Bressey, John: 210
Bridger, Mrs: 77
Brookhaven, Captain: 78
Browne, Joseph: 97–9, 101–2, 105, 259
Buckingham, Duke of: 67, 69
Bulley, Kelham: 133
Burbidge, George: 83
Burn, Baron: 236
Burn, William: 211
Burnett, Colonel Sir Leslie: 219
Burrow, Edward: 153–6
Busby, Thomas: 25–6, 44, 52, 54
Byfield, Mrs: 104, 107
Byrde, Edmund: *44*
Byrde, Richard: 42

Capel, Henry: 160, 166, 171, 183, 195, 198, *plate 9*
Carpenter, Edward: 220
Carter, Benjamin: *124*
Carter, Robert I: 124
Carter, Robert II: 147–50, 152, 154–6, 164, 166
Carter, Robert III (son of Robert Carter II): 166–7, 175, 179, 188, 215
Carter, Robert IV (son of Robert Carter III): 215
Catherine, (Queen), of Aragon: 34
Chalmers, Alexander: 199

267

Champion, George: 120
Chantler, Alfred: 194, 198
Charier, Benjamin: 44
Charles I, King of England: 67, 69, 99
Charles II, King of England: 67, 81, 88, 97, 99, 101–2, 108
Charley, John: 2, 4, 19, 26, 30, 37–9
Charley, Richard : 25
Checkett, William: 67
Chell, Miss Sarah: 161
Cheslyn, Robert: 70, *78*, 79
Christian IV, King of Denmark: 63
Clark, J. W. S.: 238
Cleeve, Ambrose: 84
Clever, J.: 189
Cleves, (Queen) Anne of: 23, 34
Cloker, Henry: 59, 168, 215, 233
Cloker, John: 4, 17, 59
Cloker, William: 17
Cock, Richard: 15
Codd family: 163
Codd, Edward: 133
Comenius: 72
Cooke, Richard: 25
Coultman, William: 102
Crompe, Hugh: 4, 17
Cromwell, Jasper: 50
Cromwell, Oliver: 67, 74, 79, 81
Cromwell, Thomas: 34
Curtis, H. F.: 224

Danby, Lord: 98
Dance, George: 121
Dean, Richard: 152
Delabarr, Frances: 114
Denman, Lord: 176, 178
Devon, Richard: 101
Doane, William: 52, 60
Dodson, George: 25, 44, 50, 61
Drake, Sir Francis: 8
Draper, Adam: 48
Dugleby, John: 130, 132, 163
Dunn, Newton: 211
'Dutchmen': 19, 32

Eaton, Peter: 119
Edison, John: 144, 146
Edward VI, King of England: 27, 31, 34
Edwards, John: 25
Edwards, Richard: 65

Elizabeth I, Queen of England: 27, 32, 41–2, 47, 61, 99
Elizabeth II, Queen of England: 236
Elkington, George: 192, 202–3, 205, 215, 259
Elkington, Vivien: 222
Elletson, John: 60
Elliot, Edward: 54
Elnore, Thomas: 17
Esdaile, James: 140
Esdaile, Sir Peter: 176
Essex, Earl of: 47, 74
Eykyn, Roger: 181

Ferris, William: 163
Firman, Thomas: 85, *104*
Firth, James: 147–9, 153–8, 163–4, 166, 168, 172, 174, 181, 215
Flamsted, Francis: 77
Flamsted, George: 77
Fleet, Sir John: 97, 101, *104*, 107–8, 111, 113, 119
Ford, A. S.: 224
Foster, Henry: 45
Foster, Richard: 48
Foster, Sir William: 216, 259
Fox, Murray: 225–6, 234, 237–8, *plate 12*
Fullwood, John: 63–4

Gamble, Henry: 41, 42
George I, King of England: 113, 119
George II, King of England: 120
George III, King of England: 127, 152
George VI, King of England: 220
Gibson (later Lady Knyvett), Avice: 35–9, 54, 62, 86, 94, 105, 217, *plate 1* (see also RATCLIFFE CHARITY)
Gibson, Nicholas: 5, 35–7, 86, 160, 246 (see also RATCLIFFE CHARITY)
Gibson, Stephen: 44
Gilling, Percy: 199, 213
Gilling, Robert: 215, 219
Glenny, C. F.: 237
Glenny, Malcolm: 220, 231
Gorsuch Browne, M. H.: 237
Gorum, John: 118
Grant, Allan: 228
Grey, Lady Jane: 39
Griffin, David: 138
Griffin, Harold: 213, 216, 225, 235
Grosvenor, Lady: 133
Grosvenor, Sir John: 118–20

INDEX OF PEOPLE

Gurney, Alderman: 56
Gurney, Sir Richard: 72

Halden, John: 65
Hall, G. H.: 224
Hamlet, William: 50
Harrison, Richard: 64
Harrod, Mr: 238
Hart, Mr: 156–7
Hart, Robert: 190
Hart, William: 163–4, 190
Harvey, John: 17
'Hary' the Dutchman: 29
Hatchett, Edward: 227–8, 245
Heath, John: 4, 27, 30, *31*, 35, 37, 39, 62
Heath, Stephen: 26, 39, 42, 44, 54, 61
Henry VII, King of England: 7, 33
Henry VIII, King of England: 7, 23, 31–3
Herring, Henry: 111, 115–7, 121, 127 (*see also* EGHAM CHARITY)
Herring, John: 109–10
Highes, Lewis: 68
Hoare, Alice: 242
Hobhouse, Mrs: 104
Hodgson, Peter: 72
Hopkins, Reverend George Adolphus: 152, 167
Horsman, Lawrence: 20
Hosier, Stephen: 60, 63–4
Howard, John: 228, 243
Howell, Michael: 243
Hudson, James: 101
Hudson, Thomas: 65
Husbands, A. Newton: 234
Hutchinson, Roger: 38
Hynde, Humiliacion: 68

Ireland, Daniel: 83

Jackson, John: 211, 215
James I, King of England (and James VI of Scotland): 61, 63
James II, King of England: 97, 101, 103, 106, 108, 113
James, Duke of York: 81, 88–9, 98–9, 173 (*see also* James II)
James, Helen: 20
James, John: 20
Jeans, Dr Thomas: 150–2, 167, 175
Jeffreys, Lord: 102

Jephson, Alexander: 106–8
Johnson, Thomas: 176–7
Jones, William: 128–9, 143
Joughin, L. (Jo): 244–5, 254

Kem, Anthony: 67
Kempe, William: 101
Kitchen, Hezekiah: 68
Knapp, Joseph: 70, 78
Knyvett, Dame Avice *see* Gibson, Avice
Knyvett, Sir Anthony: 35, 94, 217

Lambe, Dr John: 69, 74
Lambert, Daniel: 120–1
Landell, William: 215
Laud, (Archbishop) William: 68, 72
Legg, Cyrus: 160, 191, 194
Looker, John (jnr): 97
Looker, John (snr): 76, 97, 108
Lufton, John: 64–5

Manning, Thomas: 56
Mary (Tudor), Queen of England: 27, 35, 39, 40–1, 47
Mason, Thomas: 93
Matson, Malcolm: 247–8
Meare, John: 61–2
Mills, Richard: 102
Milton, John: 78
Molde, Robert: 44
Monck, General, Duke of Albemarle: 67, 80
Monsell, Dr John: 194
Moore, John: 1, 18
Morris, Roger: 79, 81–2, 89–90, 92, 96

Neale, Henry: 135
Nelson, Lord Horatio: 143
Nelson, Thomas: 68
Newell, George: 128
Newland, Robert: 64
Newton, James: 199, 209
Newton, John: 238, 242
Nicholas, James: 25
Nicholas, Thomas: 50
Norfolk, Duke of: 27, 49
Norman, Ian: 243
Norris, Harold (Bertie): 227–8, 231
Northumberland, Earl (later Duke) of: 27, 32, 39
Nottingham, Mr: 56

269

Ogle, W. S.: 204, 207, 210–11

Paget, John (jnr): 128
Paice, William: 207
Palmer, E. P. (Bunny): 229, 236, 238, 243–5
Palmer, Edward: 91
Palmer, Judith: 94
Peel, Sir Robert: 143, 172
Pember, Gregory: 166
Pennington, Issac: 72
Pepys, Samuel: 67, 81, 87–9, 91
Perkins, Thomas: 52, 57
Perrin, Commander C. R.: 235
Petyt, John: 46
Philip II, King of Spain: 40–1
Phillipps, Francis: 115
Pibble, John: 48
Powell, William: 68
Prince Charles Edward: 121
Prince Regent: 175
Princess Alexandra of Denmark: 166, 176
Putley, James Edward: 199, 213
Pym, John: 67, 99

Queen Elizabeth, The Queen Mother: 220

Randall, Tobias: 86
Ratcliff, Oldfield: 214
Rawlinson, Thomas: 77
Reed, J. L.: 234
Richardson, Thomas: 137
Roades, Henry: 64–5
Roberts, Gerard: 68, 95
Rochdale, Hamlet: 60
Rowe, Thomas: 113
Rupert, Prince: 73–4, 76
Russell, Barnabas: 219, 222
Russell, Herbert: 199
Russell, Major J. N.: 237

Saint, T. W.: 224
Salomons, Sir David: 176–7, *178*, 234, *plate 8*
Salomons, Sir David L.: 208–9, 211
Sandiloe, Edward: 103
Sapcote, Gilbert: 52
Scherman, John: 15
Scott, Alderman: 132
Scott, Caleb: 84
Scott, Robert: 117
Shaftesbury, Lord: 81, 99

Shaw, Robert: 48, 55–9, 64–5
Shrewsbury, Earl of: 49
Shuter, Leonard: 192, 198–9
Skelton, Frank (Bill): 219, 243
Skippon, Philip: 74
Smith, Digby: 243
Smith, George: 181
Smith, James: 146, 167
Smith, Jonas: 68
Smith, Reverend John: 155
Speed, William: 86–7
Staines, William: *41*, 47
Stamp, John: 64
Starr, Baptist: 54, 56
Starr, Richard: 39, 42
Stepkin, Peter: 98
Stileragge, Edward: 62
Stonarde, John: 58
Stone, David: 177, 179–81, 209
Stow, John: 55–6
Strode, Henry (jnr): 94, 109–11, 113, 115–18, 128, 136, 150–1, 164–5, 195, 201, 205–6, 208 (*see also* EGHAM CHARITY)
Strode, Henry (snr): 94, 95
Stutzberry family: 68, 91
Surrey, Earl of: 49
Swayne, George: 47, 57–8, 62, 74, 105
Swayne, Robert: 25
Swift, William: 10

Tayleure, Michael: 128–9, 136
Thelloe, Peter: 60
Thelloe, Thomas: 50, 60
Thompson, John: 41
Thompson, William: 68
Thornborrow, William: 176
Thurgood, Robert: 15–17
Topper, John: 20
Trinder, David: 139, 155
Turk, John: 65
Turnbull, A. W.: 222
Turner, Carey: 151
Tuttye, Robert: 47, 56
Tyrrys, Roger: 4, 17

Venner, Thomas: 68, 79–80
Vernon, Robert: 48
Victoria, Queen of England: 143, 176

Waller, Edmund: 75

Walpole, Sir Robert: 113, 120
Warde, Thomas: 45–6
Watson, John: 38
Weir, Alexander: 168, 172
Wellington, Duke of: 143, 174
Wellock, P. M.: 215
Wentworth, Lady: 38, 53
Wentworth, Lord: 37–8, 54
Westmorland, Earl of: 27, 32
Wheeler, Thomas: 52
Whitehead, John: 25
Whitnall, Peter: 43, 51
Whitnall, Thomas: 43
Wildey, Captain: 78, 83, 106
Wildey, Richard: 118
William, Prince of Orange: 102

Williams, Barnes: 206
Williams, G. B.: 186
Williamson, John: 10
Willimott, Robert: 120–1
Wilson, Samuel: 65
Wilson, Thomas: 52
Wimberry, William: 101
Winch, Richard: 84, 85
Wolsey, Cardinal: 18, 49
Wood, Thomas à: 4, 37
Wood, Tobias (Toby): 56, 86
Wrenne, Thomas: 52
Wright, William: 26
Wyatt, Robert: 40
Wylles, John: 25

Index of Subjects

Numbers in *italic* type refer to illustrations in the text. Cross references in SMALL CAPITALS refer to the INDEX OF PEOPLE (page 267 onwards).

accounts, of Coopers' Company: 17–18, 24, 27, 30, *36*, 39, 42, *43*, 45, 53, 67, 59, 63–5, 99, 106, 110, 114, 116, 118, 128, 136, 138–9, 146, 151, 158, 167, 186, 209–11, 234, 243 (*see also* audit)
Acts of Parliament (*see also* City of London (Ward Elections)):
   1523: 18
   1531: 18–19, 42, 114, 134
   1565: 42
   1589: 48
   Chantries: 35
   Charities, 1812: 152, 160, 171
   Endowed Schools: 160
   Nuisances Act, 1852: 186
Advisory Group: 242
Aire and Calder Bottle Company: 187
Albion Tavern: 174–6
Aldermanic Court: 48, 50, 247
Aldermen: 7, 33, 79, 100, 110
Aldgate: 40, 69, 90, 177
All Hallows, Staining: 69, 107
All Saints, Barking: 38
almshouses and almspeople (*see under* Egham Charity; Ratcliffe Charity)
'Ancients', the: 17, 26, 45, 56, 81 (*see also* Assistants)
annuities: 56, 117, 137, 143, 167
   Annuities Committee: 167
Apothecaries' Company: 243
apprentices: 1, 4, 10–11, 13–16, 34, 40, 69, 108, 136, 220, 230, 242, 253, *plate 15*
   bequests to: 21
   in Bridewell: 31
   in Civil War: 71–2, 76, 78
   geographical origin: 20–1, 252
   gifts of silver spoons to Company: 44–5
   indentures: 14, 45, 64
   May Day 1517 riot: 49
   orphan tax: 136
   presentation to Court of: 20–1, 23–4
   register of: 50
   registration scheme: 213–14

   'set over' of: 20–1, 50
Armada, Spanish: 8, 47, 58, 63
arms:
   of City of London: 23, 174
   of Coopers' Company: 9, 10, 23, 33, 43–4, 93–4, 122, 152, 164, 214, 222
   Royal: 44, 58, 63, 93
Assistants: 22, 26, 82, 87, 91, 94, 100–2, 110, 119–20, 123, 128, 147, 149, 156, 217, 253–4
audit: 24, 53, 63, 96, 128, 136–8, 146, 254 (*see also* accounts)
Audit Day: 83, 103, 138, 258

Baltic Exchange, bomb blast at: 245–6
Banfield bequest: 148 (*see also* Ratcliffe Charity)
banners of Coopers' Company: 10, 23, 30, 33, 63, 122–3, 174, 177, 179–80, 209
barges of Coopers' Company: 33–4, 62–4, 88, 95–6, 113, 122–3, 140, 176–7
bargemaster: 34
barrels: 4, 8, 13, 83, 85 (*see also* casks; firkins; kilderkins)
   ale: 24, 30, 252
   gunpowder: 83
   soap: 11, 24
   'tight': 4
Bartholomew Fair: 40, 124
Basing House, siege of: 74
Basinghall Street: 1–2, 7, 27, 28, 29, 39, 58, 87–8, 93–4, 99, 153, 179, 181–2, 193, 209, 217, 221
Bassishaw Ward: 1, 173, 179
Beadle: 2, 18–19, 22–4, 42–3, 47–8, 50, 53, 82, 87, 90, 94, 104–5, 114, 119, 134, 143–5, 158, 166, 177, 179, 205, 209, 238, 242
Beckenham: 214, 216, 219
Becton Gas and Lighting Company: 169, 188
Becton Road: 188, 203, 210
Bell Watergate Inn: 170
bequests to Coopers' Company: 35, 59–60, 62, 158, 172,

INDEX OF SUBJECTS

Bevis Marks: 228
Billeter Lane: 39
Birchin Lane: 60
Bishopsgate: 30, 89
    bomb blast in: 222, 246
Blackman Street: 119, 186, 208
Blantyre Street: 225
Bow Road: 161
brewers: 11, 18, 41, 85, 97, 114, 134, 144, 203
Brewers' Company: 134–5
Bristol: 10, 76
Broad Street: 55, 170, 187–8, 197, 214, 225
Broderers' Company: 42
Brookhead: 214
Burlington Mews: 170

Cable Street: 225
Carpenters' Company: 92
casks: 3–4, 7–8, 11, 13, 18, 21, 24–5, 41, 43, 48, 50–1, 68, 75–7, 83–5, 110, 113–15, 134, 144–5, 212, 218, 252, 255 (*see also* barrels)
Charities of Coopers' Company: (*see also* Egham Charity; Ratcliffe Charity)
    Benevolent Fund: 211, 235–6
    Charity Committee: 235, 243–4
    City Parochial Foundation, donation to: 173 (*see also* loan charities)
    Coopers' Livery Housing Fund: 246
    Harold Griffin Charity: 244
    loan charities: 173
    Old Coopers' Livery Fund 211, 235
    Palmer Foundation: 236, 243–5
    William Alexander Fund: 235
Charity Commission: 153, 159, 171–3, 187, 189–90, 193, 195–7, 201, 204–6, 215, 228, 235, 254
Charters of Coopers' Company: 70, 100–1, 138, 147, 209
    1501: 3–4, 7, 15–17, 81–2, 246, 257–8
        confirmation of: 41
    1661: 81–2, 148, 255
        surrender of: 100
    1685: 100, 102, 105, 108
Cheapside: 2, 4, 13, 28, 33, 88
Chief Commoner: 237
chime, of a barrel: 21, 218
Christ's Hospital: 45, 111
Church Commissioners: 228
Church Settlement, 1559: 10, 68
City and Guilds Institute: 194, 198

City Chamberlain: 50
City of London (Ward Elections), Private Members' Bill: 247
Civil War: 67, 69–70, 76, 78–9, 86, 97, 99, 103, 106
    American: 173
Clerk: 1–2, 18, 30, 45, 62, 64, 72, 84, 87–9, 93–4, 103, 105, 113, 119, 133, 136, 141, 143–4, 147, 169, 195, 203, 230 (*see also* BOYER, HENRY PELHAM; BROWNE, JOSEPH)
    accommodation for: 94, 182, 217
    Assistant: 197, 210, 222, 238, 242
    collecting rents: 128
    loans to Company from: 146
    ill-health of: 207, 210–11
    new appointments of: 76, 97–8, 100, 102, 164, 210, 238, 242
    oath of: 82
    responsibilities of: 88–9
    split in duties of: 167–8
Cloker service: 216–17, 219, 233
Clothworkers' Company: 121, 217
Coldharbour: 109
Coleman Street: 68–9, 72, 79
Commissioner for Sewers: 181
Committee for the Outworks: 75
Committee on the Accounts: 146, 163
Common Council: 72, 75, 91–2, 119–21, 180
Common Hall: 4, 27, 33, 138, 148, 175, 182, 196, 209, 212, 219, 221, 230, 233, 238, 257
Compter, Lord Mayor's: 23, 25, 50, 52
cooperages: 7, 10, 17, 19, 40, 47–8, 69–70, 90, 114, 199, 244
Coopers' Court, Bow: plate 14
Cordwainer Ward: 177
Cordwainers' Company: 221
coronations: 33
    of Anne Boleyn: 23, 33
    of Henry VIII: 23
    of James VI: 63, 82
    of Prince Regent: 175
    of Queen Mary: 40, 50
Corporation of the City of London: 15, 31, 60–1, 63, 71, 91, 100, 102, 176, 181–2, 193, 198, 221–2, 225, 237, 247
Counsel, Standing, of Coopers' Company: 56, 60, 99, 105
Court, of Coopers' Company:
    arbitrations of: 25–6, 153–4
    attendance at: 50, 54, 67, 87, 119

273

behaviour in: 49, 52, 95
conduct of: 42
committees of: 85, 118, 172, 174, 210, 224, 226, 231, 235
composition of: 81–2, 100–1, 105, 147, 185, 209
decisions of: 53–4, 58, 77–8, 84, 108, 117, 130, 132, 137, 156, 159–62, 165–6, 169–70, 189, 201–3, 207, 213–4, 221–2, 228, 243
divisions within: 99, 101, 109
dinners: 62, 75, 104, 124, 136, 146, 175, 193, 199
elections to: 120, 140, 179, 181, 232, 241–2
finance court: 242
first court: 23–4
legal actions and: 65, 70, 113–14
meetings of: 22, 24, 29, 30, 64, 71, 83, 86, 88, 90, 107, 217, 222, 238–9
minutes of: 17, 46, 58, 72, 86, 93, 99, 109, 115, 129, 140, 149
quarterly courts: 79, 87, 103, 129, 132, 157, 167, 177, 197
relations with Livery: 127, 135, 137–41, 148–9, 233, 248
resignation/retirement from: 166, 232, 241
Court Room: 93–4, 181, 217, 219, 222, 229, 246
Court of Chancery: 54, 60, 65, 99, 105, 116–17, 128, 150–1, 164, 168, 171, 208, 225
Crimean War: 173, 177
Crooked Lane: 17, 39, 59, 68, 91, 168
Customs, Board of: 187

damask: 23, 38, 44
Default Books: 114
Dowhill: 11
Drapers' Company: 91
Dunstan Place: 153, 159, 170, 186, 208

East India Company: 97, 107–9, 119, 130, 155–6, 158, 167, 170–2, 187
Eastcheap: 119, 214
Edgware Road: 214
Edgwarebury Lane: 225
Egham Charity (*see also* Staines; Plaistow: 94, 163, 175, 186, 209, 235, *plates 2, 6*
accounts of: 139, 146, 193
almshouses: 115–16, 128–9, 150–2, 164–5, 205–7, 243
almspeople: 111, 128–9, 151–2

annual inspection of: 164
closure of: 201–2
Egham Eleemosynary Pensions Charity: 207
grammar school: 201, 206–8
grantees of: 236, 244
gravel digging at: 168, 173
pensions of: 116–17, 128–9, 151–2, 165–6, 210–11, 244
Plaistow development: 173, 187–90
re-building of: 149–52
Sion Villa: 188
speculative development of: 153, 188–9, 202
Staines development: 205–6
triennial view of: 190
Egham Urban District Council: 206
Election Day: 16, 22–3, 41, 44, 52, 62, 67, 82, 97, 135–6, 138–9, 174–5, 199, 230, 258
Election dinner: 103
exhibitions, to Oxford and Cambridge Universities (*see also* Gibson scholarships; schools and schooling): 43–4, 105
exhibition of coopering: 199

Farriers' Company: 213
Fenchurch Street: 11, 39, 69, 91, 132, 153, 168, 170, 186, 217
Feoffees for Impropriations: 69
Fifth Monarchists: 68, 79
Finance and Property Committee: 224
Finance Committee: 205, 213, 215, 224, 226–7
fines: 82, 254
breaking rules: 24–6, 50, 52, 75, 77, 103
defective work: 3, 13, 25, 84
entry to Livery: 14, 95, 109
entry to office: 108, 121, 149, 230
entry to lease on property: 38, 58, 60, 163
legal fine: 97–8
royal fine: 70, 74
steward's fine: 124, 174
Finsbury Court: 42
Finsbury Fields: 69
Fire Court, of City of London: 91, 130
Fire Court, of Coopers' Company: 91
firkins: 4, 5, 13, 24 (*see also* barrels)
First World War: 201, 211–14
air raids: 212
Fleet Street: 63
'foreigners': 15–16, 18–19, 41–2, 45, 48–9
fortifications, of the City of London: 74

274

INDEX OF SUBJECTS

Fraternity of Coopers: (before 1501) 1–4, 7, 10–11, 13–17, 26
freedom of the City of London: 14, 21, 242, 256
freedom of the craft: 14, 21, 75, 121, 124, 135, 198, 229–31, 242
freemen: 13, 59, 102, 146, 255, 256–7

Garlickhythe: 60, 91
gauges: 18, 48, 113
    standard: 134
Gentlemen of the Trade: 135
Gibson foundation (*see* Ratcliffe Charity)
Gibson scholarships (*see also* exhibitions): 158
girdles: 15, 30
glass: 4, 57
    in the hall: 29
Golden Lane: 169
Goldsmiths' Company: 94
gowns: 2, 22, 30, 238
Gracechurch Street: 33, 40
grantees (*see under* Egham Charity and Ratcliffe Charity)
Great Fire of London: 79, 81, 88–92, 94–6, 102–3, 113, 129–30
Gresham's Buildings: 182
Grocers' Company: 35, 59, 94, 109
ground rents: 153, 186, 193, 203–4, 214, 225
Guildhall: 7, 15, 22, 28, 40, 72, 74–6, 88, 147, 166, 175–6, 180–2, 212, 217, 221–2
Guy's Hospital: 215

Haberdashers' Company: 120
Hall of Coopers' Company: 4, 221, 225, 228
    Committee: 221, 238
    'Common Hall': 4
    First Hall (1547–1666): 7, 23, 27, 28, 29–31, 34, 39, 44–5, 48, 52, 58, 69, 71–2, 75–6, 78–9, 87, 89–90, 92, 95
    Second Hall (1670–1868): 92, 93–8, 102–4, 107, 113, 120, 122, 132, 138, 140, 143–4, 148, 164, 175, 177, 181–2
    Third Hall (1868–1940): 183, 193, 196, 209, 211–15, 217, 219, *plate 11*
    Fourth Hall (13 Devonshire Square) (1957–): 222–4, 228, 229, 233, 234, 238, 245–6, *plate 13*
    commercial leasing of: 227
Hand-in-Hand Insurance Company: 130

hangings, painted: 4, 29, 58
Harp Lane: 214, 225
Hatfield Street: 119, 149, 169–70
Hazlitt House: 214, 245
hearse cloth (*see also* pall cloth): 43
Honourable Artillery Company: 73, 179, 237
hoods: 2, 30, 49
hoops: 8, 24, 51
householders: 15, 21–4, 32, 47, 70, 79, 100, 114, 132, 256

indentures: 20–1, 45, 145, 213
inflation: 18, 21, 42, 57, 59, 62, 86, 144, 219, 221, 224–5, 227, 230
Informer: 47–8, 77, 98, 114, 256
Innholders' Company: 176
inventory, of Coopers' Company possessions: 23–4, 211
Ireland: 47, 60–1, 67, 73, 97–8, 106–7
iron chest: 24
Islington: 18, 75, 119

Joiners' Company: 18
Joint Industrial Council: 213
journeymen: 5, 10, 18, 21, 25, 32, 34, 47, 50, 53, 71, 78, 114, 117, 199, 256

Kensington: 186
kilderkins (*see also* barrels): 4, 13, 24
    'naughty': 24
King Street: 92
King's Bench: 120, 124, 139, 149

Ladies' dinners: 193
Lady Fair: 19, 114
Leadenhall Street: 33, 90, 186, 216, 228
linen: 38, 44, 89
Little Tower Street: 119, 144, 168, 171, 183, 186
Livery, of Coopers' Company: 2–3, 40, 45, 120, 176, 179, 182, 213, 221, 224–5, 228, 231, 243, 248
    admissions to: 24, 75, 86, 129, 230, 243
    calls to: 70–1, 78–9, 90, 95
    committees of: 227
    Court-Livery gap: 141, 232–3
    decisions of: 31, 212
    dinners: 34, 75, 94, 123, 160, 174, 180, 199, 213, 219, 234
    elections to: 22
    expulsion from: 50, 52
    fines: 14, 95, 109

275

lists of members: 102, 136, 147
protests by: 134–40
radicalism: 70
re-calls to: 101, 105
size of: 4, 22, 113, 119, 230
Wardens from: 81–2, 148–9
women and 243
Liverymen: 43, 138
London Bridge: 17, 33, 39–40, 59, 88, 168
London School Board: 201
London Tavern: 174, 177
London Wall: 28, 87, 89
Lord Chancellor: 17, 49, 102, 116–17, 151–2
Lord Chief Justice: 54
Lord Mayor's Court: 7, 11, 13–14, 51, 53, 84, 95, 103–4, 109, 124, 256
Lord Mayor's Day: 44, 50, 62–4, 70, 75, 88, 90, 95, 103, 121, 124, 136, 138, 174, 176–7, 180, 199
Lord Mayor's procession: 33, 122–3, 140, 176, 238
lottery, drawn at Coopers' Hall: 143–4, 171, *plate 7*
Ludgate: 40, 45, 97

Maldon: 117, 164, 192
Mansion House: 121, 177, 234, 238
marks, coopers': 13, 15, 21–2, 42, 102, 140, 256–7
Massachusetts Bay Company: 69
Master's apprenticeship: 242
May Day: 49
Merchant Taylors' Company: 94, 199
Merralls, builders: 188–9, 193
midsummer: 25, 32, 34–5, 191, 194
Mile End Road: 161, 195, 247
Miles Lane: 59, 144, 168, 170, 186, 214
Moorgate: 42, 69
motto of Coopers' Company: 10, 23, 33, 35
Mowbray Road: 225

napery: 23, 104
Napoleon: 143–4, 175
Naval Commissioners: 113
New Barnes: 115 (*see also* Plaistow)
New England Company: 69
New Model Army: 76, 103
New River Company: 93

oath, of Coopers' Company: 22
obelisk, to commemorate William Alexander: 164, *plates 4–5*
ordinances: 11, 13, 16, 41–2, 47–8, 82, 144, 256, 258

orphans of coopers: 2, 11

pall chest: 3, 58, 211, 217
pall cloth: 1–2, 10–11, 42, 58, 104
Parliament: 19–20, 45, 47–8
  Company support for during the Civil War: 74
  Long Parliament: 72
  'Short' Parliament: 71
Parson Woodforde's diary: 150
patrimony: 14, 16, 230–1, 233–4, 242–3
pensioners (*see* grantees *under* Egham Charity and Ratcliffe Charity; Woodham Mortimer)
pewter, of Coopers' Company: 4, 23, 89, 93, 104
plague: 21, 29, 42, 44, 47, 49, 63, 65, 81, 87–8
Plaistow: 115, 151, 164, 168–9, 173, 187–90, 193–4, 202–8, 210 (*see also* Egham Charity)
plate, of Coopers' Company: 76, 82, 89–90, 104, 212, 215, 217, 237
Plumbers' Company: 199, 213
Port of London Authority: 208
Portsoken Ward: 176–7
Poulter and Co.: 198
prices of barrels, control of by Coopers' Company: 13, 18–19, 42
Prince Regent Lane: 188, 204
Privy Council: 20, 42, 47–8, 97, 99–100
Protestants: 10, 27, 34, 40–1, 47, 61, 67–9, 72–3, 76, 97–8, 106, 113, 140
Puritans: 67, 122

Quakers: 68, 83, 85, 91, 95–6
Quarter Day: 136, 157, 257
quarterage: 3, 12, 14, 24, 42, 47, 49, 70, 110, 158, 257
  quarterage book: 14–15, 45, 59, 158
Queen's bench: 54
quincentenary of Coopers' Company: 246–8

railways: 143
  effect on Coopers' charities: 168–70, 173, 185–6, 189, 205
Ratcliffe: 18, 44, 47, 53, 55, 57–8, 106–7, 154, 160, 212, 246 (*see also* GIBSON, NICHOLAS)
  foundation at: 35–9
  Old Wool Quay: 36–9
  powder house at: 83
  fire at: 129–30, *131*, *132*

INDEX OF SUBJECTS

wharves at: 60, 63, 106, 119, 130, 155–6, 167, 171, 180, 187–8, 208, 214, 216, 225
Ratcliffe Charity: 39, 45, 54, 55, 56, 86, 90, 105, 108, 118, 146, 149–50, 157, 163, 165–8, 180, 186–8, 193–4, 196–7, 201, 214, 217, 225, 235, 243–5, 252, *plate 10* (*see also* Schools and Schooling)
   accounts of: 139, 146, 167
   almshouses: 36–9, 50, 57, 60, 88, 99, 106, 110, 119, 132–3, 149, 153, 165–7, 195, 197–8, 254
   almspeople: 53, 59, 65, 86, 104, 129–30, 153–4, 197–8, 201
   bequests to: 59, 60, 111, 136, 171
   Cosh's Buildings: 208, 214
   expansion of: 156–8
   fire at: 129–30, 131, 132
   grantees of: 236, 244
   income of: 59, 137, 156, 171, 187, 245
   inspection of: 62
   pensions: 39, 50, 53, 59, 86, 90, 105, 111, 153, 166–7, 201, 205, 211 (*see also* grantees *above*)
   property of: 145, 153, 155, 158–9, 168, 170, 172, 186, 193, 208, 213, 225
   rebuilding of: 132, 137, 143, 159–60
   repairs to: 148, 152–3, 173
   School House Lane: 60, 129–30, 132, 153
   triennial view of: 189
redemption: 3, 14, 16, 135, 230, 243
Reformation, the: 10, 34
Registered Coopers' scheme: 213–14
religious radicalism: 68, 70, 79
rental: 39, 45, 58, 90, 94–6, 119, 159–60, 168, 186–7, 193, 214, 219
Roundway Down: 76
Royal Navy: 32, 48, 58, 113, 115

Saddlers': 217
St Aldgate's: 11
St Anthony Cross: 18
St Augustine, works of: 62
St Botolph Aldgate: 69
St George's Bar: 33
St Katherine Coleman: 69
St Katherine's liberty: 47
St Lawrence Jewry: 69, 217
St Lawrence Pountney: 88, 110
St Luke's: 169
St Magnus the Martyr: 33, 220

St Michael's Bassishaw: 1, 22, 28, 105
St Michael's, Crooked Lane: 68, 168
St Olave's: 62, 69
St Paul's Cathedral: 11, 33–5, 41, 50, 58, 63, 65, 80, 123, 216, 219, 234
   Fire of London and: 88–9
   Lady Chapel of: 14
   'Newerk' of: 10
St Stephen's, Coleman Street: 68–9, 72
Schools and Schooling (*see also* Egham Charity; Ratcliffe Charity; usher):
   Coborn Boys' School: 196–7
   Coborn Girls' School: 162, 196, 215, 236, 254
   Coborn School: 196, 197, 198, 216, 219–20, 233, (*see also* Coopers' and Coborn School)
   Coopers' and Coborn School: 233, 236
   Coopers' Girls' School: 162, 196 (*see also* Girls' School)
   curriculum: 156–7, 159–61, 185, 202
   Egham School Board: 206
   Endowed Schools Commission: 160
   grammar school: 156, 158–9, 194–5, 201–2, 207–8, 237
   Girls' School: 160–2, 196, 216, 254
   North London Collegiate School: 161, 216
   Prisca Coborn education foundation: 196, 210
   prizes and prize-giving: 129, 158
   schoolmasters at Egham: 115–16, 128–9, 143, 150–2, 166, 175, 183, 194 (*see also* BEATTIE, JOHN; PAGET, JOHN)
   schoolmasters at Ratcliffe: 38–9, 45, 59, 65, 86–7, 105–8, 130, 132, 150, 153–6, 175–6, 183 (*see also* SPEED, WILLIAM; WARDE, THOMAS)
   Strode's school: 151, 206, 220, 233
scrivener: 14, 23, 30, 38, 45
seals: 18, 70, 77, 114, 134
Sealer: 18, 24–5, 47–8, 70, 77–8, 83–7, 90, 102, 113–14, 134, 257
   searches by: 13, 18–19, 42, 45, 47, 57, 62, 114
Second World War: 215–19
   air raids/blitz: 158, 216, 259
   bomb damage: 216, 221, 225
   War Damage Commission: 219
serjeant: 13, 18–19, 23
Sheriff, of City of London: 5, 35–6, 107–8, 118, 120–2, 140, 174, 176–81, 238
Silver Jubilee, of Queen Elizabeth II: 236

277

sisters of Coopers' Fraternity: 12, 15
Smithfield: 19
soap-barrel makers: 11
soap-boilers: 13, 84, 85
Society of the Livery: 148, 181, 209, 213, 243, 248 (*see also* Livery of Coopers' Company)
South Western Railway Company: 171 (*see also* railways)
Southwark: 11, 18–19, 40, 47, 62, 70, 74–5, 77, 109, 114, 119, 168, 186
Spectacle-Makers' Company: 213
spoons, given to Coopers' Company: 21, 45, 76, 78, 82, 93, 104
Staines: 115, 128, 164, 168–9, 188, 190, 202, 205–7, *plate 6* (*see also* Egham Charity)
Staines Lodge estate: 190, 206 (*see also* Egham Charity)
Standard, the (water conduit): 4, 13
standings of Coopers' Company: 33, 40, 63, 123, 148, 176
staves: 8–9, 13, 23–4, 40, 63, 85, 212
Stepney: 35, 37, 39, 45–6, 53–4, 73, 86, 99, 105, 120, 154–7, 159, 162, 167, 174, 195–6, 198, 201, 210, 225, 235, 243
Stepney and Bow Foundation: 196, 201, 225
Stepney Causeway: 156
stewards: 75, 90, 104, 124, 138, 174
Stone House: 37–8
strangers: 15, 18–20, 25, 41–2, 47–8, 53
Strode's College boat club: 236
Strode's Foundation: 201
strong room: 181, 211, 217, 229
surveyor of Coopers' Company: 149, 182, 189–90, 202, 204, 206, 209, 216, 222, 237
Surveyor to the City: 91
sweating sickness: 21

Tallow Chandlers' Company: 177
taxes: 20–21, 25, 31, 40, 58, 70, 76, 78, 82, 115, 118, 120, 132–3, 144, 192
    corporation: 234
    land tax: 110, 118, 149
    Orphan tax: 136
    ship money: 58
    wine duty: 115
Tees Union Shipping Company: 188
Temple Bar: 40, 119
Thames Street: 36, 39, 88, 132, 170, 216, 225
Thessaly Square: 216, 225
Thornley Coal Company: 156

Thrale and Company: 144
Three Cranes Wharf: 18, 123
tools, coopers': 3, 8, 9, 11, *51*, *145*, *212*, *218*, *237*, *238*, *plate 16*
Tower Bridge: 186
Tower Hamlets: 235, 243–6
Tower Hill: 11, 18
Town Clerk: 147, 166, 182
Treasurer, of Coopers' Company: 224, 226, 228, 257
Turners' Company: 199
Turnham Green: 74

United Guilds service: 219, 234
Upminster: 233, 236
ushers: 38–9, 59, 65, 86–7, 105–6, 108, 110, 150

Vintners' Company: 71, 77, 97, 120

Wardens: 1–3
    Junior: 3–4
    Renter 39, 51, 60–1, 108–9, 136, 139, 183, 232, 238, 257
    Senior: 4
    Under: 17, 22, 24, 26, 58, 61, 64, 70, 81–2, 95, 102, 109, 139, 147–8, 158, 232, 234, 237, 258
    Upper: 4, 15, 20, 22, 24–5, 27, 52, 57, 60–1, 63–5, 82, 110, 119–20, 139, 141, 147–8, 199, 215, 258
Wax Chandlers' Company: 16
West Ham: 159, 195–6, 202–4, 207
Westminster Abbey: 33
Westminster Hall: 72
Whigs: 81, 97, 99–102, 120
Whitefriars: 11
Whitehall: 87, 99
    palace of: 71
widows: 2, 11–12, 15, 44, 53, 60, 105, 114, 167, 233
wine-coopers: 68, 71, 79
wives: 11, 39, 64, 123–4, 161
Woodham Mortimer: 117–19, 133, 143, 146, 149, 158, 163–4, 185, 190–3, 208, 210, 212–14, 216, *plate 3*
    agricultural depression, effect on: 190–2, 202
    commutation of tithe of: 164
    pensions from ('London' Pensions'): 133–4, 146, 165, 193
Woolwich: 164, 170, 189, 199, 204–5

About the Author

PAMELA MARYFIELD was educated in the North of England at Skipton and Sunderland. She read history at Girton College, Cambridge and spent a career in education, latterly as Principal of a Surrey Further Education College. In 1994 she wrote *Henry Strode's Charity*, a history of one of the Coopers' Company Charities. She has published a number of articles on education and history and is currently researching Yorkshire monasteries. She lives in Berkshire and Yorkshire and enjoys wasting time watching cricket.

Moore gate

Coleman St.

Guild Hall

Alderm: bery.